THE INFAMOUS
SOPHIE DAWES

THE INFAMOUS SOPHIE DAWES
NEW LIGHT ON THE QUEEN OF CHANTILLY

ADRIAN SEARLE

PEN & SWORD HISTORY

AN IMPRINT OF PEN & SWORD BOOKS LTD.
YORKSHIRE - PHILADELPHIA

First published in Great Britain in 2020 by
PEN AND SWORD HISTORY
An imprint of
Pen & Sword Books Ltd
Yorkshire – Philadelphia

Copyright © Adrian Searle, 2020

ISBN 978 1 52671 749 8

The right of Adrian Searle to be identified as Author of this work has been asserted by him in accordance with the Copyright, Designs and Patents Act 1988.

A CIP catalogue record for this book is available from the British Library.

All rights reserved. No part of this book may be reproduced or transmitted in any form or by any means, electronic or mechanical including photocopying, recording or by any information storage and retrieval system, without permission from the Publisher in writing.

Typeset in Times New Roman 11.5/14 by
Aura Technology and Software Services, India.
Printed and bound in the UK by TJ International

Pen & Sword Books Limited incorporates the imprints of Atlas, Archaeology, Aviation, Discovery, Family History, Fiction, History, Maritime, Military, Military Classics, Politics, Select, Transport, True Crime, Air World, Frontline Publishing, Leo Cooper, Remember When, Seaforth Publishing, The Praetorian Press, Wharncliffe Local History, Wharncliffe Transport, Wharncliffe True Crime and White Owl.

For a complete list of Pen & Sword titles please contact
PEN & SWORD BOOKS LIMITED
47 Church Street, Barnsley, South Yorkshire, S70 2AS, England
E-mail: enquiries@pen-and-sword.co.uk
Website: www.pen-and-sword.co.uk

Or
PEN AND SWORD BOOKS
1950 Lawrence Rd, Havertown, PA 19083, USA
E-mail: Uspen-and-sword@casematepublishers.com
Website: www.penandswordbooks.com

Contents

Introduction		vi
Chapter 1	Fall and Rise: The Smuggler's Daughter	1
Chapter 2	A Life Off-kilter: The Bourbon Aristocrat	24
Chapter 3	Entrapment: A Web of Outrageous Fortune	41
Chapter 4	*Ménage à Trois*: Scandal at the Château	63
Chapter 5	Power Grab: Chantilly's Queen Assembles Her Court	80
Chapter 6	Intrigue: Sophie's Pact with the Orléans Prince	103
Chapter 7	A Will of Infamy: The Condé Inheritance	127
Chapter 8	Tragedy at Saint-Leu: The End of the Condé	143
Chapter 9	Deadly Suspicions: Suicide or Murder?	158
Chapter 10	End Games: The Scarred Spoils of Victory	184
Endnotes		196
Acknowledgements		206
Selected Bibliography		208
Index		211

Introduction

The Isle of Wight has produced, or been strongly linked with, a cast of truly remarkable women whose extraordinary life stories have fascinated, shocked, amazed and, in some cases, titillated an appreciative audience extending far beyond the shores of the island that was once their home.

These women have included top-drawer characters such as the beautiful Seymour Fleming, Lady Worsley, whose high-octane adulterous sex life scandalised English society late in the eighteenth century and stretched the boundaries of 'criminal conversation' to their absolute limits. At the other end of the scale was dowdy seaside landlady Dorothy O'Grady, sensationally sentenced to death for treachery in the Second World War after playing the part of an enemy spy 'for a giggle'.

Their stories are scarcely believable. You could not make them up. And yet they pale in comparison to the tale of Sophie Dawes, the smuggler's daughter who experienced the ultimate rags to riches life to rise from abject poverty and the island's workhouse to the dizzying heights of post-revolutionary royal French society, eventually claiming a form of royal status for herself as she ruled the household of a fabulously wealthy Bourbon prince as the unofficial Queen of Chantilly. This was a reign of terror. It led to scandal, an outrageous pact with the King of the French and the very suspicious death of her Bourbon lover.

Further deaths in mysterious circumstances would follow as Sophie ensured her lasting infamy in France. But how could any of this have happened? There have been some outstanding biographies, in France and Britain, tracing the extraordinary life story of Sophie Dawes. The most reliable were the works, in the early decades of the twentieth century, by the French writer Violette Montagu and the English author Marjorie Bowen. They provide magnificent sources of reference today for anyone looking afresh at Sophie's story.

Introduction

Yet there were gaps in these otherwise excellent works. There was a particular need to know more about Sophie's formative years in order to establish a clearer understanding of the triggers to her later infamy. This book sets out to fill those gaps and provide new perspectives on some of the story's key events.

Sophie Dawes has never had a 'good press'. But her unique place in history has always provided the basis for a good – a *very* good – story. Hopefully this book has used that basis to good effect.

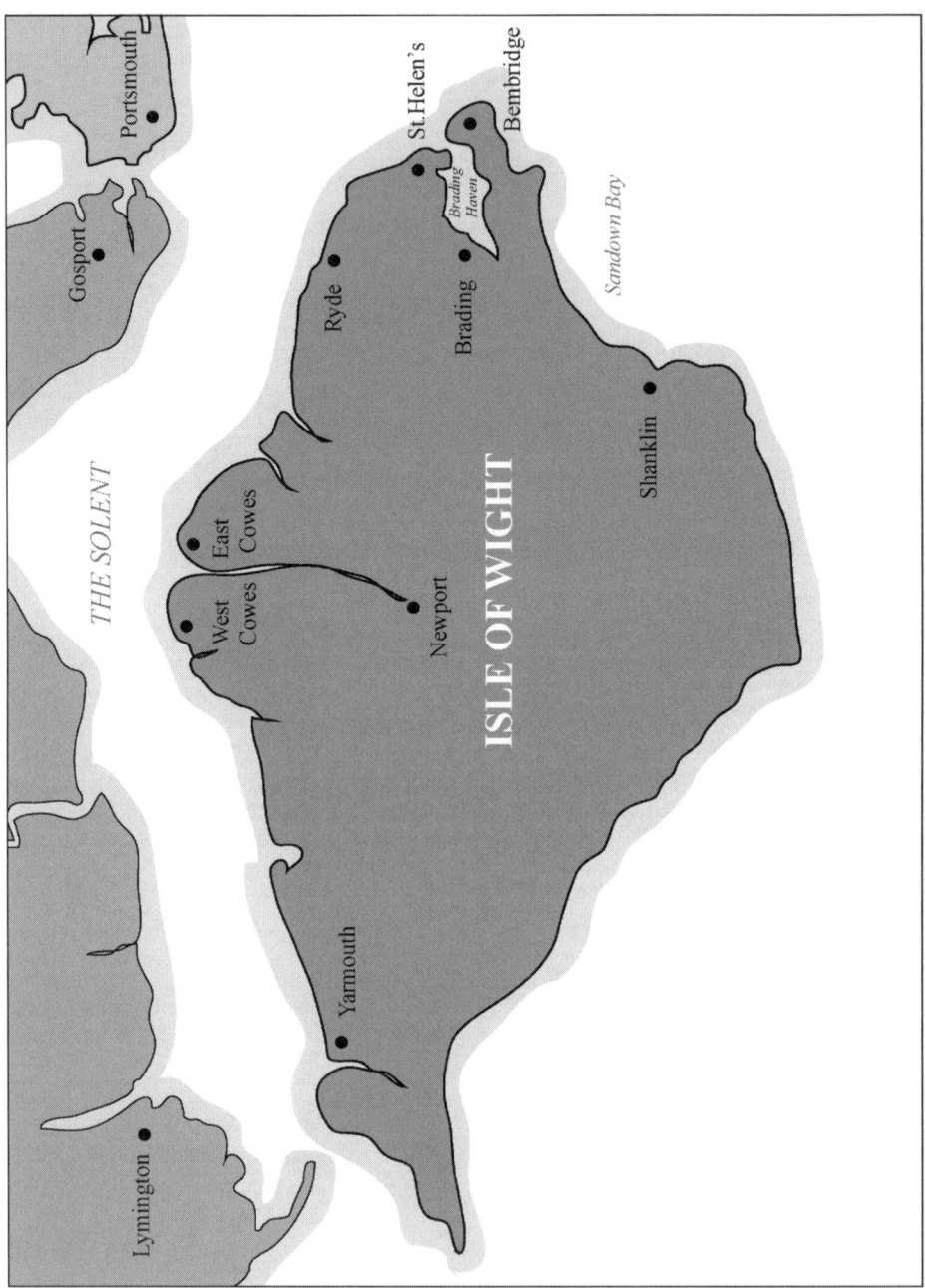

Map of the Isle of Wight showing principal locations during the period of Sophia Daw's childhood in the late eighteenth century and her St Helen's birthplace near Brading Haven before its reclamation from the sea. (Sarah Searle)

Chapter 1

Fall and Rise:
The Smuggler's Daughter

The formative years of the Englishwoman whose rags to riches story would so spectacularly stamp an indelible mark on the history of post-revolutionary France held little in the way of promise. Indeed, there was nothing at all to suggest, at best, anything other than a life of drudgery and servitude; one devoid of recognition beyond the narrow confines of a humble existence amid the relative obscurity and rural remoteness of her birthplace on the Isle of Wight.

Any biographical account should, of course, begin with the date of the subject's birth. Yet all attempts to establish with certainty the year, let alone the precise date, of Sophie Dawes' low-key start to a life which would prove to be anything but modest or restrained have been frustrated by the absence of a baptismal record in infancy – the usual source for determining the age of a child born in England before the introduction of birth registration in 1837 – and a subsequent catalogue of conflicting documentary evidence. We are left with the vague conclusion that she was born sometime between 1789 and 1793. The commemorative plaque which today adorns the front wall of her village home in Upper Green Road, St Helen's[1] proclaims that the future 'Queen of Chantilly' was born there 'around 1792'. It seems a safe bet.

Name styling, too, is something of a problem when recounting Sophie's story. Neither her given name nor the family name corresponds precisely to how she is remembered today. Called Sophia at birth – the adaptation to Sophie, the Gallic form of the name, was a much later consequence of her time in France – she was the eighth of the ten children born to fisherman Richard Daw, popularly known and always recalled as Dicky, and his wife, the former Jane Callaway. Despite early biographical insistence that theirs was a union never blessed with the sanctity of a wedding ceremony, the couple had been married at the village church in 1775. Again, the longer expression of the surname as Dawes, subsequently adopted by most of her family and generations since, came in Sophia's adulthood.[2] Not untypically for the period, she was one of only four offspring of Dicky and Jane to reach maturity, each of the remaining six children succumbing to a tragically early death as an infant or young child.

The first of the Daw children was James Richard, believed to have been born at St Helen's in August 1777, although if his birth was sanctified by baptism there are no surviving records to confirm this. James would emerge safely from childhood. Not so fortunate were William, whose birth in July 1779 was followed almost exactly two years later by his death, and Richard, a Christmas Day arrival in 1780 who survived only until his thirteenth month in 1782. By December of the following year Jane had given birth once more, this time to a girl, Mary-Ann, the second child destined for a full life. Sadly, this was in stark contrast to Sarah, born in 1785, who lived for just nineteen months, dying three days after Christmas in 1786, five months after the birth of a second Richard, who seems to have lived only long enough to acquire a name. More heartbreak was to follow for Jane Daw following the birth in July 1788 of another daughter, Charlotte. By the start of November 1791 Charlotte was dead, aged 3.

So, if we opt for the likelihood that Sophia was born as the eighth child 'around 1792,' her only surviving siblings would have been James and Mary-Ann. However, in February 1793 she acquired a younger brother, the second to be called William, and in November 1795 Jane Daw gave birth to her tenth and final child, a second sister for Sophia, baptised as Charlotte Mary. The St Helen's household thus contained five children (if we extend that definition to include the 18-year-old James) as the century neared its conclusion. However, the twin terrors of financial hardship and ill-health, sadly common in that period among the lower reaches of English society, would soon combine to hold the family of Dicky Daw in a vice-like grip.

For these reasons we must first examine the known character of the father and that of the village environment which provided the setting to this part of Sophia's story. Dicky Daw may have been an established fisherman, along with many others in the locality at that time, but the bulk of his income came undoubtedly from a second, entirely illicit,

Fall and Rise

profession. As was the case elsewhere around the island's coastline, and at English coastal areas in general, smuggling contraband was energetically pursued in a village a short distance uphill from the Solent shoreline in the north-eastern corner of the Isle of Wight, close to the banks of the town of Brading's inland tidal haven, which would not finally be reclaimed from the sea until 1881.

On the opposite side of the haven lay Bembridge, most easterly of the island's coastal settlements. Together, the waterside neighbourhoods in Wight's northeast constituted a smuggling hub. The small boats of their free-trading mariners made frequent trips southwards across the seventy-odd miles to Cherbourg, Harfleur and other ports in Normandy to replenish their vessels with the ill-gotten cargoes of spirits, tobacco and other highly-desired consumables before, heavily laden, setting off on their return journey to the island's distant shores.

Within their own communities these men were not seen as social outcasts or despised as criminals. For centuries smuggling foreign imports which would otherwise have attracted a high levy of customs duty had been regarded in coastal areas as something of a right, the benefits of which extended to, and were seized without demur by, an established chain of local residents, embracing all sections of a community's social stratum. Smuggling had long claimed a degree of morality, fired by deep resentment at the high rate of taxation imposed by successive governments seeking ever greater sums of money to finance foreign wars.

This shared interest would have sheltered Dicky Daw and his free-trading colleagues from the law – that and the general inadequacy (and in some cases, complicit dishonesty) of the official forces that were put in place to thwart the illegal trafficking. There can be little doubt that the latter had a particular problem with Dicky, who seems to have more than made his mark as a mariner, as devious as he was skilled, hugely capable of outrunning and outwitting the revenue men. So renowned was his seamanship, the core of his smuggling capabilities, that the narrow channel he used to navigate through the treacherous rocky outcrop of Bembridge Ledge on reaching home waters became enshrined on Admiralty charts as Dicky Daw's Gut – a name that, while initially bestowed out of grudging respect, has stuck ever since!

Of the many colourful tales that used to be told of the smugglers' nefarious antics in St Helen's, perhaps the most memorable, and ghoulish, was centred on the remains of the old church on the shoreline, a battered reminder of a rich ecclesiastical heritage dating back to the late arrival in the eighth century of Christianity on the island. The church, replacing a wooden Saxon predecessor, had occupied a small peninsula on the Duver (an Isle of Wight dialect word for a sandy coastal strip, usually with dunes) at the mercy of the sea, which had eventually ripped it apart. By the eighteenth century the only remnants of the stone-built church on dry land were the tower, still intact today as a sea mark, and the former churchyard which held the graves of several generations of villagers. It was a spooky place at the best of times.

In their highly readable 1977 parish history, *Twelve Hundred Years in St Helen's*, co-authors David Low and Sheila White described how the free-traders made good use of this forbidding place: 'Some of the tops of the tombs in the churchyard were loose and, after the attentions of the smugglers, became looser still and would move fairly easily to allow kegs of brandy and other smuggled goods to be hastily stuffed inside to await collection when the coast was clear.'

Another ruse was particularly useful if there were any simple village folk around. The smugglers would disguise a man in a white sheet and seat him on a tombstone playing a drum. This gave rise to the legends of dead drummers in churchyards, which in turn gave local people a horror of passing such places at night and thereby witnessing the clandestine antics!

Added the village historians:

> Smugglers were up to all kinds of tricks and one of the most ingenious was to use long poles with horse-shoes nailed on the ends. These were stamped into the sand in the opposite direction to that in which [the smugglers] were going, in order to mislead the Excise Men. Equally clever ways of bringing in the brandy were devised: a great deal of it was towed through the harbour entrance in ten-gallon tubs lashed together and weighted.

Such was the dark underbelly of village society at that time, but what of St Helen's itself? Named as a consequence of the old Duver church's rebuilding in the Norman period and its subsequent dedication to the fourth-century Roman Empress, Saint Helena, mother of Emperor

Constantine the Great, the Daw family's home village in 1795 contained around forty small houses. These were built primarily from the stone abundant in the neighbouring quarries, roofed with thatch and clustered around an expansive area of rural greens, known previously as Eddington before St Helen's inland retreat away from the land around the old church. Today, the spacious verdant heart of the village constitutes one of the largest village greens in England.[3] Back in 1795 the population was recorded as 210, a figure that would grow significantly during the lifetime of the girl destined for celebrity status as far removed as possible from the lives of the remaining 209 residents recorded in that eighteenth-century survey.[4]

The cottage in which she and her family jostled for living space was among those lining the sloping village green's higher (northern) perimeter. The earliest surviving photographs of the building, although considerably post-dating the period of the Daw family's occupancy, provide a clearer idea of its likely appearance in the late eighteenth century than a glance at the property today allows. There are descriptive references to it as 'nought more than a fisherman's hut' back in the 1790s. Judged on the photographic evidence, these seem ridiculously dismissive of its true dimensions, but those early images do indicate a home with a markedly shorter front elevation than exists on the charming house that survives today in Upper Green Road. It is known as *Freefolk*, a name which may or may not offer a nod to its free-trading past.

The present owners believe the original house may account for only the right-hand portion of *Freefolk* when viewed from the road. This seems likely. Certainly the brick-faced upper floor, adorned with the commemorative plaque, is a more recent addition, replacing the rooms whose windows protruded from the steeply sloping roof which would have provided cover for the Daws' home. So the front of the property has changed substantially since Sophia's childhood. But step inside and the curious visitor is transported immediately back to the period of her upbringing alongside the cart track which would later evolve into Upper Green Road.

Commendably conscious of the building's historical tradition, owners Mark and Rosy Hickman have peeled back the centuries, combining careful restoration with sensitive substitution to reveal as far as possible the distinctive flooring, both stone-flagged and wooden-planked, the timber beams and the inglenook fireplaces which would have been familiar features of the smuggler's home as his family struggled to make ends meet in turn-of-the-century St Helen's. The house exudes an air of comfort, cosiness and charm today. Would Sophia have felt those sustaining qualities of family life back in the days of her infancy?

Along with her siblings, she would have spent some of her childhood propping up her father's legitimate trade by picking shellfish from the shore. Probably she took for granted – or was otherwise preoccupied in the company of the competing young pickers from neighbouring families – the idyllic coastal vista which formed the backdrop to her child labour. It was largely unchanged a half-century or so later when the writer W. H. Davenport Adams, in his *History, Topography and Antiquities of the Isle of Wight*, published in 1856, drew attention to 'the many beautiful views – the English Channel sweeping away to the eastward, Bembridge and its elm trees on the opposite point, the surrounding Downs, the Haven, and the old town of Brading.' Did Sophia scan that vista in search of her father's boat?

How she would have reacted to a first siting of Dicky Daw's homecoming vessel, heavily laden with his catch of the day, legitimate or otherwise, is open to question. All the evidence, and the folklore too, points to one conclusion: the home he was returning to was not a happy one.

In terms of social standing and family responsibilities, the problem with Dicky was not the way he set out to earn his income, which potentially would have been considerable; it was the way he chose or, as time wore on, probably became compelled by addiction, to fritter it away. Again, like many of his cohorts – though local legend suggests he was especially prone to this – he seems to have consumed a considerable amount of the spirits he smuggled and thereby most of the profits. It was easy for Dicky to satisfy his ever increasing need for alcohol. Sadly for his wife and children, who should have fared better than most in St Helen's from Dicky's lucrative earnings, it was just as easy for them to suffer the inevitable consequences of his chronic dependency. One preserved account of their collective slide into poverty and heavy reliance on institutional help for the destitute tells a tragically depressing story.

It comes from the pages of record books compiled at the Isle of Wight House of Industry, the island's workhouse. Noted for being among the first centralised rural workhouses in England, taking as its model the Samford House of Industry in East Suffolk which had opened in 1763, this huge edifice, its façade as gaunt as it was imposing, dominated an isolated eighty-acre site on what until then had been unutilised land adjacent to the eastern limits of Parkhurst Forest (though the workhouse survives today as the oldest part of the St Mary's Hospital complex).[5]

With the land acquired on a 999-year lease, Forest House, as it became known, was conveniently located a short distance north of Newport, the island's capital. It had been planned as the physical embodiment of a bold statement of intent by the island's ruling class to revolutionise the provision of relief for the destitute, a responsibility hitherto invested in, and jealously guarded by, each of the island's parishes. The workhouse was the key element of the Isle of Wight Incorporation for the Poor Act, which, despite opposition from several of the parishes, desperate to retain the benefits of income and cheap labour from local management of their poor, was granted Parliamentary approval in May 1771. The island's largest public building at the time of its construction, the House of Industry, although still incomplete, opened its doors for the first time in August 1774. In the years to come, many of the island's poorest would feel the cold embrace of an institution colloquially decried as the Grubber.

While there was, just about, a regular supply of food for inmates at Forest House, the term 'grubber', used progressively until it acquired the status of common parlance in the Victorian era, had no association with grub of the edible kind. It was used instead as a derogatory label for someone who routinely scavenged in drains to scratch out a pitiful living. In its early years the workhouse for some of these poor wretches possibly represented something of a sanctuary, but for most inmates, down on their luck, fallen from grace, innocent victims of others' misdeeds, ill-treatment or basic lack of adequate familial care, admission to the House of Industry marked a last desperate retreat from starvation, a final clutching of survival's straws.

On paper, at least, the aims of Forest House's founders, its governing body of guardians, were honourable, well-intentioned and neatly summarised by Jack and Johanna Jones in their authoritative work, *The Isle of Wight: An Illustrated History*, published by the Dovecote Press in 1987. Workhouse objectives, they wrote, were 'to care for the aged and infirm, to give employment to the able-bodied, to correct the profligate and idle, and to educate children in religion and industry'. But the care was basic, the environment anything but homely. Although the majority of inmates had been driven by their desperate state to seek admission, and while they were not prisoners in the accepted sense, neither were they treated as guests, free to come and go as they pleased. The gates to the Parkhurst workhouse were locked each night.

Forest House *did* offer succour for the poor but this did not extend to any appreciable degree of home comfort. The workhouse had not been planned as an easy option for the destitute. 'Support yourself in your own home or you'll end up in here' was effectively the forbidding ethos.

For child admissions in particular, the workhouse must have stirred up a whirlwind of emotions. Uprooted from their home and everything they knew, herded unceremoniously off to Parkhurst in a farm cart, cut off entirely from their family and forced to sleep in draughty dormitories – which, until reform in 1813, meant sharing the thin mattress of an iron bed with others – their regimented daily routine of working, feeding and sleeping was punctuated by the monotonous clanging of bells to denote the start or end of one or other of these precisely set procedures, every day the same. But maybe, hopefully, in time they grew to appreciate that they were almost certainly better off in the care of the workhouse than they had been at home.

All things, of course, are relative. The practically never-changing mealtime menu covering seven days at Forest House was probably markedly more nourishing than the scraps provided irregularly in the cottages of the island's poor, but it makes particularly unappetising reading today. This menu sheet from the early years of the nineteenth century serves as a good example:

	Breakfast	Dinner	Supper
Sunday	Bread & butter	Boiled beef	Potatoes
Monday	Bread & butter	Peas & beef liquor	Bread & butter
Tuesday	Bread & butter	Bread & butter	Bread & butter
Wednesday	Bread & butter	Beef soup	Potatoes
Thursday	Bread & butter	Bread & butter	Bread & butter
Friday	Bread & butter	Potatoes, peas or beans, pork fat	Bread & butter
Saturday	Bread & butter	Rice milk	Bread & butter

Over the course of nine years, three of Dicky Daw's children would be served this frugal fare, but the family's involvement with the House of

Fall and Rise

Industry actually began on 1 April 1797. By then Dicky's mental health had clearly deteriorated to such an extent – the assumption being, as a result of his alcoholism – he appears to have been no longer capable of earning any sort of living, legal or otherwise, to support either himself or his dependants. On that day he was admitted to the Parkhurst workhouse. The surviving records provide a one-word comment about his desperate condition on arrival at Forest House. It was something of a catch-all phrase at the end of the eighteenth century for people with mental instability. Richard Daw, the former expert mariner and renowned artful smuggler, was now described simply as 'insane.'

There is nothing in the records to indicate the source of this diagnostic conclusion or whether any real attempt at determining the cause of Dicky's troubled state was actually made. We know only that five weeks later, on 6 May, he was discharged from the workhouse, the reason for this left unexplained. Whether or not Dicky then returned to his St Helen's home – and there is now no way of knowing this – he was clearly still incapable of supporting his family. On 10 June the keeper of records at the House of Industry noted that two of the Daw children had that day entered the workhouse on the stipulation that their troubled father each weekend should pay 2 pence (0.83p in today's decimal currency), at a time when a labourer's average weekly income was around 17 shillings (85p today), towards their keep. The register of inmates identifies the two children admitted to the workhouse as Sophia, whose age is given as 6 – indicating a birth date in 1791 – and her 4-year-old brother, William.

They were still there a year later, now aged 7 and 5, respectively, according to the preserved records. Despite having no longer to provide for them at home, back in St Helen's Jane Daw continued to struggle against the odds. We can only conjecture about the precise nature of the revised domestic arrangements in which she found herself in 1798. The workhouse records do at least provide the basis for an educated guess, beginning with the assumption that, wherever he was actually living at the time, the dysfunctional Dicky, in his forty-seventh year, had by now wholly abrogated the protective twin roles of husband and father.

For some years Jane's eldest son, James, now in his early twenties, would have been old enough to make his own decisions and had probably assumed the role as *de facto* head of the family. In April 1798 he had married local girl Mary Crann in the village church. It is likely that he brought his new bride to live in the rapidly emptying family home. It is also probable that Mary-Ann,

Jane Daw's second eldest child, just short of her sixteenth birthday, was by then working in some form of domestic servitude, although it is impossible to be precise about this. But that would still have left Jane to fulfil, with virtually no discernible income, the role of mother to her infant daughter Charlotte Mary, who had yet to reach the age of 3.

The sad reality of Jane's plight is borne out by the next reference to the Daw family in the House of Industry record books. On 21 September 1799 it was noted that 3-year-old Charlotte had been taken from her St Helen's home to become the third child of Dicky Daw admitted to the workhouse. However, three became two on 21 December when Sophia was discharged from the House, the appended note in the relevant book making clear this was at the 'request of her brother'. The reasons behind James Daw's move to secure his young sister's release from the workhouse were not explained. One of his principal motives may have been to provide some help for their mother who had endured so much suffering and heartache over a prolonged period. Jane and Sophia were destined to share a great deal of the dramatic events which dominated the latter's extraordinary story but the reunion – if reunion there was – between mother and daughter in December 1799 unhappily would prove to be short-lived as the Daw family's declining fortunes plunged further into the realms of abject misery.

The workhouse records for 1800 note the continued existence there of William Daw, now 7, and his 4-year-old sister, Charlotte. A year on, their names were recorded again on the register of inmates, but in October 1801 tragedy reduced the family presence at the House to a single representative. Four months short of his ninth birthday, William had passed away. It was not at that time uncommon for children to die in a workhouse or, indeed, anywhere else, so it comes as no surprise to find no other details of his passing other than the one word, 'died'.

Not for the first time a single stark word had been used by a scribe at the workhouse to denote the collapse of a life in the Daw family. 'Insane' … 'died'. In a sense it comes as something of a relief to find no similarly severe references alongside Charlotte's name as her continuing residence at the House was noted in both 1802 and 1803, by which time she had reached the age of 7. The records are vague about her presence there in 1804, though the absence of any discharge note makes this a distinct probability. One thing is certain – on 24 March of that year the workhouse had renewed its acquaintance with Charlotte's sister, Sophia.

Fall and Rise

Evidently, the circumstances which had allowed her discharge a little more than four years earlier had been unsustainable and Sophia was once more an inmate of the House of Industry. It was at this point in the workhouse record-keeping that the seeds were sown for the confusion, which has persisted ever since, over the year of her birth. In December 1799 she had left the workhouse as a child whose age had been recorded earlier that year as 8. Now, in March 1804, four years and three months later, when we would expect her age to have risen to 12 or possibly 13, she is described on re-admittance as a 15-year-old!

There is nothing to explain the anomaly. Was this a correction in order to redress an earlier error? Or was the error made on readmission? Did Sophia, or a family representative, lie about her true age on readmission in the hope that this would improve her chances of more speedily escaping the grim realities of workhouse life, given that girls and boys were treated as adults in Forest House beyond the age of 13? There is no way of knowing which of these possibilities, or perhaps some other explanation, provides the most likely answer to the riddle. However, in a period far less obsessed with age than our own, such inconsistencies were common.

What is certain is that Sophia's second period of residency at the House of Industry lasted less than nineteen months. On 11 October 1805 – aged 16 or 17 if we adhere to the workhouse's re-admittance details from March 1804 – she left the House to take up an apprenticeship at an Isle of Wight farm. Since farms were a common destination for young workhouse inmates granted an apprenticeship outside its walls, it is unsurprising that Sophia's departure did not merit a mention in the House's minute book. However, inspection of the corresponding 'register of persons apprenticed by Guardians of the Poor', also preserved at the Isle of Wight Record Office, reveals that her new employment was with a farmer by the name of William Kemp at 'Cliff'. Almost certainly this was a shortened reference to Cliff Farm, which still functions today on the town of Shanklin's southwestern fringe.[6]

It is, of course, impossible to know how Sophia viewed the prospect of low-paid employment at the relative remoteness of the farm. Was she resigned to a life of drudgery with the attendant possibility that her new employer would treat her with little or no respect or kindness? Had she heard stories of the physical and sexual abuse often meted out to apprenticed girls from the workhouse, some of whom were returned to the House pregnant and, in the eyes of the guardians, disgraced? Maybe she had been told how, later, they were further abused by being housed as unmarried mothers away from the mass of inmates, forced to wear coarse 'punishment' clothing and cruelly denied some of the more palatable items from the already austere dining menu.

While we might guess at Sophia's emotional state as she turned her back on Forest House, there is no need for conjecture about the choice of clothing at her disposal on leaving Parkhurst. The workhouse carefully compiled a full 'list of waring apparel [sic] sent with Sophia Daw' on the day she departed. In fact, there were two lists, the likely explanation for this being that the first (below left) represented the clothing the Master of the House planned for, or expected, her to take while the second column (right), more hastily scribbled, listed the items she actually did take with her. The original spelling has been retained in the following copies:

1 Bonnet	1 Bonnet
4 Shifts	6 Shifts
2 Gownes	4 Gownes
2 Petticoats	3 Petticoats
3 Approns	6 Approns
2 Pr. of Stockings	3 Pr. of Stockings
8 Caps	8 Caps
4 Half Hankerchiefs	9 Half Hankerchiefs
1 Stays	2 Stays
2 Pr. of Shoes	2 Pr. of Shoes

A half han[d]kerchief was half a square of fabric, usually decorative, cut diagonally across and, in the eighteenth and early nineteenth centuries, worn usually on the head or round the neck.

These then were the clothes, a typical domestic servant's wardrobe, Sophia carried away. Intriguingly, the archived apprenticeship register adds the note, 'husbandry – 2 years', an indication that Sophia's engagement at Cliff Farm may not have been as a domestic servant, the usual assumption, but in some form of generalised agricultural labour, and that farmer Kemp had agreed to apprentice her for a two-year period. Whatever the detailed truth of that, it certainly did not work out as envisaged by the workhouse. Either through resentment at her lot, an inbred, or possibly acquired, wilfulness or a surprising spark of ambition – perhaps a combination of all of these traits – Sophia was not to stay long in farm domesticity. The other possible motivation for what happened next is that she *was*, as many have concluded, abused in some way at Cliff Farm. There is no proof of this. Most of those who tell her story do not concern themselves with reasons, noting only the one simple known fact: Sophia Daw ran away.[7]

Details of her flight from the farm – precisely when it happened, how she got away, whether she had any help and where she was headed – are impossible to verify. We may surmise that she had no desire for a return to the House of Industry, by far the most likely outcome if she were caught anywhere on the Isle of Wight. To escape a discredited retreat to the workhouse, and the horrors that potentially would follow there, she had to flee the island altogether, something that very few islanders at that time would ever contemplate – certainly not somebody with her background. Local tradition asserts that she was taken to Portsmouth in the wherry of 'old Hal Southcott'. This cannot be disproved; historical record does not rule it out.

In the days before the building of the UK's first seaside pier at Ryde in 1814 transformed cross-Solent travel to the still-developing town on the Isle of Wight's northeast coast, enabling journeys at all states of the tide, the task of ferrying passengers to and from the mainland at Portsmouth was in the hands of a makeshift fleet of Ryde Wherries, purpose-designed twin-mast sailing boats with long overhanging bows. The wherries handled the job well but at low tide, the revealed presence of the town's extensive sandbanks, stretching half-a-mile out to sea, meant that an uncomfortable transfer to and from a cart was required when embarking and disembarking at Ryde. By 1796 much of the passenger trade on the route had been taken over by a far larger vessel but the wherries were still needed as a means of transferring people from ship to cart at low tide. It was during this period that Sophia crossed the Solent in the summer of 1806, so it is possible to imagine her passage all the way to the mainland, whether or not she travelled as the *sole* passenger, would have provided a welcome boost for a wherry master whose day-to-day sailing activity was now normally confined to coastal work. Was it sufficiently unusual for him to later recall the event, thereby giving birth to the legend?

This sort of detail, the minutiae of Sophia's first great leap out of obscurity, has not overly concerned many of those who have told her story. 'She went to Portsmouth' is pretty much the only information provided by them to describe this defining event. The rarity of such an undertaking is all but ignored. Neither do they question at all the probable difficulties involved.

Sophia would have first to have made her way to her point of embarkation. Did she tackle the ten or so miles of trackway to Ryde on foot or was she fortunate enough to hitch a lift in some form of wheeled transport? If so, was this planned or was it purely a case of serendipity, of being in the right place at the right time? We might also ask if she went to Ryde at all. Might she instead have joined the wherry at a point closer to Cliff Farm, maybe in nearby Sandown Bay or, as has been suggested, in Brading Haven, close to her home village of St Helen's? It is perhaps pertinent to note that Southcott is a surname with close historical links to the village – and indeed to its smuggling heritage. Was Sophia's boatman a family friend, a free-trading partner of her father? If so, the likelihood is her voyage was pre-planned.

If 'old Hal', or whoever was at the helm that day, was *not* known to her, he is highly unlikely to have made the crossing without seeking some form of payment. If we accept this, the question is: how did Sophia pay him? Some say she handed over sixpence to Hal. If so, where had it come from? Apart from her keep – food, drink and a bed to sleep in – she would have earned, in financial terms, little more than a pittance at Cliff Farm, if she were paid at all. She might have been given the fare by a well-wisher, perhaps a family member, but the common supposition is that she stole money from her employer at the out-of-the-way Shanklin farm, a key part of a planned dash to freedom and adventure – the very first of her many life-enhancing schemes. Others, no doubt influenced by knowledge of later events but little else, suggestively imply that she paid the boatman 'in kind'. We will never know. Suffice it to say that Sophia found some way to secure her passage to Portsmouth en route to infamy.

There are no traceable further references to Sophia in the material archived at the Isle of Wight Record Office. She had left behind for good her troubled life on the island. The House of Industry records refer just once more to the Daw children, noting the discharge in April 1806 of 8-year-old Charlotte. It would appear that the only member of the family yet to break free of institutionalised poor relief was Dicky Daw. Years later we find him mentioned in connection with a court case held at Newport Guildhall on 1 March 1817 when the Guardians of the Poor complained that Dicky's son, James, described as a shopkeeper, was refusing to maintain his father. James was ordered by the justices to pay 2 shillings per week to the House of Industry. We may assume he did so grudgingly. Perhaps understandably, given the suffering he had caused, Dicky's offspring were keen to see the back of their father, who managed to cling to life until his death in August 1828 at the age of 76.

If we were to judge him according to modern attitudes towards alcoholism and mental illness, we might do so with a far greater degree of kindness and understanding. Dicky Daw was as damned by drink as, progressively, his wife and children were by the far-reaching social consequences of his addiction. It had fired him up and then it had left him to wither.[8]

By the time of his death, of course, Sophia had long since turned her back on her father. Unlike her relationships with most of the other members of her family, once she had left the Isle of Wight following her flight from Cliff Farm, Dicky was to play no further part in her life. Ironically, perhaps, it is possible that she clambered off the wherry on arrival at Portsmouth alongside the Quebec Tavern in Bath Square, which served in the early years of the nineteenth century as the mainland terminal point for an augmented ferry service from Ryde. Close to the tavern stood the Customs-house, where the revenue officers Dicky Daw had once delighted in evading on his smuggling runs from France kept a close watch on all vessels entering the port. If the wherry came into Portsmouth this way her master would more than likely have been hailed and asked to explain the purpose of his arrival there – possibly the closest the revenue men ever came to apprehending a member of the arch-smuggler's family!

It is widely accepted – and there is no reason to query this – that, initially, Sophia did not venture far on the mainland once she had stepped ashore from her Solent transport. We can imagine a torrent of emotions cascading through her mind: the relief of having got this far without serious mishap colliding with rippling thoughts of hopeful expectation, excitement and nervousness as she walked alone from the unfamiliar quayside of Portsmouth's old town, bound, whether it was by design or a case of chancing her luck, for the doors of the George Hotel. Good fortune, it seems, was on her side. The hotel needed a chambermaid. Sophia got the job.

But which George Hotel was this? There are two candidates. To reach the first would have meant a walk for Sophia of a mile or so northwards to arrive at Queen Street in the Portsea district, close to the gates of the naval dockyard. Today, the George Hotel at this location has a claim to be the last surviving eighteenth-century public house in Portsmouth. Its listing as a tavern in a 1784 directory supports this. Whether paying guests at the time of Sophia's arrival were accommodated there in sufficient numbers to necessitate the need for a chambermaid is something of a moot point. The more likely option is that Sophia found work even closer to her point of disembarkation. An easy walk along the nearby High Street of Old Portsmouth would have brought her to the George Hotel which occupied a prominent site there at that time and had recently accommodated the guest who would ensure its enduring fame to this day.

This imposing hotel, well-established as a favourite haunt for naval officers in Portsmouth, had provided Horatio Nelson with his last meal on English soil. Having left his Surrey home in Merton and travelled overnight by post-chaise, he breakfasted there on the morning of 14 September 1805 prior to setting sail aboard HMS *Victory* to engage the combined might of French and Spanish foes in what would prove the most famous sea battle in British history. Lord Nelson's epic finale to an outstanding naval career off the Cape of Trafalgar on 21 October was, of course, pre-destined as a defining moment in the Napoleonic Wars, whatever the outcome. The crowds of adoring well-wishers who, aware of his presence, flocked to the George on the morning of his departure, necessitating a back door exit for Nelson to preserve their safety as he made his way to his flagship, was indicative of the importance of his mission.

Those same wars with Bonaparte's French empire – and, in her case, the sequence of events which unfolded in the wake of the emperor's eventual downfall – would later have an effect on the life of the young girl from the Isle of Wight as profound, in relative terms, as it had been for Lord Nelson. Perhaps in her own mind, having escaped the workhouse as the vice-admiral was en route to Trafalgar, and having now entered the George Hotel, possibly by the very same door Nelson had used a year or so before to avoid the masses, she dreamed of better things to come. Yet there was certainly nothing of great import predestined for Sophia

Daw as she took up her duties cleaning the bedrooms and bathrooms at Portsmouth's grand hotel.

If historical records of employment at the George were ever kept there it is likely they were lost when, in 1941, the hotel was severely damaged in one of several devastating Luftwaffe bombing raids on the city that year – and then demolished.[9] In the absence of factual information it is possible only to surmise about the details of Sophia's stay at the hotel and its relevance to her story. Her duties at the George would certainly have brought her into contact, albeit fleetingly, with guests from a markedly higher rank in society than her own. Did this lead to admiration, perhaps provoke envy, within her, giving impetus to a burgeoning desire to haul herself up the rungs of social standing, to share in the apparent good fortune of the hotel's guests? Did she, now in her teenage years, begin to recognise a certain interest among the male clientele in her youthful good looks – and how she might just be able to use this asset to very good effect if she were canny enough to harness it in her favour?

Whatever the innermost emotions, Sophia's sojourn in Portsmouth seems to have been a short one. Her next move would transport her, along a route paved with undulating fortune, to the ultimate date with destiny. Again, the usual references to this part of her story state merely that she 'went to London'. The only accessible historical fact that can usefully be added to this is that the George Hotel was the start point for the *Rocket* stagecoach service to the capital, Sophia's most likely mode of travel from Portsmouth. When and why she left the George, how the coach journey was paid for and whether or not she travelled alone remain as unanswered, and probably unanswerable, questions, but it *was* to London that Sophia had gone.

For a girl from the Isle of Wight's workhouse to have reached Portsmouth had been remarkable enough. For her to have subsequently travelled on to London was extraordinary. Sophia might have been celebrated historically for this fact alone had her story reached its climax at this point. But she had only just begun to earn her colours as the highly-ranked adventuress historians, for want of a better, more rounded noun, would later delight in labelling her.

That she was resourceful at this stage cannot be doubted but it is difficult to imagine her arriving alone in the sprawl of London and securing immediate employment as an assistant in a milliner's establishment, which is where she next turns up in most biographical accounts. The likelihood is that, by now, she had learned how best to use the key resources at her disposal – her youthful prettiness, developing sexuality and the beguiling, wide-eyed disposition that would be so evident when she posed for her first known portrait a few years later.

To have found a good job with prospects in a high-class London milliner's shop she must surely have received some help, the sort of assistance a well-connected gentleman, smitten or at the least enchanted by her feminine wiles, might well have provided for her. Sophia was proving good on her own but it is probably true that simultaneously she was unleashing a talent for snaring targeted admirers possessing the wherewithal, financial and otherwise, to advance her cause.

And Sophia's cause was no doubt elevated several notches higher by coming into contact with the wealthy clientele who sought to top off their fashionable clothing with the expensive headwear so temptingly portrayed in the hand-coloured plates of *The Lady's Magazine,* from exotic turbans with strong African influences to the far simpler hats, a trend exported from social upheaval in post-revolutionary France, which adorned the coiffured hair of high society women in Georgian Britain as the nation awaited the Regency of the future George IV.

It is probably safe to assume that Sophia's involvement in dressing the decorative hair of the millinery shop's 'high-end' customers, menial though this might have been at the start, stirred still further the powerfully intoxicating emotions of admiration and envy which coalesced to fire a burning ambition to escape the lot of a shop-floor servant, no matter how good at her job she was, and aspire instead to the status of those who would be served. Perhaps there was a dangerous element of frustration and resentment, too. This might explain why Sophia, who since leaving the Isle of Wight House of Industry had displayed such a determined prudence in making her progression up the initial rungs of social improvement, should now risk falling heavily backwards and throwing it all away. Sophia Daw fell in love. It knocked her off course

That, at least, is the usual, kindest, interpretation of the relationship which, the story goes, cost Sophia her job. Taking into account what is now known about the general character of her liaisons with men, it may be that the physical desire for male company was more to the fore than anything to do with a truly romantic yearning. Possibly it was a combination of the two. Or it could be, as some sources sympathetically suggest, that she was the victim of a serial seducer. Whatever it was, her reputed attachment to a water-carrier, who presumably delivered water he had drawn from a nearby well or pump to the milliners' shop, was quite unlike anything that had gone before, or would develop later, in the annals of Miss Daw's dalliances with men. Whoever this man was, his humble station in life would have presented no discernible advantage to Sophia's social climbing ambitions. In fact, the opposite was the case.

Most accounts of this murky episode, which appear to originate from *Les Secrets de Saint-Leu*, French writer Adolphe de Belleville's work of 1831, suggest that Sophia's employers, having learnt of the affair, felt it was inappropriate for a member of their staff, no matter how insignificant her precise status. Others imply the discovery of the relationship was a physical revelation rather than a case of hearsay. In other words, the couple were caught *in flagrante delicto* on the premises. Irrespective of Sophia's true emotions at the time, the latter does seem the more likely. Whether Sophia was seduced or whether she did the seducing is a moot point.

Sophia was down – but she was not quite out. How much of the next part of her story is fact and how much, convenient legend is arguable – like a great deal of the events in her teenage years – but we next find her acting the part of a Georgian Nell Gwynne, selling oranges to London theatre-goers at Covent Garden in an attempt to scratch some sort of living. Where she lived at this time, and to what extent a probable renewal of domestic hardship affected her, is lost to history but there is a suggestion that her waning fortunes were lifted when Sophia charmed her way into 'bit part' employment as an actress at the very theatre where she had plied her meagre trade in citrus fruit. Proof of this is hard to find. A. E. Billault de Gerainville, writing in 1871 of Sophia's later role in the life of the last King of the French, *Histoire de Louis-Phllippe,* is prominent among those who doubt the authenticity of this brief stage career. Other French (and later British) writers, notably Violette Montagu in 1912, are far less dismissive, pointing with some justification to later evidence of an acting talent – or at least a discernible stage presence not usually associated with amateur dramatists – in the future Queen of Chantilly. Whatever Sophia managed to achieve at the theatre in Covent Garden, it appears to have stood her in good stead for the next act in her remarkable life story.

We might say she had been talent-spotted, although precisely which of her emerging talents proved the magnet for her next male conquest is hard to say. It might not have mattered much to her – the man was snared and Sophia, the girl from the workhouse, was about to reap the rewards of a sudden, dramatic elevation into a world far removed from anything that had gone before. The consistency of the telling and re-telling of this next episode is compelling but, once again, the available factual information is sketchy and devoid of some key points of reference – most glaringly, the identity of the man at its heart. Violette Montagu describes him as 'a rich officer (whether in the English army or not is uncertain)' in her classic book, *Sophie Dawes: Queen of Chantilly*, published in London and New York by John Lane in 1912. In her own account for the same publisher in 1934, *The Scandal of Sophie Dawes*, English author Marjorie Bowen calls him 'a well-to-do foreign gentleman'. Both are markedly more precise when it comes to the detailed geographical setting for this part of the story.

They accept the tradition that Sophia's latest admirer installed her in an 'elegant villa' amid the then pastoral surroundings of Turnham Green, now part of Chiswick in the west London borough of Hounslow. The clear inference is that the man was her lover, protector and benefactor, and that she lived in the house within convenient reach – whether this was sporadic or on a more permanent basis – of his affections. And, one might add, his money. It is said that while she was there she was able, for the first time, to satisfy expensive tastes in both dining and fashionable clothing, and was even equipped with a servant to carry out the sort of domestic duties she had herself formerly undertaken. Had this rags to riches story reached its pinnacle at this juncture it would already have been amazing – but there would be many more dramatic twists and turns before destiny had finished with the remarkable Sophia Daw.

The next would see her ambitions dramatically tumble from the luxury of high living at somebody else's expense to land once more at the bottom of the social pile – and that is putting it mildly! That Sophia had learned how physically to please a man can be regarded as a given. It seems that she made full use of this in managing to hold her wealthy lover's affections for a reasonable period. But at this stage she may have had very little else to offer. By all accounts she was blessed with an above average intelligence and a sharp wit but, with only her rudimentary education at the workhouse to fall back on, and yet to acquire either conversational skills or an appreciable degree of social etiquette, her chances of hanging on indefinitely to his admiration were probably minimal. His ardour eventually left him – and so too, on his probable command, did Sophia. If we believe one version of the tale, he agreed to pay her an annuity of £50, a generously hefty sum in those days, though it is thought probable that it came nowhere near to the amount of money she had grown accustomed to receiving as his 'kept woman', the archetypal lady of leisure, at Turnham Green. Apparently, her spending while in residence had been incautious, to say the least, and now she set about squandering her parting gift. It is difficult not to be led to that conclusion when we learn what happened next.

Actually, it is far from clear what *did* happen next if we take this to mean the period immediately after her dismissal from Turnham. The legends and traditions which support so much of Sophia's story as a young woman in England provide not a flicker of illumination to guide us. But most accounts agree where she ended up – and this next stage in her amazing journey through life would initially degrade her status and ambitions before upgrading both to an unimaginable degree so staggeringly sensational that it is scarcely believable to this day.

Before we consider the rise, we must first address the fall. It was so profound that it is surely stretching the imagination to suggest that even someone possessed of the most scheming of natures would have planned it as a murkily convoluted means to an end. For her story now takes us to a house of ill repute in London's Piccadilly. Nobody has suggested that she was engaged there in overt prostitution. The perceived wisdom is that she worked instead in some form of domestic servitude. Quite what was expected of a domestic servant in this early nineteenth-century London brothel is open to interpretation, especially if we accept the tradition that, while there, Sophia came into close contact – some say *very* close contact – with several of the wealthy clientele. Whether there was extracurricular activity on her part or she was just a provocatively eye-catching ornament in her servant's garb, whether she had, after all, planned the whole episode in a fit of devious cunning, she certainly made the most of it.

History was on her side. Since 1789 revolution in France and the subsequent imposition of Napoleonic rule had unseated from their country of origin – those who had escaped the fatal embrace of *Madame Guillotine* – thousands of emigrants who sought refuge in the calmer waters of neighbouring states. Many had fled to royalist Britain, among them members of the aristocratic elite. As New Zealand academic historian Kirsty Carpenter, a well-respected specialist on this aspect of French revolutionary turmoil, reminds us in her study, *Refugees of the French Revolution: Émigrés in London 1789–1802*, not only was Protestant Britain the one European country to provide the Catholic French *émigrés* with financial assistance, it was unique as a host nation because the British had nothing to gain politically from offering their support.[10]

London was the chosen destination for most *émigrés*. While some were reduced for the first time to earning a living from employment, others had sufficient time on their hands, and enough money, to enjoy some of the earthier pleasures the British capital had to offer. Many frequented the brothel in Piccadilly where, it appears, Sophia Daw was a notable attraction. Into her story, and the bordello, walked a Frenchman recalled today only as Monsieur Guy.

If we follow this strand of tradition, had it not been for M. Guy's peek (if that's all it was) into Piccadilly's promised land of lusty fulfilment, Sophia probably would not have gone on to claim the fame, and then the notoriety, for which she is remembered today. There is, however, more than one version of the events that followed Guy's fateful visit to the brothel. The first seems highly plausible; the second, although it cannot be ruled out as an optional truth, is the stuff of wonderful legend, beloved of many who delight in relating Sophia's story.

Whatever the prime reason for Guy's presence at the brothel, he was already embarked on a mission – to find a pretty playmate in London for his aristocratic French *émigré* master, with whom he had travelled as a loyal body-servant to various European destinations in the revolution's wake before his employer reached the haven of a tolerant England. If we were to compile a pecking order for Gallic *émigrés* of the period, Guy's master would be very near to the top. Louis Henri Joseph, Duke of Bourbon, was heir to the even grander title held by his elderly father, the Prince of Condé, when, fortuitously for both parties, he was introduced to Sophia by Guy, who had picked her out at Piccadilly as the perfect partner for the libidinous duke.

It was a little less straightforward than a simple introduction if the second version of this episode is to be believed. This claims that Sophia was made the subject of a wager at a game of whist played between the exiled French duke and two English aristocrats, the Earl of Winchelsea and Prince Edward, Duke of Kent, the fourth son of King George III and, later, father of Queen Victoria. Louis Henri emerged triumphant and duly claimed his prize! The possibility of both versions of the tale being true – with Louis Henri risking the loss of Sophia's attentions in the card game following an initial encounter with her – cannot be ruled out.[11]

It is usually written that Sophia was 20 at the time she first set eyes on Louis Henri and that he was 52. Since it is known that the duke was born in April 1756, that would point both to 1808 as the year of their meeting and to 1788 as the year of Sophia's birth. But if we factor in the complication of the conflicting workhouse records and opt for the earlier references to her age, we must remove around three years from her maturity, leaving us to contemplate a girl of 17, possibly only 16, who had crammed in an extraordinary wealth of experience, both good and bad, since leaving the workhouse a mere three years earlier.

Unpalatable though this might seem to us today, there is historically absolutely no hint of reluctance on Sophia Daw's part to submit to the Duke of Bourbon's overtures. Undoubtedly she was canny enough to spot the positives from entering into a liaison with a man considerably older than she – and *very* considerably richer in terms of both status and monetary worth. The duke's willingness to install the young enchantress as his 'official' London mistress, with her mass of brown hair, sparkling blue eyes and, it is said, the clearest of complexions, probably needs no further explanation. And thus began the relationship that would, in time, shake to its core the very structure of the post-Napoleonic monarchy in France.

Chapter 2

A Life Off-kilter:
The Bourbon Aristocrat

In one sense the early years of Louis Henri Joseph de Bourbon mirrored those of Sophia Daw's in being seemingly set in stone from the outset. As was the case with Sophia, there was no hint that, in the years to come, his preordained hard-sculpted route through life would be chiselled away to deflect him down a path of destiny wholly unforeseen at the time of his birth in Paris on 13 April 1756. In every other respect the two parts of this fantastically unlikely Anglo-French pairing had absolutely nothing in common, as diametrically opposed as it is possible to imagine. In a metaphorical sense, the distance travelled by the pair along the path to the eventual, and ultimately cataclysmic, collision of their respective worlds was vast.

It was at the Hotel de Condé, principal Paris seat of the princes of Condé, that Louis Henri first saw the light of day. His birth ensured the continuance of the male line of his illustrious family, a cadet branch of the ruling House of Bourbon, represented on the throne of France at the time by King Louis XV – Louis the Beloved – who in April 1756 was in the forty-first year of a reign that was destined to last until 1774. The Bourbon-Condé line descended from the princely house's sixteenth-century founder, the noted Huguenot leader and soldier, Louis I de Bourbon. This first prince had set in train a lineage which would sparkle through the course of several succeeding generations with star-studded achievement, both on and away from the battlefield. In the eighteenth century it was the hardest of acts for Louis Henri to follow.[1]

He was the second child of Louis Joseph, the current Prince of Condé, and his wife, Charlotte de Rohan, following the birth in 1755 of a sister, Marie, who died eight months short of her fifth birthday. While a third child, Louise Adélaïde, was born to the couple in 1757, this was less than three years before Charlotte herself died, aged just 22, following a long illness, leaving Louis Henri to emerge from childhood as the sole male inheritor of the 200-year-old Bourbon-Condé title held by his father. That, in the eyes of his sternest biographical critics, he was seldom to distinguish himself in any particular activity, capability or mindset, other than a talent for mediocrity, was probably not helped by a forced introduction to adulthood – or at least, adult responsibilities – when he was still in his childhood years. It cannot have helped his natural development towards maturity that, in April 1770, when he was only 14, he was married to his distant cousin, Bathilde d'Orléans, six years his senior.[2]

The wedding ceremony was certainly a distinguished affair, held in the presence of the assembled French court in the chapel at the palace of Versailles. In terms of status the couple were well matched. Both were descended to the same degree from Louis XIV, *Le Roi Soleil*, as their respective paternal great-grandmothers were sisters, two of the seven children from the Sun King's relationship with the most celebrated of his mistresses, Madame de Montespan.[3] As a prince and princess of the Bourbon royal blood, they were both entitled to be addressed in the style of *Altesse Sérénissime* (Serene Highness). But the marital union of Louis Henri and Bathilde was certainly not blessed with any lasting degree of serenity.

That a young boy of 14 would find it impossible to adjust to married life with a partner of far greater maturity is hardly surprising, especially as Bathilde had acquired an aura of deepening spirituality born of her father's decision, at the prompting of his mistress, to send his daughter to a convent following the death of her mother in 1759, when Bathilde was just 8.

Shared royal blood status was the only thing she and Louis Henri had in common. It is often written that he 'quickly tired of her' but it is surely just as likely that Bathilde had as much difficulty as he did in adapting to this convenient – to the respective families if not the unhappy couple – marital alliance between prominent branches of the Bourbon dynasty. From all accounts they managed just six months of recognisable wedded harmony – and that's probably an overstatement – before the relationship drifted into one of occasional contact. Nonetheless, in August 1772 Bathilde gave birth at the château of Chantilly, principal country retreat of the Bourbon-Condé princes, to the couple's only child, Louis Antoine, destined to be far better recalled today for his infamous death than he was for his birth.

The arrival of Louis Antoine, Duke of Enghien, a title inherited from his father, appears to have done nothing to repair the fractured relationship of his parents, who had since his birth borne the ducal Bourbon title. As he approached the age of 20 Louis Henri, tall in stature with a long face to match – his portraits have led some to suggest his countenance was not entirely dissimilar to that of a sheep! – had developed a need for the kind of sexual gratification he was denied, and very probably no longer bothered to seek, from a wife whose devotions might well by then have been rooted primarily in the mind rather than the body. Either that or she had simply had enough of his many youthful indiscretions, an obvious embarrassment to her.

By 1778 those misdeeds had descended into scandalous acts of adultery on his part. But it seems there may have been more to the young duke than immediately meets the eye when consulting the historical record. Constructing a more rounded perspective of his character during his brief period of marriage is perhaps helped by studying reports of a bizarre incident said to have occurred two years before his adulterous behaviour came to the notice of Bathilde.

Differing, often conflicting, accounts exist. According to *The Gentleman's Magazine*[4] in London, reporting – as part of a generously sympathetic tribute – the death of the duke in 1830, Louis Henri was 'not deficient in military spirit' as a young man. And neither, judged on this appraisal, was he lacking in chivalric valour when it came to challenging a perceived slur on the reputation of his wife in 1776 when a courtly masquerade ball had been undermined by a dispute which arose between Louis Henri and his slightly younger Bourbon kinsman, Charles Philippe, Count of Artois, son of the late Dauphin of France – and future king.

Adopting its accustomed flowery prose, the magazine described the contretemps and how it spiralled into a dispute with honour – and the potential for bodily injury – at stake as Louis Henri squared up to the man who, half a century later, would sit on the French throne as Charles X:

> The Count, having a lady with him, was followed by the Duchess of Bourbon. She seized his mask by the beard, and the strings snapped; the Count seized the Duchess's mask, and broke it. The Duke of Bourbon, conceiving that the sex of the Duchess should have preserved her

A Life Off-kilter

from rude retaliation, sent the Count of Artois a message [challenging him to a duel]. The duel took place at the Bois de Boulogne [forest], near the Port des Princes. They fought with swords, and the Count of Artois, having made a lunge in which his sword seemed to pass under the arm of the Duke of Bourbon, the Chevalier de Crussol, who was one of the seconds, believed the Duke to be wounded; and on the seconds interfering, the parties were reconciled.

Since guessing, or trying otherwise to establish, the identity of guests was a popular feature of most masquerade balls, this odd episode comes across to the modern-day reader as ridiculous overkill, alleviated only by the fact that neither of the combatants was actually killed! However, if we make allowances for the social mores and demands of the period, we might view the actions of Louis Henri in springing to his wife's defence, or at least that of her honour, in a more favourable light. But there is little evidence of further expressions of support for Bathilde from her husband as the marriage foundered. His adultery had punctured a hole in their relationship every bit as sharp and wounding as a penetrating sword. By 1780 the ill-starred couple had split. Reconciliation was never on the cards and, while sexual dalliances would continue to punctuate the life of Louis Henri, the duke would never marry again.

The patriarchal norms of the day dictated that it was Bathilde, rather than Louis Henri, who suffered the harsh immediate consequences of marital separation in high French society. Cruelly, her reduced domestic status effectively left her banished from the court of Louis XVI – who had succeeded to the throne on his grandfather's death in May 1774 – and very much on her own. It was an isolation which saw her granted initial refuge at the château of Chantilly before the ties with her departed husband's family were finally broken when she found accommodation elsewhere. Life, eventually, would become more interesting for her, thanks in no small part to her financial worth. But it followed a curious route, taking in ownership at various stages of grand Parisian mansions, including the Hôtel d'Évreux (which she renamed the Élysée Palace, now the official residence of the President of France); the secretive birth of an illegitimate child, the product of a liaison with a young naval officer (a clear demonstration, if ever there was one, that she, too, was not averse to the physical manifestation of *l'amou*r); a flight abroad to escape the terrors of the French Revolution; and a conversion from her once deeply-held Christian faith to a belief in, and dedication to, the occult.

Her separation from the Duke of Bourbon in 1780 left him free to pursue – now very publicly – his lengthy affair with the opera singer Marguerite 'Mimi' Michelot which resulted in the birth of two illegitimate daughters, Adélaïde (Adele), addressed as Mademoiselle de Bourbon, who was born in November 1780, and Louise, whose birth followed in September 1782.

The arrival of Louise came a month after Louis Henri had joined the forces of the Bourbon allied nations of Spain and France in their protracted bid to wrest control of Gibraltar from the British. Part of the European theatre of the American Revolutionary War (1775–83) and recalled as the Great Siege of Gibraltar, it was one of the longest sieges in military history, having begun in June 1779. Contemporary references note the presence of both Louis Henri and his princely Bourbon relative (and former duelling rival), the Count of Artois as part of a greatly augmented allied siege force. They record the men's arrival at the allied military camp in mid-August 1782, in time to inspect preparations for the forthcoming 'grand assault,' a huge, final bid to force the surrender of the vastly outnumbered British garrison on the Rock.

The perceived importance of the royal pair's arrival was underlined in an exchange of letters between the military leaders of both sides at the siege, delivered under flags of temporary truce and reproduced in *History of the Siege of Gibraltar 1779–1783*, Captain John Drinkwater's classic account, the first edition of which was published from Edinburgh in 1839.

Sent from his camp at Buena-Vista on 19 August, allied commander, the Duke of Crillon's letter to General George Eliott, who commanded the besieged British garrison in his role as Governor, was, on the face of it, full of respectful courtesy and was accompanied by the present of 'a few trifles for your table, of which I am sure you must stand in need as I know you live entirely on vegetables'. For the commander of a garrison which had been under siege for more than three years, it is not difficult to imagine how such a gift might have tempted a man of lesser integrity than Eliott to surrender to his, and his men's, hunger – and give up the fight.

In case this was not enough, the Duke of Crillon had opened his letter with another solicitous gesture:

> His Royal Highness, [the] Count of Artois, who has received permission from the king, his brother, to assist at the siege as a volunteer in the Combined Army, of which their Most Christian and Catholic Majesties have honoured me with the command, arrived in this camp on 15th instant. The young prince has been pleased, in passing through Madrid, to take charge of some letters which had been sent to that capital from this place, and which are addressed to persons belonging to your Garrison; his Royal Highness has decided that I would transmit them to you, and that to this mark of his goodness and attention I should add the strongest expression of esteem for your person and character. I feel the greatest pleasure in giving this mark.

Later, in similar soft-soaping vein, the wily Crillon assured General Eliott of 'the pleasure to which I look forward to becoming your friend, after I shall have learned to render myself worthy of the honour by facing you as an enemy'. He then referred to the arrival in the allied camp of Louis Henri. 'His Highness, the Duke of Bourbon, who arrived here twenty-four hours after the Count of Artois, desires also that I should assure you of his particular esteem.' In this round-about way, Eliott had been left in little doubt that a major offensive was imminent and warned that he should seriously consider surrendering. The allies were moving in for the expected kill and two princes of the Bourbon royal blood (who would very soon be joined by numerous other French and Spanish nobles among a host of sightseers) had come to watch.

Eliott did not take the bait. Entreating the duke not to 'heap any more favours on me of this kind' in his reply of 20 August, he used a similarly gracious tone to play Crillon at his own game:

> I find myself highly honoured by your obliging letter of yesterday, in which your Excellency was so kind as to inform me of the arrival in your camp of His Royal Highness, the Count of Artois, and the Duke of Bourbon, to serve as volunteers at the siege. These princes have shown

their judgement in making choice of a master of the art of war, whose abilities cannot fail to form great warriors. I am overpowered with the condescension of His Royal Highness in suffering some letters for persons in this town to be conveyed from Madrid in his carriages.

It is not hard to imagine a contemptuous smile spreading across the face of General Eliott as he continued his response to the allied commander: 'I flatter myself that your Excellency will give my most profound respect to his Royal Highness, and to the Duke of Bourbon, for the expressions of esteem with which they have been pleased to honour so insignificant a person as I am.'

There would be no surrender. Whatever Eliott really thought of the young Bourbon nobles in the allied camp, their presence would not shift him – and neither would it make any difference when the massive assault of 13 September was unleashed by the Duke of Crillon's forces. It was a spectacular failure for the 65,000-strong Spanish-French alliance. In terms of both men and ships, their casualties were far greater than the losses inflicted on Eliott's garrison. It was the beginning of the end for the drawn-out siege. By February 1783 it was over.[5]

General Eliott's effusive tribute to the abilities of the young Bourbon aristocrats, 'which cannot fail to form great warriors', was, either by design or mistaken belief, wide of the mark in the case of the Count of Artois. It is generally accepted that Charles Philippe had attended the siege 'for the ride', a mere distraction rather than a genuine desire to further a military career. Such a motive would have been entirely in keeping with the life of idle dissipation he had pursued as a young man. However, judged on later events in which he displayed a courageous relish for military endeavour, the same can probably not safely be said of Louis Henri. There are reports, supported with little in the way of factual detail, that he took an active role in the siege and was among the huge number of allied combatants wounded in the fighting.

The wound he sustained appears to be have been to his right shoulder, the result of a musket ball passing through it, a disabling injury which, certainly in later life, restricted movement of his arm so that he needed help with dressing his hair, knotting his cravat and undertaking other tasks which would normally require him to raise the arm above his shoulder. This was the first of three significant injuries suffered by Louis Henri during the course of his life – and considerably relevant today when considering the controversial nature of his death in 1830.

Seven years after the siege the Bourbon dynasty in its entirety collapsed. The extraordinary backdrop to the storming on 14 July 1789 of the medieval fortress and prison at the Bastille in Paris, mighty symbol of French royal power – *abuse* of power in the eyes of the revolutionary insurgents who attacked it – and attendant aristocratic privilege is an event as well-chronicled, and debated, as any in the eighteenth-century history of Europe. In the years that immediately followed, France was a nation in the grip of tumultuous turmoil, the period historians would later call the Reign of Terror. And *la Terreur* was about as bad as it could possibly get for any member, close or outlying, of the humbled royal house of the *ancien régime*.

This left the Bourbon-Condé dynastic branch very much in the revolutionary firing line or, to put it more accurately, in the menacing glare of *Madame Guillotine's* overworked blade. Since 1740 the Prince of Condé, Louis Joseph, had fulfilled the role of *Grand Maître de France*, head of the royal household, as close to the royal family as anyone at the Bourbon court.

Whichever precise date is preferred for the start of *la Terreur* – and there is no real consensus among historians – the three generations of the Bourbon-Condé male line did not hang around to witness its bloody progress. Louis Joseph, his son, Louis Henri, and grandson, Louis Antoine, together with the remainder of the prince's family and his long-time mistress, Maria Caterina Brignole, estranged wife of Prince Horace III of Monaco, had all joined the flight from France of those among the aristocratic elite who, no matter the cost to their dignity and wealth, were determined to deny the revolutionary executioners in Paris the pleasure of lopping off their respective noble heads. They had wasted no time getting out of the heat, leaving at the first outbreak of civil disturbance in that momentous month of July 1789.

They would not witness the king's enforced period of constitutional monarchy at Versailles, a concept despairingly alien to the Bourbon notion of absolute rule by divine right, which lasted until the abolition of the monarchy itself in September 1792, and the subsequent executions the following year, on 21 January and 16 October respectively, of the 38-year-old Louis XVI and his 37-year-old queen, Marie-Antoinette.

Instead, the Condé nobility had sought out, and were receiving, the protection of those European nations willing to offer them exile.

Leaving Versailles on the night of 19 July in a procession of three carriages and a small escort of horsemen, the prince's entourage had initially headed for the relative, but declining, security of Chantilly. Having rested at the château, the fleeing Condé party then continued north via Péronne, Valenciennes and Mons to reach Brussels, a city then part of the Southern Netherlands. Apart from a short period of French rule in the 1740s, Brussels had been under the control of Austria since the transfer of sovereignty from Spain to the mighty House of Hapsburg in 1713. For the escaping Condé nobles the city was the first of several major staging posts along the route of their flight from Paris, a journey that would eventually take Louis Joseph's refugees to the Rhineland and the safe royalist haven of Coblenz.

While self-preservation was understandably the prime motivation for moving this far from the French capital – a distance of around 400 miles, without taking into account lengthy detours en route – this was in no sense a cowardly retreat. The Prince of Condé had served his country with distinction as a general in the complex hostilities of the Seven Years' War (1756–63), France's final involvement as a monarchical state in a confrontation between coalitions of the great European colonial powers. In that epic encounter, a virtual world war fought on five continents, Louis Joseph had more than proved his military credentials. Now, exiled and deprived of access to most of his vast fortune, he had resolved to organise from afar an army of resistance to the new order in Paris. By 1791 he had set in being the *Armée de Condé*.

Coblenz (the modern-day German city of Koblenz) was as good a place as any for Louis Joseph to raise his army. The city was presided over by Prince Clemens Wenceslaus of Saxony, since 1768 the Archbishop-Elector of Thier – the last to hold the office in what would prove the dying years of the centuries-old Holy Roman Empire. Louis XVI was Clemens Wenceslaus' nephew. Deeply worried by the removal of the French monarchy and the threat it posed to his territory, the elector opened the doors of Coblenz to forces opposed to the republican regime. Coblenz duly became a hotbed of resistance, a magnet for the exiles.

While it was one of several *émigré* field armies, the corps assembled by the Prince of Condé, 25,000-strong at the outset, would be the only

A Life Off-kilter

one to survive the War of the First Coalition, the initial (1792–97) period of what are recalled as the French Revolutionary Wars, a prolonged series of engagements which pitted several European monarchical powers, often fighting with a serious dearth of co-ordinated strategy, against the French First Republic. The eventual inclusion within its officer ranks of Louis Joseph, Louis Henri and Louis Antoine, three directly descending generations of the same noble family, was remarkable enough; the fact that at times they fought together in the same campaigns endowed the *Armée de Condé* with a uniqueness of composition which can rarely, if ever, have been matched in any other war.

Jacques Delille, the contemporary poet known as 'France's Virgil', was sufficiently moved by this remarkable feat to wax lyrical in rousing lines of verse which recalled the famous May 1643 victory for a French army led by Louis II de Bourbon, *le Grand Condé* (1646–86), who, as the Duke of Enghien, defeated Spanish forces at the Battle of Rocroi near the end of the Thirty Years' War, a decisive outcome which had saved France from invasion by its enemy:

> *Condé, Bourbon, Enghien, se font d'autres Rocroi.*
> *Et prodigués d'un sang chéri de la victoire,*
> *Trois générations vont ensemble a la gloire.*

An English translation, while lacking the rhythmic quality of the French, still conveys its spirit:

> Condé, Bourbon, Enghien, make another Rocroi;
> And, lavish with the cherished blood of victory,
> Three generations go together to glory.

Unfortunately for Louis Joseph, a prince in need of closely aligned foreign partners if he was to carry the fight to the enemy, his army also bore what amounted to a uniqueness of purpose, one that was largely shunned by those it fought alongside. There was no shortage in Europe of anti-revolutionary allies for the prince's corps but the principal aims of these nations was to keep the republican revolution firmly within the confines of France while, hopefully, gaining new territory from a vanquished foe as they prosecuted the war. There was markedly less allied interest in launching a full-scale invasion of France in a bid to topple the revolutionary government and restore the monarchical status-quo – the overriding aim of the prince.

This divergence of purpose led increasingly to a maelstrom of friction and mistrust in the *Armée de Condé* among those countries from whom Louis Joseph sought not only military partnership but also the funding to secure the continuation and development of his *émigré* force. This was especially true when it came to the prince's relationship with Austria, the Condé army's principal battlefield partner during the war. It soured to such an extent that at one stage the Holy Roman Emperor, Francis II, ordered the arrest of Louis Joseph for insubordination. Knowing their place as an exiled band of aristocrats fighting from within a foreign army was evidently a problem for the Condé corps, laden as it was with a wealth of some of the highest-ranking French nobility and – in common with the other *émigré* forces – led by officers of the former French royalist armies who had fled the revolution to oppose it from afar. It did not assist their cause, nor ease relationships with foreign allies, that many insisted on being paid on a par with the remuneration they had previously enjoyed in the service of their deposed king.

At their vanguard the three Bourbon-Condé nobles, father, son and grandson, fought with no small degree of valour in the campaigns of 1792 and 1793 at several battles in the Black Forest region. For the Duke of Bourbon, upon whom our focus must again fall, the fighting towards the end of 1793 at the village of Berstheim (today part of the Bas-Rhin department in north-eastern France), a notable engagement in the Rhine Campaign of 1793–94, may have represented his finest hour in the revolutionary wars but it came at a heavy personal cost. Accounts published early in the nineteenth century tell how Louis Henri was at the head of the second and third division of cavalry during an offensive led by his father against massed republican forces. They describe how he launched a spirited charge against the enemy's own cavalry.

Recalling the battle as part of its obituary reportage in 1830, *The Gentleman's Magazine* wrote that, 'impelled by the ardour of the moment', he had 'rushed forward with only a few followers when the Republicans, taking advantage of the circumstances, immediately surrounded him. The contest was bloody and the Duke was severely

A Life Off-kilter

wounded but, the rest of his troops coming up, the enemy took to flight, leaving their artillery in possession of the Royalists.'

Assuming this to be an accurate account of the incident, and not one overly respectful of Louis Henri's aristocratic status and thus prone to exaggerated praise, we may conclude that, in this period of his life at least, the Duke of Bourbon was possessed of both gallantry and a dedication to serve the cause of his father and the deposed French monarchy. The wound he sustained at Berstheim, the result of a sabre slash, was certainly serious. His left hand was mutilated, with, according to some sources, 'several fingers' removed. It was another disabling wound, inevitably restricting use of his hand. As with the shoulder injury sustained earlier at Gibraltar, it would later acquire considerable added significance at the time of his death.[6]

Yet it seems not to have overly hindered him as the revolutionary wars closed in on the nineteenth century. He was at the head of cavalry in his father's *émigré* army until 1796.

However, in 1795 we find him temporarily in England. Having landed on the Isle of Wight (see chapter 3) he went to London to help prepare for the ultimately ill-fated counter-revolutionary invasion of France, launched on 23 June that year with a combined French *émigré* and British naval crossing of the English Channel to the Quiberon peninsula in Brittany. Organised in support of the royalist uprisings of Chouannerie and the Vendée, the invasion – culminating in the bloody Battle of Quiberon – was a disaster for the royalists, with more than 11,000 of the monarchists either killed or taken prisoner by the revolutionary forces.

While the Condé army was represented at this botched attempt to aid the royalist cause, Louis Henri did not sail with the invasion fleet to Brittany. But his role in helping to plan the attack, and his commitment to the counter-revolutionary struggle in general, meant that he was held in high esteem by his Bourbon peers. This much is evident from a letter sent to him on 24 June, the day after the Channel crossing, by the exiled king, Louis XVIII, the former Count of Provence, writing from Verona in the Republic of Venice. Just sixteen days had elapsed since Provence had succeeded (in the eyes of the monarchists) his tragic young nephew, Louis XVII, as titular ruler of France. Tuberculosis had led to the death of the imprisoned 10-year-old boy whose own nominal reign had lasted a little over two years since the execution of his father, Louis XVI – during which period Provence had 'ruled' as a self-appointed *émigré* regent.

This king without a throne was clearly in melancholic mood as he penned his letter to Louis Henri:

> My cousin,
>
> I am very sensitive to the part you take in my just pain; it sweetens the bitterness a little bit. I am well [aware] that you fought for the late king, my lord and nephew, but I hope that it is not at the same price; your blood is too precious for the State and for me, so that I do very much desire God to spare it. Always count on the true esteem and friendship with which I am, my cousin, your very affectionate cousin,
>
> Louis

Whether or not the Duke of Bourbon found the content of this somewhat despairing letter inspiring is a matter for conjecture. Certainly, no amount of rallying from a monarch in name only was going to help the military endeavours of the armies now fighting under his banner. In 1796 Louis XVIII would be forced to flee Verona for a further period of harried refuge elsewhere when French republican forces under Napoleon Bonaparte invaded the Republic of Venice.

The active strength of the Condé corps varied according to the demands placed upon it by the allied armies. It underwent several reorganisations and was passed from one paymaster to another, in service with the Russians from 1797, then transferred to the pay of the British. The latter dissolved the corps in 1801 as the revolutionary wars that had spiralled across vast tracts of the European continent – and well beyond – neared conclusion, just a few days short of a decade after they had begun, with the ending of the War of the Second Coalition (1798–1802).

Amid the plethora of territorial changes confirmed by the treaties of Lunéville (1801) and Amiens (1802), the French republic emerged intact, unbowed and strengthened under its new First Consul, and soon to be emperor, Napoleon.[7] For the *Armée de Condé*, despite its comparative longevity and undoubted valour across several campaigns, the whole venture had proved a vainglorious failure, the corps' involvement in the

A Life Off-kilter

wars against the republicans succeeding only in heightening ill-feeling and violence in France towards the aristocratic elite.

While the three Condé nobles – the prince, his son, Louis Henri, and grandson – Louis Antoine, all survived the wars, the status of their once mighty familial house had been shaken to the core. Their own futures were again at stake, exposed once more to the exigencies and savage desires of the anti-monarchists in their native land. A triumphant return to France was now no more than a distant – a *very* distant – dream. For the Prince of Condé, the Duke of Bourbon and the Duke of Enghien the fighting was over. But further, bitter, misfortune lay cruelly in wait.

A new land of royalist refuge had beckoned for Louis Joseph and Louis Henri; it offered them rest and recuperation. By 1802 they were exiled in Great Britain. Two years later, while residing with his father at the Palladian magnificence of Wanstead House, near Chingford in Essex,[8] Louis Henri learnt that his son, the 31-year-old Duke of Enghien, had been arrested by French revolutionary forces at Ettenheim. It was April 1804 when Louis Henri read the disarming news in *The Morning Herald*. By then events had already moved on at a startling pace, too quickly for the London paper to keep up. Soon afterwards, the increasingly anxious Duke of Bourbon heard from the similarly exiled Count of Artois, paying him a visit at Wanstead, how devastatingly dramatic those events had been. On 21 March Louis Antoine had been executed – murdered in the eyes of many – by a firing squad in the torch-lit moat of the Château de Vincennes, near Paris, his body bundled unceremoniously into a pre-dug grave.

Like his father and grandfather, the young duke had commanded units of the *Armée de Condé* with courageous distinction. Unlike them, he had not sought refuge in Britain. Instead, having secretly married Charlotte Louise de Rohan, niece of the Cardinal de Rohan, a matter of weeks before his arrest, he had set up home just east of the French border at Ettenheim in Baden-Württemberg, Germany. That proximity to France and Louis Antoine's aristocratic pedigree combined to snare him in a web of intrigue which falsely linked him with a new royalist conspiracy to overthrow Napoleon and restore Bourbon rule – a trumped-up charge of treason.[9]

Despite lacking proof of Louis Antoine's involvement in the plot, and allegations that he several times made secret trips into France as part of its preparations, the order for the duke's arrest was issued from Paris. It was not long before dragoons of the revolutionary forces, crossing the Rhine in secret and surrounding his house, had taken Louis Antoine prisoner. By March 1804 he had been moved, via Strasbourg, into the château at Vincennes to await his fate.

The duke was tried by a hastily-convened military commission under General Pierre-Augustin Hulin. A staunch republican, the general had taken part in the storming of the Bastille. On the face of it, Louis Antoine represented everything he had despised about the old order in France. The fact, eventually recognised by his captors, that there was no evidence of the duke's complicity in the conspiratorial bid to reinstate monarchical power was not enough to save him. Louis Antoine's status as a Bourbon aristocrat who had fought against the French republic in the recent wars and was believed, or at least said, to be lending his support to a new European coalition planning to oust Napoleon, was enough to keep him in the dock. And yet Hulin was prepared to forward to Bonaparte an appeal by the duke for mercy.

It is usually accepted that the general was in the act of drawing up the appeal document when he was stopped summarily from doing so by the higher authority of Anne-Jean-Marie-René Savary, the general commanding the body of gendarmes specially set up to guard the First Consul. While he later denied this, Savary is frequently credited with condemning the duke to death.

But on whose authority was *he* acting? Did the order to kill Louis Antoine, no matter what the evidence against him dictated, come from Napoleon himself? Not according to one contemporary source. More than a decade after the infamous execution at Vincennes, Irishman Barry O'Meara was serving between August 1816 and July 1818 as Napoleon's doctor during the toppled emperor's imprisonment by the British on the remote South Atlantic island of St Helena. His letters and journals from this period offer a fascinating historical perspective – but come with a warning. O'Meara, whose high-profile feud with Hudson Lowe, governor of St Helena, has been discussed at length during the past two centuries, was an out-and-out Bonaparte sympathiser, a champion of the once mighty French ruler.

According to O'Meara in his two-part 1822 book, *Napoleon in Exile or A Voice from St Helena*, it was while recalling the controversial events of 1804 that Napoleon told him a letter of appeal *had* been dispatched from Vincennes on behalf of the Duke of Enghien. O'Meara added:

> Bonaparte observed: "The Duke had written to me offering his service, and asking [for] a command in the army from

me which that scelerato [villain], Talleyrand did not make known until two days after the execution. Talleyrand is a briccone [crook], capable of any crime. I'd caused [the duke] to be arrested in consequence of the Bourbons having landed assistance in France to murder me." Talleyrand had proposed to cause all the Bourbons to be assassinated and even offered to negotiate for its accomplishment. He demanded a million of francs for each.

So, if this was an accurate account by O'Meara of his discussion with Napoleon, and the fallen emperor was himself correctly recalling the sequence of events leading to Louis Antoine's death – and not merely venting his disdain for a man he had come to regard as 'shit in a silk stocking' – it was Talleyrand, France's Foreign Minister, who was entirely to blame for an execution which had left monarchist regimes across Europe reeling in shock and disgust. The impression given by the Irish doctor's recollection is that Bonaparte would have spared the Duke of Enghien and might well have welcomed him into the French republican army.

The accuracy of events as presented by O'Meara, with support from other like-minded sources, is, at the least, debatable. Other versions insist that Napoleon, despite pleas for Louis Antoine's pardon by the First Consul's wife, Josephine, was adamant the young duke should die.

Whatever the truth behind Louis Antoine's infamous death, it came as a savage blow for his father when the news reached him at Wanstead House in 1804. His wounded pride at the outcome of the revolutionary wars – and with it his chances of reclaiming the status and trappings he had once enjoyed in royalist France – had been compounded by the disfiguring physical injury inflicted at Berstheim. Now, the metaphorical knife had been twisted heartbreakingly further into his being by the shocking loss of his son. Some have described his life in the years of exile which followed in London as one characterised by apathy, social withdrawal and a combination of odd and dissolute behaviour, with little, if any, saving graces. While the facts do lend support to this view, on its own it seems a judgement too harsh for a man who had lost so much. It is hard not to feel some sympathy for the broken Bourbon duke.

It is from this period that the pen-portrait of him as being 'of mediocre taste, intelligence and character', the description applied in Marjorie

Bowen's 1934 book, *The Scandal of Sophie Dawes*, comes into play. He was, she added, 'weak, amiable, vicious, lazy, with deep strata of obstinacy, pride and prejudice beneath his complacent exterior'. Even the concession that he was 'amiable' struggles to stand out from Bowen's list of adjectival barbs as a redeeming feature, suggesting his amiability might just have been another indication of his lack of moral fibre.

However, setting to one side his youthful, and arguably understandable, breaches of marital fidelity, there is no real evidence of the above character traits prior to the death of Louis Antoine. With the exception of his dubious intellectual abilities, which were hardly of his making, the dismal assessment by Marjorie Bowen, and others before her, of a fault-ridden 'mediocre' man seems only to fit in with his life from the unhappy early days of English exile.

But from this point the gallant, loyal warrior duke had become a thing of the past, betrayed by his increasingly louche and miserly behaviour in London. Largely shunning the company of his aristocratic peers, seeking out the sort of basic, low-cost accommodation they would have considered very far beneath the norm for a man of his breeding, dining on the cheap meat served in the city's chop houses, skulking around theatres until a performance was part-way through and admission was offered at a reduced rate, and retaining only one servant, the reliable Guy, to attend to everything else, Louis Henri, the exiled Duke of Bourbon, had become a drab caricature of his former self, in dire need of a lasting pick-me-up to add colour to his existence. It was fortunate for the duke that Monsieur Guy was on hand to pick it up for him.

He had acquired a taste for the companionship of low-class young women of easy virtue. Sophia Daw is highly unlikely to have been the first temptress talent-spotted by the assiduous Guy at the London brothels for his master's enjoyment, though she was probably the first among them recruited from the realms of domestic servitude. That said, these are, and will always remain, matters for conjecture. But one thing is devoid of doubt. Sophia would never again perform the duties of a servant. While she would more than capably fulfil for Louis Henri the potential for entertainment that had seen her plucked from the Piccadilly gutter, it was more her purposes, her needs and, above all, her ambitions that would now be served by him.

Chapter 3

Entrapment:
A Web of Outrageous Fortune

That Monsieur Guy had chosen well there can be no doubt. Not at the outset, at least. Louis Henri was clearly entranced with his young English charmer who seems to have had no difficulty playing the role of mistress to her noble new benefactor, irrespective of his advancing years and any disappointing consequences this may have brought to the bedchamber in which they were increasingly wiling away the hours. It is possible, as some have suggested, that Sophia's youthful bloom might by now have already lost a little of its sheen considering her life experience up until this time. If, despite the lack of any real evidence, this was the case, there was obviously more than enough glitter left to shine on His Grace.

Sophia had long since mastered the art of seduction – and how to use it fully to her advantage when the opportunity arose. She had learnt that nothing in life was perfect; sacrifices were sometimes required in order to obtain the riches that lay, potentially at least, tantalisingly ahead at the end of that normally elusive rainbow. We will never know the extent of her expectations on realising the Duke of Bourbon was smitten with lust and longing for her. He was a French aristocrat. One day, surely, he would return to France. Before that, he might quickly tire of her, tempted away by another pretty – prettier than she? – playmate. She might not have a lot of time; it made sense to get what she could from him while she had the chance.

This assumes that she had no real affection for the duke, that she was cold-hearted, selfish and grasping at this stage of her life. It may be an assumption too far. We might also conjecture whether Louis Henri, highly experienced in the art of sexual love for his own gratification thanks in part to his many dalliances with 'women of the night', also had the capacity, whatever his physical condition, to please his young mistress's own sensual desires. There is no way of knowing whether there might have been more to their relationship than is generally supposed, though the suspicion remains that there was little commonality of purpose within their respective needs. Be that as it may, it was not long before Sophia had a string of very good reasons to, at the very least, feel a warm sense of gratitude towards Louis Henri.

Once she had proved the lasting worth of her talents in the bedroom, the money began to flow her way. Her lover, generously provided with funds by his father, showered expensive gifts on her so she could begin to look the part of the courtesan. By 1811, three years into their relationship, and despite his own preference for living cheaply, he had found her a suitable place to live, a very fine home indeed in Queen Square, the eighteenth-century metamorphosis of the baronet, Sir John Cutler's former garden in Bloomsbury. Here, Sophia Daw could survey – with immense satisfaction, no doubt – the open landscape to the north of the square formed by the hills of Hampstead and Highgate, rising in apparent tribute to the distance travelled and the heights now reached by the former workhouse girl from the Isle of Wight.

While it would not have been seen as *de rigueur* for the exiled aristocrat and his low-born mistress to co-habit the house in Queen Square's Gloucester Street, it may be supposed he visited this comfortable London address on a regular basis. But if that supposition is extended to allow thought of the house as a 'love nest', a difficulty immediately arises. Sophia was not the sole resident. Her mother came too! Probably for the first time in her sixty years of life, Jane Daw had left the Isle of Wight for onward transportation to what must have seemed a wholly alien world amid the fashionable homes of Bloomsbury. Probably, this was Sophia's idea.

There is plenty of evidence of a close relationship between Jane and Sophia, despite – or maybe because of – the lengthy periods of separation during the latter's teenage years. It would be perfectly understandable if Sophia now felt in need of her mother's companionship and love. Apart from that, she was thinking ahead. She needed to keep Louis Henri onside if she was to hang on to the many tangible benefits the relationship provided. At the same time, it seems she may have been growing tired of playing the one-dimensional role of a rich man's easy lover, who might at any time decide to look elsewhere for his pleasure and cast her aside. Having her mother in attendance was probably as good a way as any of cooling his ardour, making her less available for his sexual gratification, when her thoughts were elsewhere, keeping him at arm's length while being careful not to risk forcing him out of her life.

In this sense, just by being there, Jane Daw probably did fulfil the role of the *duenna* that has been ascribed to her by a succession of writers. But it seems doubtful that she was in any real sense 'in charge' of her daughter's moral behaviour – the horse had well and truly bolted on that a long time before – or, indeed, any other aspect of the ambitious Sophia's life in London. She was there as a companion and confidante, certainly, but surely not as a governess. Miss Daw had reached the stage when nobody aside from her was calling the shots.

And while, no doubt, it felt good to be able to indulge anew in the life of luxury she had earlier enjoyed at Turnham Green as the grandly-kept woman of a besotted male admirer, she was canny enough to know that there was a lot more to be gained from her new circumstances. She had come far but she was not yet the finished product. We cannot be sure whether it was she, seeking to mould her social skills to fit more aptly with her new domestic situation, or the duke, perhaps edging towards frustration at his lover's lack of learned discourse, but the decision was taken: education should be the semi-literate concubine's next step.

She was, of course, starting from a very low base, her formal education at that point having been restricted to whatever she had managed to glean from her workhouse tutors in the basics of preparation for life as a servant. Sophia had lived thus far on her wits. She was certainly not stupid, nobody's fool, and, much to her credit, she seems to have embraced the opportunity to broaden her intellectual horizons. At her noble lover's expense and, it would be good to think, his encouragement, she was tutored not only in the modern languages of English and French but also in Greek and Latin. Her surviving exercise books prove how assiduously she applied herself to the daunting task of assimilating the works of Xenophon and Plutarch, surely an extraordinary feat of learning. No doubt she enjoyed far more the tuition she also received at home in deportment, music, dancing and, in particular, dramatic art.

For two years she kept at her studies, regularly visiting her well-paid tutors at a school in the southwest London district of Chelsea. How many, or few, windows of opportunity were left open for Louis Henri during that period is impossible to say. Did it leave him frustrated, jealous of the time she was spending with her tutors rather than with him? We have no knowledge of the duke's inner thoughts at this time but we may conclude that he remained firmly under the spell she had cast over him. From 1812 he was paying her a hefty annuity of £800, worth somewhere in the region of £54,000 today, to spend in whichever way took her fancy.

Maybe it was she who in that same year commissioned a miniature of herself by the Anglo-French artist Jean-François-Marie Huet-Villiers.[1] Now hung in the *Musée Condé* at Chantilly, it is a charming portrait of the young Sophia, perhaps idealised to an extent but still conveying to the beholder the face of an engagingly pretty country girl, an unfussy image quite unlike any of the grander portraits of her which survive from her later life. Beneath the clusters of auburn curls, her round face is dominated by the large dark blue eyes, crowned by prominent brows, above a handsomely distinctive nose and a pair of wide, thin lips – regular features which have an uncanny ability to hint both at mischief and the innocence that might be expected of a young woman rather modestly attired in a securely fastened simple muslin dress. The muscular shoulders betray a stockily-built girl who is no stranger to hard, domestic toil.

Spellbound the duke may have been, but in 1814 he had departed London and returned to France with his now-ailing father following the dramatic overthrow of Napoleon Bonaparte's French Empire by the combined forces of Russia, Austria and Prussia. Massively outnumbered, the French army had surrendered on 31 March after a day of decisive fighting in the Parisian suburbs. Talleyrand, Napoleon's former foreign affairs minister, long at odds with the emperor's military strategy, had seized control, handing the keys to the city to Tsar Alexander I, allowing the triumphant allies to enter the capital of war-weary France the same day. The Battle of Paris, the final action of the War of the Sixth Coalition, had been brought to a close.

On 1 April the French Senate had set up a provisional government through the prompting of Talleyrand, who was elected its president. A day later the senate had agreed to depose Napoleon from his imperial throne. By 11 April the Treaty of Fontainebleau had formally ended the emperor's rule, forcing his immediate abdication, a prelude to exile on the Mediterranean island of Elba. The official armistice had been agreed and signed on 23 April by the allies and Charles, Count of Artois, on behalf of the French. Talleyrand, acting on behalf of the senate and now firmly pursuing the return of monarchy, had persuaded the coalition powers that Bourbon restoration should be implemented under Louis XVIII, the first, as it turned out, of the brothers of the executed Louis XVI to succeed to the reinstated throne. Twenty-five years of armed opposition to Europe's elitist status quo appeared at an end.

And so the way had at last been cleared by this fast-moving sequence of momentous events for the return of the Condé aristocrats to their native land. As they were reunited with the shattered remains of their old domain at Chantilly, a casualty of the revolutionary years, beginning the first stages of its restoration while finding time to indulge once more in their shared favourite pastime of hunting with hounds, Sophia Daw had been left behind in Bloomsbury with her mother. There had been no invitation from Louis Henri to join him in the land whose language she had so diligently mastered in the hope of one day setting foot there.

Had the drain on his purse of so expensive a mistress – when others could have been obtained at much lower cost and minus their mothers – finally broken the hold she had over him? Had it led to a parting of the ways? Again, we are left with guesswork. The fact was that the duke had left her behind and the indications are he had no intention of ever seeing her again. This had not been part of her scheming for an even better future than the one she had carved out, thanks to Louis Henri's influence, infatuation and income, in London. Sophia wanted more but now, her annuity terminated, she was forced to move out of Queen Square and before long was feuding over money, or the lack of it, with the landladies of the lodging houses in which she sought refuge. It was not going well for Miss Daw; somehow she had to put that right. There was only one way. Sophia determined to win back the affections of her noble lover

But in France the Duke of Bourbon had his mind on other matters. The restoration of the Bourbon monarchy had been agreed on the understanding that Louis XVIII introduced a new constitution for the French state, a condition imposed by the senate and in line with the strategy of the coalition of European powers which had brought Napoleon to his knees. The king had accordingly issued a charter in which many promises were made for progressive policies and structures to reflect the huge swing in attitude and society brought about by revolution and Napoleonic rule. Chief among these was Louis' agreement to a new two-tier legislature, with a chamber of elected deputies sitting beneath an upper chamber of hereditary and life peers nominated by the king. This nod towards an imperfect democracy was to be supported by freedom of religious expression (although Roman Catholicism, badly diminished during the revolutionary period, would again be recognised as the *official* State religion)[2] and, up to a point at least, relaxation of censorship to allow a partial freedom of the press.

The rewards for submissive acceptance of these and a host of other constitutional reforms were, however, substantial. Under the terms of the Treaty of Paris in May 1814 Louis XVIII had been offered a platform from which to rebuild the French nation in the wake of its Napoleonic defeat. The victorious allies of the Sixth Coalition (Austria, Great Britain, Portugal, Prussia, Russia and Sweden) had permitted France to retain its augmented 1792 borders and had imposed no war indemnity measures on the vanquished foe. Just as generous had been a promise to withdraw occupying coalition forces from French soil as soon as Talleyrand, representing the king, signed the Paris treaty to formally end hostilities on 30 May.

But the return of monarchy, albeit in modified form, was widely resented by those yearning instead for the anti-elitist populism of the country's fallen military dictator. Bonapartism, as it would later be defined, remained a huge threat to the introduction of a partial constitutional monarchy. It was not a time to throw caution to the wind, but Louis XVIII failed to tread carefully, quickly alienating his people by reneging on a particularly sensitive promise made in his charter. In a bid to redress a war-depleted French exchequer, he had swiftly gone back on his word to abolish on his restoration deeply unpopular taxes levied on wine, tobacco and salt.

Breaking this key promise, no matter the fiscal arguments he might bring to the table, was an unpalatable move for a populace wary of a return to Bourbon absolutism. While the king's charter had provided for all French citizens to be regarded as equal before the law, it was very wide of the mark in terms of meaningful equality. The document's retention of a substantial prerogative for Louis and his nobles, and the fact that voting for the legislature would be severely restricted to citizens over the age of 40 who paid at least 300 francs a year in direct taxes, were obvious stumbling blocks to a peaceful transition to the new royal order.

It was all to fall dramatically apart in 1815. In late February, Napoleon Bonaparte escaped from his Tuscan exile on the island of Elba just 300 days after being taken there in captivity. Louis XVIII completely underestimated the threat to his throne and Napoleon's assembled troops, greatly inflated by mass defections from the royalist army, marched on Paris, where little armed opposition was offered. The king fled the capital and slipped out of the country,[3] leaving the emperor to make a triumphant return to the city on 20 March.

The Bourbons had been humbled – again. No doubt the shame and misery was felt keenly by the Duke of Bourbon. The exiled king asked him on 13 March to rouse Vendée and other departments of the west in the royalist cause. But Louis Henri found very little enthusiasm there for an uprising against Bonaparte. His powers of persuasion having so lamentably failed, he gave up the fight. Instead, he persuaded himself to take a short sojourn in Bourbon Spain.

Fortunately for him, Napoleon's return to power in France lasted only until 8 July when the monarchy under Louis XVIII was restored for a second time following the emperor's defeat the previous month to Wellington and his coalition allies at the Battle of Waterloo. The Hundred Days, as history would a little imprecisely round it up in recall, was over. In its wake the king would face a host of new challenges as a very different France emerged from what would prove the final chapter of Napoleonic warfare. A new Treaty of Paris, far harsher than its predecessor, saw the nation's borders cut back to those of 1789 and this time the allies of the victorious Seventh Coalition (Austria, Britain, the Netherlands, Russia, Prussia, Sweden, Switzerland and several German states) *did* impose war indemnity measures on the French and left an occupying force of 150,000 in parts of the country, with France bearing the cost.[4]

With wise pragmatism, Louis XVIII pardoned the vast majority of those who had taken Napoleon's side during the emperor's return, guaranteed meaningful religious and press freedoms, embraced wide-ranging constitutional reforms which diminished his monarchical power and saw the wily Talleyrand – for whom the Hundred Days had represented a rare period in the diplomatic doldrums – returned to power in the elevated role of France's first prime minister (*Président du Conseil*).[5] Meanwhile, for Napoleon Bonaparte the days of empire this time had truly crumbled – and he with it. Forced once more to abdicate, he headed for renewed exile, this time on remote Saint Helena, from which he was never to return.

In contrast, the Duke of Bourbon was back in Paris by September – and facing overtures of persuasion every bit as unwelcome for him as his own coaxing had seemed to most of the peasants in the Vendée six months earlier. He may have managed to push his relationship with Sophia Daw to the back of his mind while on his travels. But she had been thinking of little else. Determinedly she had made up her mind to follow him across the English Channel. And in Paris she had waited for him. On the duke's return from Spain, she was ready to pounce.

Shaken by knowledge of her proximity, but unmoved, he studiously ignored the many letters she sent to her 'dearest friend', the lengthy messages of implied devotion she had written, in both English and French, to her 'poor dear', imploring him to take her back. She had learned tact and diplomacy among her proud list of newly acquired skills. She sought to convey to her estranged lover the attributes of a lady of learning, with demure, ladylike manners to match. Her carefully prepared charm offensive was matched by a surprising willingness to wait. And a large degree of patience was, it transpired, a very necessary virtue for Sophia in Paris.

It is a testament to her extraordinary determination, ambition and willpower that she waited as long as she did, spinning her silken web of entrapment time and again in the hope of snaring her prey. Stubbornly, resolutely, he continued to snub her for almost eighteen months. For a woman who, despite her recently hard-won social elevation and apparent courtesy and calm in her repeated entreaties to the duke, was subject to fits of undignified violent temper, it was truly remarkable that she never seems in this period to have exploded in frustrated anger at the rebuffs with which she was constantly confronted. Or perhaps there *were* angry outbursts at his treatment of her, but others were around to feel the heat of her wrath.

For Sophia was not alone in Paris. Jane Daw is adrift from this part of the story, the assumption being that she had returned to the Isle of Wight when her daughter sailed for France. But it seems Sophia travelled, and then lived, with (or close to) a male companion by the name of 'Barry'. Whether that was his first name or surname is lost to the vagaries of history. Marjorie Bowen floats the idea in her book that the full name of this mysterious companion may have been Barry Lyndon, but offers no explanation for this, a hint that the author might have offered it with tongue in cheek. If not, it may be that there has been confusion by someone at some stage with the fictitious character in William Makepeace Thackeray's 1844 serialised magazine story, *The Luck of*

Barry Lyndon, based on the life of the Anglo-Irish rake and fortune-hunter, Andrew Robinson Stoney and later released as a book.[6]

The real-life Barry may well have been a rake himself but the fortune at stake when he arrived in Paris with Sophia was the one she was set on securing from the Duke of Bourbon. Nothing more about Barry, or the nature of his relationship with Sophia, is known. Presumably, he served as her protector and, given the parlous state of her funds at this point, might well have financed her Parisian adventure – bed, board, bonnets *et al.* What he received in return – or perhaps was promised when her fortune was settled – must be left to the imagination but it is likely he did not stay with Sophia for the whole period of her waiting game.

There are reports of angry clashes, possibly over rent arrears although this has never been proven, with the landlady of a boarding house and a consequent eviction ahead of short-term moves to lodgings at 5 rue La Pelletier and on the left bank of the Seine at 7 quai Malaquais. There is no hint of help, financial or otherwise, from the shadowy Barry by this stage. Somehow, as the restored Bourbon monarchy reasserted itself, Sophia managed to find the resources, both practical and emotional, to cling to the ever-lengthening quest for her own Bourbon restoration – the rekindling of her seemingly burnt-out relationship with Louis Henri.

She was unaware that his flames of passion had been burning fiercely for some time, his frustration boiling over at the missing of his English rose. Sadly for Sophia, it was not for her the duke was pining. He had not only found a mistress to replace the troublesome Miss Daw, he had comfortably housed her in the northwest of London at Lisson Grove, Marylebone. From the limited evidence available, we learn that this was another Sophia (though the French variant of Sophie is the more usual form recorded) with the surname of Harris. While it is omitted from many accounts of his life, there are those who tell of Louis Henri, unsettled and restless in France, returning temporarily to London within two years of leaving the city in 1814 and renting a house for a short period in Hertford Street, near Hyde Park. Researchers in France have concluded that it was then, around 1816, that he had met his new love in London, a theory based on the letters of lustful devotion he was soon writing to her from France.

Another explanation is that, prior to his 1814 departure from London, very soon after falling out with Sophia Daw, either by deliberate searching or serendipity he had come across, and fallen for,

Miss Harris. Whenever they met, the duke was smitten – as this letter to her makes clear:

> Alas! How wretched I am now that I am no longer near you. I neither sleep nor eat; indeed, I am in despair and overwhelmed by business. How different from the time when, as soon as I woke, my first thought was to produce [for] you some pleasure! You can be certain that I shall never overlook you and that I shall return to England. But God knows when this will be possible and also how much I desire it, for I suffer cruelly here. And meanwhile, tell me everything that you find of interest. Take care of your precious health. You are so pretty, so lovable! I embrace you thousands and thousands of times. Do not forget your old friend; I am always so attached to you!

Research by French genealogists clouds the details of this relationship by suggesting that Miss Harris twice gave birth to illegitimate children fathered by Louis Henri. According to them, the first child, a girl, lived for only a few days following her birth in December 1817 while the second, a boy, was stillborn in May 1819.[7] These dates sit awkwardly with the known events involving the duke and Sophia Daw between 1817 and 1819, a period in which Sophia finally broke Louis Henri's resistance to her entreaties and then cemented the bond between them in a manner disgracefully unorthodox yet entirely in keeping with her evolving story.

We do not know which of her many letters to Louis Henri crushed his resolve to stay clear of her, whether she beguiled him into believing he was her true and only love, tempted him with pretty promises of specific sexual pleasure, or simply wore him out so that it was, in the end, easier to throw in the towel of surrender rather than continue to wrap himself in the cloak of delusion that she would eventually give up and go away. Whatever it was, he replied to her letter and was soon paying her a visit. It was the first of several. In 1817, as he approached his sixty-first year, the Duke of Bourbon had stumbled feebly into the spider's well-prepared trap.

Sophia had grabbed what she could from life since fleeing the unpromising strictures of her Isle of Wight childhood. To a degree, she is deserving of our admiration for what she had achieved against all odds. Certainly she had used her feminine wiles, and the succession of gullible men who had fallen for the clever tricks of her trade, to get this far. We might forgive her for this. But she was about to take things a huge step forward into the realms of pure, unadulterated self-interest and unabashed personal gratification. Sophia Daw had stars in her eyes.

As the reinstated mistress of a wealthy aristocrat on the verge of a princely inheritance from a father whose life was ebbing away, a man positioned very close to the revived French monarchy, she could see her way to fulfilling an outrageous fantasy – access to the royal court of Louis XVIII. But she could not go there as Louis Henri's commoner English concubine. She needed respectable status. Happily for her, the duke was fully appreciative of this. Indeed, it seems it was he who insisted she must adopt a wholly different persona with a history to match. To do so, she had also to acquire another name. Sophia by now had already gone part-way towards this by lengthening her surname from Daw to what she perhaps considered the more genteel form of Dawes. Her first name, at least among the French, had already, after several years in the country, begun to take on the Gallic form of Sophie with an 'e'. The conversion of Sophia Daw to Sophie Dawes was but an intermediate step. A more fundamental name change was required. To put it another way, she must now agree to be wed.

The plot was hatched. Sophie henceforth would masquerade as the duke's illegitimate daughter and, as such, would find – or have found for her – a well-connected man willing or, if necessary, persuaded to become her husband. It was a means to an end for them both. For Louis Henri it ensured his mistress would always be close at hand, posing as the devoted daughter. For Sophie, it would be her ticket to the court of King Louis. All they needed was a dupe.

More than willing to pursue this deceitful course, Sophie assured the duke that finding a husband would not be difficult. She had, she said, already received one proposal of marriage in that very year, but had turned it down. This was almost certainly a lie but no doubt it reassured Louis Henri that the task of marrying her into 'respectability' would not be a problem. She was soon receiving a great deal of help in this regard. Once she had been presented in courtly circles as the duke's natural daughter she attracted a lot of attention and, at least on the surface, respect from women of high rank. They were possibly a little disturbed by the residue of coarseness, the hint of vulgarity, which she could never quite dispel from her demeanour, but they were prepared nonetheless to make allowances for this chink in her armour.

The story goes that it was the wife of a colonel in the royalist army who first put forward the name of Adrien de Feuchères as the ideal match for Mademoiselle Dawes. A distinguished army officer himself, he certainly stood out from the crowd – and was soon drawn into the web.

In stark contrast to Sophie Dawes' self-serving, duplicitous character, Adrien de Feuchères seems to have been a man of the utmost integrity, devoted above all else to serving his country in his chosen military career. While the family name was taken from that of a town in the north-eastern Ardennes region (a municipality which in 1828 would merge with neighbouring Sapogne to form the present-day commune of Sapogne-et-Feuchères), Adrien was the son of Parisian parents Jean Nicolas de Feuchères and his wife, Jeanne (née Thomas), comfortably well-off members of the city's aspirant upper bourgeoisie. He was born in the capital on 20 November 1785 during the final tumultuous years of Louis XVI's ill-starred absolute monarchy. Baptism had followed at the city-centre church of Saint Barthélemy a few years before the edifice, having recently been expensively part-rebuilt at the behest of the king, was confiscated from the Catholic Church authorities for the 'national good' and then demolished as revolution gripped France. By the time Feuchères had enrolled for officer training at the newly-founded military academy within the magnificent château of Fontainebleau in 1804 the French state was at a crossroads, having undergone the profound social and constitutional upheaval of the revolutionary years. Now, under its expansionist new 35-year-old emperor Napoleon, it was locked in the renewed hostilities of a war-torn Europe.

Leaving the academy as a 2nd lieutenant in the 105th Infantry Regiment for immediate service with the *Grande Armée* in the Napoleonic Wars, Adrien fought at the Battle of Jena, a major success for Bonaparte which contributed significantly to his rout of the Prussian forces in 1806. In February of the following year Feuchères was again in action with his regiment at the bloody, inconclusive two-day Battle of Eylau against the Imperial Russian Army. In the warmer weather of June 1807 the 105th helped inflict a decisive defeat at Friedland on the forces of Count von Bennigsen, a veteran German general long in the Czar's employ, forcing the Russians into treaty negotiations with Napoleon and leaving the rampaging Bonaparte seemingly omnipotent on the European continent without, for a while at least, an enemy in sight.

Feuchères had served his regiment with distinction. His reward was promotion to the rank of captain and a posting to Spain, initially on the staff of the army in Aragon during the opening exchanges of the Peninsular War. Napoleonic forces were now pitted against a new tripartite coalition of allied armies from Spain, Portugal and Great Britain in the struggle for Iberian dominance. Once more the young officer distinguished himself in combat as Spanish forces were soundly beaten by the French under Marshal Jean Lannes in November 1808 at the Battle of Tudela. In July 1809 Feuchères was decorated for his outstanding service and valour, becoming a chevalier (knight) of the *Légion d'honneur*. In September 1813, towards the end of the Peninsular War, he was wounded as French imperial troops mounted a successful night assault against an allied British and Spanish force at the Battle of Ordal. However, he survived the war in Iberia and had been promoted further to the status of battalion commander by the time the Napoleonic Wars finally came to an end at Waterloo in 1815.

The second restoration of the Bourbon monarchy saw him retained in military service, now a highly-rated officer in Louis XVIII's Royal Guard. It seems to have been a smooth transition from the imperialist army of Napoleon I for Feuchères, whose family was aligned to the royalist cause. His transition from eligible bachelor to the prospective husband of Sophie Dawes is more difficult to define. Adrien's motives for pursuing a match with the smuggler's daughter from the Isle of Wight, under the implanted impression that she was actually the progeny of the Bourbon aristocrat who would very soon inherit the title of Prince of Condé on his father's death, have always been a matter for conjecture. This is obscured by his apparently easy acceptance of her situation – he seems to have asked very few questions – and the lure of significant financial gain, with the duke proffering a dowry of 140,000 franks, roughly the equivalent of nearly £7,000, which would equate to more than £500,000 today. Also on offer was an enviable position for M. de Feuchères as the soon-to-be prince's *aide-de-camp*.

On the face of it, securing the hand in marriage of Mademoiselle Dawes must indeed have seemed a very good catch to the ambitious soldier. His precise feelings at the time, however, have never amounted to anything more than an educated guess. Was it ambition pure and simple, infatuation, lust or love? Or maybe, given the complexities of human nature and the manipulative forces the scheming bride-to-be would undoubtedly have employed to get what she wanted, it was a torrent of mixed emotions on his part. Certainly, Adrien de Feuchères appears wholeheartedly to have embraced his impending marital union with the beguiling Sophie.

We can imagine equal enthusiasm on her part. Considering Sophie's voracious sexual appetite there can be little doubt that she would have relished the prospect of marriage to the dashing 32-year-old officer. His portrait confirms he was a man of obvious military bearing, just a handful of years her senior. However, Adrien's good looks and potential as a lover were of secondary importance. He would serve her primarily as a pawn, a dupe, a cuckold. He was the means to an dishonourable end, a convenient pathway, as downtrodden as it gets, to her ultimate fantasy of recognition, status and power way beyond the dreams of virtually all her female contemporaries and wholly unimaginable for the average English workhouse graduate.

The preparations for the nuptials, indelibly stamped by the manipulative hand of Sophie Dawes and lacking any apparent meaningful input from Feuchères, were truly a curious affair. In order to achieve her social aspirations in France – for her, the whole point of the marriage – Sophie had first to ensure legal recognition in that country for the impending union. To do this she had to prove her identity to the satisfaction of the civil authorities in Paris. It was tricky. Hiding the true facts about her birth and early life on the Isle of Wight was essential to the masterplan. Revealing, or even hinting, that she was the daughter of an alcoholic fisherman-smuggler and, as a child pauper, had received her initial education in the island's House of Industry en route to an expected servant's career was out of the question for someone seeking the very highest degree of social acceptance in what was now her adopted land.

But neither, for fear of being caught out, could she swear to the Parisian authorities that she was a bastard child of the Duke of Bourbon, despite having previously assured her future husband, among a good many others, that the Bourbon-Condé aristocrat really *was* her father. Her chosen method for getting round these seemingly intractable obstacles stands as one of the most extreme examples of the extraordinary lengths she would go to in order to fulfil her ambition. To describe it as audacious is simply not enough. Flabbergasting is the far better fit!

Entrapment

Sophie was now a practiced liar. Her devious mind came up with its greatest feat of mendacity yet as she gave the city authorities a hugely fictionalised account of her background in a statement dated 4 June 1818. About the only truthful fact she provided was her city centre home address (thanks to the generosity of Louis Henri) in Paris – at No. 9 rue Neuve des Capucines. The rest were lies. Insisting she was actually 'Mme. [Mrs] Sophie Clarck', she claimed nevertheless to be the *daughter* of Richard Clarck and Jeanne Walker, formerly of Southampton. She was, she said, the widow of William Dawes, an agent of the British [East] India Company, who she claimed had died at 'Cap' [the French word for Cape] on 16 June 1812. For anyone unaware of her true history this would not have seemed a doubtful truth.

The likelihood is that 'Cap' was a reference to the Cape of Good Hope. If so, it would have appeared entirely plausible for her 'late husband' to have concluded his life there in 1812, six years after the British, at the Battle of Blaauwberg, had wrestled back control of the Cape colony from the Batavian Republic, then a Dutch vassal of France. Britain had continued to occupy the colony, formerly under Dutch East India Company rule, until 1814 when it was ceded to the country from the Netherlands on a permanent basis. If Sophie's former husband actually had existed and really had been an agent of the British East India Company, he might well have been in the colony at the stated year of his death. *Prima facie*, her story seemed credible.

As for Sophie's age at the time, her earliest biographers seemed convinced that she had lied about this as well in claiming to be a full three years younger than she actually was. It is fair to say that she could have 'plucked from the air' just about any year for her birth that suited her. It was widely believed she had done exactly that in October 1817 when presenting herself for adult baptism in the Protestant faith at St Mary's Church, Newington, in central London, and had maintained this apparent deception in subsequent discussions about her marriage settlement and in dealing with the civil formalities which preceded the union. What is missing from these accounts is the precise age she was claiming to be. In 1817 the parish registers from St Helen's had been scoured in vain for a record of her birth. Neither at the time of her baptism nor in the period prior to her marriage a year later was there anything to disprove what she insisted was her year of birth.

It is safe to assume Sophie would not have pointed anyone in the direction of those tell-tale record books at the Isle of Wight House of Industry. This was a part of her life she was determined to bury for good. The workhouse books, anyway, would only have resulted in utter confusion had the searcher been sufficiently diligent to study the *whole* record of Sophie's extended relationship with the Newport workhouse. Whether she would have felt any certainty herself about her true age is, as discussed in the opening chapter, something of a moot point. At this stage of her life it would almost certainly have suited her to 'remove' the three additional years she had mysteriously acquired on leaving the Isle of Wight institution in 1805 – thereby confusing historians ever since!

The issue of her true age apart, had the Paris authorities dug a little deeper it would have become clear that, despite William being a name commonly given to male members of her extended Isle of Wight family, Sophie had never been married to a William Dawes, or to anyone else. She was not a widow at all. Dawes was her maiden name, taken from that of her real father, Richard (Dicky). As for Richard Clarck and Jeanne Walker, the couple she declared to be her parents, they were pure invention. True, there *was* a Dawes-Clarck connection within her family, but this had come about through the recent marriage of her elder sister Mary-Anne to a man named Bernard Clarck. It was a highly convoluted deception and a high-risk act of daring.

Despite the questions it begged, Sophie apparently was never challenged by the Parisian officials. Was it sloppiness on their part or an aura of credulity on hers? Perhaps there was inducement, financial or otherwise. All are possible. Having got away with this outrageous misrepresentation of the facts in France, she set sail for England where she had determined the wedding would take place. There was much to do and very little time to do it, such had been her desire to get the whole thing behind her as quickly as possible and avoid delaying a day longer than necessary the glittering gateway it would open to her promised land of plenty. But there would be no low-key, quick and easy wedding ceremony. English law at that time demanded a religious celebration to sanctify the marriage but there was, Sophie calculated, no time for banns to be read in London. It had to be a church wedding but still she wanted it all done within a matter of a few weeks. A marriage by licence would achieve this goal.[8]

Entrapment

On 25 July she presented herself to the Church of England authorities in the London diocese ready to complete, on behalf of herself and Feuchères, the form of 'allegation' which served as the pre-requisite for obtaining a licence to marry. What was going through her mind as she swore under oath that she knew of no lawful impediment to prevent the union? Technically, of course, there was no impediment – neither party was already married, nor were they related or in any other way prevented by canon law from being joined in matrimony. Their names were entered correctly on the form, although Sophie reverted to the English form of her first name, Sophia with an 'a', when signing the document. The problem, had it been spotted, was that she quite clearly used the surname *Dawes* rather than signing as the invented Mrs *Clarck*.

We are left to ponder whether, as the declared widow of the late – and entirely fictional – William Dawes, she had meant in Paris to describe herself as Madame Dawes rather than use the surname of her – similarly conjured up – parents, the Clarcks. Or maybe the Parisian scribe, in attempting to record in writing the information she'd fed him back in June, had simply misinterpreted the family details she had provided. Given the extent of its intricate weaving, Sophie's web of deceit was always vulnerable to ending up in a tortuous tangle.

Happily for her, there were no awkward questions from the London diocese about her background. She was merely asked to confirm that she had been living for four weeks in the parish where the wedding was to take place – at St Martin-in-the-Fields' neo-classical parish church. This, at least, would be the venue for the principal ceremony under Protestant rites. Adrien de Feuchères' Roman Catholic faith meant a second service with Catholic solemnities would be required. With the form-filling completed, the soon-to-be bride wrote to Louis Henri, her French lover, protector and partner in shameful subterfuge, happily telling the duke that she was 'only awaiting the arrival of M. de Feuchères to conclude this important match'.

From Sophie's grasping perspective, this impatience to wed had no doubt been heightened by the news that Louis Henri had succeeded to the august title of Prince of Condé following the death of his father on 13 May, three months short of his eightieth birthday. Louis Joseph's physical and mental health had declined rapidly in the years since he and his son had returned prematurely triumphant to France in 1814. His glory was in his past and, when he was awake, which was not very often, the past was where he preferred to reside in his final years. A telling depiction of the old prince at Chantilly was drawn in 1906 by the French author Raoul Arnaud. It was a sad comment on the once-proud Bourbon *émigré* who had hastened out of France in 1789 to organise royalist resistance to the revolutionary regime which had taken the Bastille, and to lead his fellow emigrant troops into a battle-royal for Bourbon monarchical restoration. Misguidedly, he had believed it might prove every bit as glorious as the stunning military achievements of his seventeenth-century ancestor Louis II de Bourbon, *le Grand Condé*.

Arnaud wrote that the prince 'revered the word emigration as if it were a household god ... he was not quite sure as to whether he had ever had a grandson; he only knew that his family had somehow inherited the glory of a long-departed Condé whose name he could no longer remember.'[9] Added Violette Montague in *The Queen of Chantilly*: '[Louis Joseph] called King Louis XVIII M. de Provence and still bore him spite because hr had not been one of the first to emigrate.'

At least the prince had lived long enough to be told, whether he comprehended it or not, of an event of massive symbolic importance for the restored Bourbon monarchy. On 21 January 1818 the remains of the executed Louis XVI and Marie-Antoinette had been exhumed from obscurity at the Madeleine cemetery in Paris and taken for re-burial with due ceremony at the Basilica of Saint-Denis, for centuries the final resting place for the monarchical rulers of France.[10]

Out of respect for his father, Louis Henri shunned the princely Condé title, preferring to be addressed, as before, as the Duke of Bourbon. But for all intents and purposes he *was* the new Prince of Condé and he had, of course, inherited the substantial material benefits – land, property and a vast financial fortune – which accompanied it. With virtually no prospect now of him marrying again and producing an heir, it seemed certain he would be the last of the Bourbon-Condé line This was the icing on the English fortune-hunter's proverbial cake. We can therefore imagine the news of Louis Joseph's death reaching Sophie in a mood of disrespectful elation. She was now the mistress of a royal prince, whether he was using the title publicly or not. The potential rewards for her patience and persistence were now sky-high.

In London, as her wedding day approached, it is probable that she maintained to those who knew nothing of her history, the pretence of her manufactured background – repeating to an equally unquestioning audience of inquiring officialdom in the English capital the same invented farrago of her story she had told in Paris. It suited her purpose; that was all she cared about.

She saw herself as an actress and this was a flawless performance. That there was collusion on the part of her family appears certain. They were not about to muddy the waters which would soon be flowing liberally from the reservoir of their favoured relative's deceit. A prosperous Sophie potentially would stand them all in good stead – if they kept their mouths shut. There is, unsurprisingly, no mention of the Daw family being invited to the nuptials. According to most sources, the Duke of Bourbon would travel from France to give Sophie away in his sham role as her father, there being no Mr Dawes, nor indeed a Mr Clarck, around to do the honours. In reality, 'giving Sophie away' was the last thing on the duke's mind!

It is much harder to determine the mindset of Adrien de Feuchères as his wedding day beckoned. How much, if any, of Sophie's pre-marital cover-up was he party to? The available evidence suggests only that, having convinced himself his bride was the illegitimate offspring of the new prince, he had learnt something of her deceitful declarations – and that something had roused in him a state of sufficient doubt or, at the least, confusion, to seek reassurance from Louis Henri that Sophie was indeed who she had said she was. We can assume he worded his enquiries in a tactful manner; it cannot have been the easiest of tasks. The prince rose to the challenge. The reply he dispatched to his protégé's future husband must have had the desired calming effect on Feuchères, who seems to have made no other attempt to clarify the worrying situation vis-à-vis his future wife.

But Feuchères had been fed a huge lie by the prince. 'I have known the lady from her tenderest infancy; any man of honour may marry her,' Louis Henri had insisted in his response. The gallant soldier's limited resolve in the matter was over. Much later, Feuchères would reveal that he had also received a letter of false reassurance from Sophie, 'informing me that His Serene Highness, the Duke of Bourbon, had brought her up and paid for her education, and that she had every reason to believe that she was his daughter'.

In recent years it has been suggested that Louis Henri might *not* have been lying in his claim to have known Sophie Dawes from her infancy. Moreover, he might really have been her father. The seeds for this fundamental twist in Sophie's story were sown by French historical writer Dominique Paladilhe in his book, *Le prince de Condé: Histoire d'un crime*, released in 2005. Paladilhe referred to the future Prince of Condé arriving in the Isle of Wight's western port town of Yarmouth in 1795, en route to London to help prepare for the cross-Channel invasion of republican France (recounted in chapter 2). This was three years after the most favoured date for Sophie's birth in St Helen's, at the opposite end of the island. The author saw this simply as a coincidence, a view shared by most of those who have studied Sophie's life. However, this has not stopped speculation that far greater significance should perhaps be attached to Louis Henri's brief presence on the isle.

It is probably unwise to rule out anything as impossible when recounting Sophie's extraordinary story, but this particular curve in the road is a particularly sharp one. The theory put forward is that she and her elder brother, James, the only two Daw children for whom no infant baptismal records can be traced, arrived on the island with Louis Henri – if not as his own offspring, then perhaps as those of another French noble – and for some reason were then left in the care of the St Helen's fisherman's family, persuading Sophie in later life to pursue reclamation of a supposedly true aristocratic birth-right in France! Quite why the exiled aristocrat should seek out a humble, albeit locally well-known, fisherman-cum-smuggler on the Isle of Wight to deposit two apparently unwanted children is not addressed, a glaring obstacle to credibility but perhaps no more fantastical than the rest of Sophie's story.[11]

That story now takes us to 6 August 1818, the day of the wedding at the magnificent church of St Martin-in-the-Fields, Westminster, arguably the greatest work from the hugely influential eighteenth-century British architect, James Gibbs. There had been a church on the site since the medieval period before Gibbs' masterpiece was built in 1722–26. While it would become a splendid feature in the northeast corner of Trafalgar Square when this was developed in the 1820s, the church was largely hemmed in by a motley collection of other buildings in 1818. But choosing it as a venue was a bold statement of Sophie's own grand design.

It may be thought a delicious irony that the church of St Martin's, before the rebuilding, was the final resting place of Nell Gwyn, long-time mistress of the Stuart monarch, Charles II. Nell had been buried there in 1687. But was this just coincidence? Or was the choice of St Martin's for the wedding at least part-influenced in the mind of Sophie by this historical link with the woman who had risen so spectacularly from obscurity to personify the spirit of the seventeenth-century English Restoration? While some may view this suggestion as little more than an airy-fairy notion, it could be argued that knowledge of the Gwyn connection to the church may well have been a factor in its selection by the Englishwoman who had so fervently set out to stamp her own extraordinary mark on the spirit of the French monarchical restoration in the early nineteenth century. Did Sophie regard Nell Gwyn as the perfect role model?

If the suggestion that Sophie sold oranges to London's theatre-goers in her teenage years is true, she may already have set out to emulate the Nell Gwyn of popular, albeit unproven, tradition – and especially so if the version of her story which suggests she actually performed on the Covent Garden stage is also a fact. Certainly, Sophie had received some tuition in the dramatic arts and would later aspire to the status of an accomplished actress, but she could never hope to match to any appreciable degree the stage presence of the professionally trained and hugely talented Nell. If there was any comedic element discernible in Sophie's reported thespian repertoire, it seems at times to have been an unintentional by-product of her limited theatrical ability! Sophie's best dramatic performances were always reserved for real life.

Compared with the magnificent setting for the Anglican wedding ceremony, the location for the Roman Catholic equivalent, held earlier in the day on 6 August, was markedly less showy. It took place at the chapel on the corner of Spanish Place and Charles Street (now known as George Street) in Marylebone. Built in the final decade of the eighteenth century, the chapel's existence owed much to the prompting of the Catholic bishop Thomas Hussey in his role as chaplain to the close-by Spanish Embassy. Considering its setting in the heart of England's capital and its strong links to the diplomats of Spain, with whose military forces he had only a few years earlier been engaged in combat, Adrien de Feuchères may well have wondered if his interests and standing as a proud Frenchman had properly been taken into account when the arrangements for the wedding were laid before him by his bride-to-be and her obsequious protector. Whatever his feelings, again he seems to have accepted it without demur.

Given the extent of the skulduggery which underpinned her marriage, Sophie and her family were wise in resisting the temptation, great though this may have been, to spread the word to a wider British audience on her upwardly mobile wedding. Choosing the splendour of the church at St Martin-in-the-Fields for the main ceremony had certainly risked drawing attention to it, but the heyday of the 'scandal sheets', which might have feasted on what would have been a delicious story had they known the real facts behind it, had yet to flourish, Among the respectable news outlets in 1818, the well-established chronicler of current affairs, *The Gentleman's Magazine*, failed to note the event at all in its regular list recording the 'marriages of eminent persons'. It would not be until the death of the Prince of Condé twelve years later that Sophie would be accorded the status of eminence sufficient for inclusion in this popular, well-read monthly digest of news and comment for the educated masses.

But in France, within a few months of her London wedding, Sophie's status in society had been elevated to a degree which carried her 'rags to riches' story into the realms of a fairy tale. As befitted his impending role as *aide-de-camp* to the Prince of Condé, Adrien de Feuchères was in 1819 granted by Louis Henri the title of baron. Thus his wife, the erstwhile workhouse inmate from the Isle of Wight, could now progress her outrageous ambition amid the politest of French society as *la baronne de Feuchères*. Sophie Dawes had never been an *ugly* duckling but her transformation had been every bit as great as the swan in Hans Christian Andersen's celebrated tale – and in one sense of the phrase she was now more than ready to 'swan around' in France, as grandly as she could, as she strove to impress all around her.

Chapter 4

Ménage à Trois:
Scandal at the Château

Chantilly had presented a sorry spectacle when the Bourbon-Condé aristocrats returned. The revolution had dealt the harshest of blows on the magnificent French Renaissance architecture in the château's two constituent parts. Only the *petit château* of 1560 remained habitable, and that to a very limited degree until the start of a modest programme of repair work had begun to restore much of its functionality as a residence. The older, original, *grand château* had been reduced to a monumental pile of rubble. Chantilly was still a great house but the debris of revolutionary fervour served as a mockingly sad reminder of what had been, in the seventeenth-century glory days of *le Grand Condé*, second only to Versailles in palatial rank.[1]

By way of contrast, it seems it was at first a mutual state of happy domesticity for the *ménage à trois* who, incredibly, set up home together in 1818 at the wounded Condé palace thirty miles north of Paris, where Adrien de Feuchères, in his dual role as his master's *aide-de-camp* and, so he had been led to believe, his son-in-law, was installed in a suite of rooms with his new wife. The young baron at this stage was no doubt toasting his good fortune at Chantilly. But the doors elsewhere in the château, frequently opened on request or demand, were all that stood between the house's aristocratic owner and his young role-playing English mistress; the windows into the true nature of their relationship remaining closed to all except the deceitful pair.

Although she found the time to fascinate the many visitors to the château with her unusual juxtaposition of courtly Gallic manners and the hard-edged traits of the English serving girl, Sophie's personal brand of fidelity during this period of her life was to forsake all others and remain faithful to her husband and lover – a challenging task since they were two different men, but one she was energetically able to cope with! She was in her prime, on top of her game, a juggler *par excellence*. If her husband questioned her about the many hours she spent in Louis Henri's chambers, Sophie had the perfect answer. She was the prince's daughter, she would remind Feuchères; why shouldn't she pay her dear father a visit?

She went out of her way to charm everyone, and especially so when the great prize she had coveted for so long was delivered to her – an invitation to the court of Louis XVIII. Before long, she was a regular visitor to the Tuileries palace on the right bank of the Seine, the king having found it politically expedient to abandon his earlier plans to live in refurbished splendour at Versailles. It was of no consequence to Sophie where the royal court was located. It mattered only that she was there, frequently in the company of the monarch, who himself believed her to be of the royal blood, the purity diminished only by what was generally thought to have been an outcome of Louis Henri's idle dalliances while in English exile.

If any courtiers suspected that it might have been with Sophie the prince had actually dallied – the object of his desire rather than the result – they appear to have kept it to themselves. Thus, the newly created baroness was able to steer herself safely through the potential pitfalls of the unimaginably high-risk double life she was leading, both at Chantilly and, increasingly, at the prince's fine new estate of Saint-Leu-la-Foret, twenty miles southwest of Chantilly in the Val-d'Oise. He had acquired it in 1816, primarily for its location on the edge of the forest of Montmorency. It had been an ancestral possession enjoyed by the princes of Condé in unbroken sequence since 1632, until the revolutionary years intervened, and one stocked with sufficient game to satisfy even Louis Henri's indulgent passion for hunting them down.

Saint-Leu had escaped the revolutionary ravages inflicted on Chantilly. Since 1804 it had been in the hands of Hortense de Beauharnais, whose familial links with Napoleon Bonaparte were very close indeed. Hortense was not only Napoleon's stepdaughter, the child of the empress-consort Josephine by her first marriage to Alexandrie de Beauharnais, she was also married to the emperor's younger brother, Louis Bonaparte. When they bought the Saint-Leu estate two years into their marriage they had begun a transformation which endowed their new domain with an expensively sublime picturesque essence, no doubt considered entirely in keeping with their exalted status among the highest strata of the House of Bonaparte. Although there had been two châteaux at Saint-Leu, set within separate parks, Louis and Hortense demolished the older of the two and framed the newer château, dating from 1693, within a united 'English park' of around 200 acres. One of the many works of grandly artistic landscaping projects undertaken by the multi-talented Louis-Martin Berthault, the influences were many and varied. In the upper reaches, the site of the demolished château, a Swiss valley was developed, with thatched cottages, a 'devil's bridge' on a narrow road and a mock-Egyptian monument. Lower down, three small lakes were created. Other features included a river, a pier, small islands, waterfalls and a belvedere from which to admire the fabulous views.

For Hortense, enchantingly pretty, endlessly amusing, the romantic, fairy-tale backdrop of Saint-Leu was the perfect setting for someone happiest when dazzling all around her in Parisian society. Her marriage, in contrast, a concoction entirely of Napoleon's making, was a loveless disaster. Although their union produced three sons,[2] the couple spent much of their married life studiously avoiding each other – a task made the more difficult when the emperor dispatched them in 1810 to The Hague as rulers of the Kingdom of Holland, his newly-created client state in the Netherlands. Louis Bonaparte's determination to run the kingdom independently of France brought the whole enterprise crashing down in 1814 when Napoleon re-annexed Holland to the French empire. The short-lived reign of the king and queen was over – and their marital relationship with it. Hortense eventually returned alone to her French château and, with the first Bourbon restoration in 1814, was granted by Louis XVIII the title of Duchess of Saint-Leu. But she soon fell out of Bourbon favour by supporting her stepfather and brother-in-law, Napoleon's attempt to wrest back control of France in 1815. Banished from the country, she left Saint-Leu for good for a life elsewhere in Europe.[3]

And so, with Louis Henri's 1816 purchase of the estate – wholly unnecessary and extravagant, with Chantilly in need of so much attention – the door had opened for another to dazzle at the château in the Val-d'Oise. It is probable that Sophie felt Saint-Leu's exquisitely charming completeness was even more suited to her constantly evolving grand ambition to grab whatever she could from her life in France than the patched-up ancestral home of the Bourbon-Condé princes at

Chantilly. If she ever reflected on the profound contrast between Saint-Leu's proximity to the woods of Montmorency and the grim forest-edge location of the Isle of Wight House of Industry at Parkhurst, contemplating how far she had travelled between the two, in every sense, it was surely with a broad smile of satisfaction and unbridled joy.

It was not, however, all plain sailing for the smuggler's daughter in France. Sophie might flutter those deep blue eyes in feigned innocence and attempt to make a virtue of her evident lack of sophistication when, despite her best efforts, it caught her out in conversation. It was not her fault, she would imply; circumstances had not allowed the prince, her dear father, to properly take care of her upbringing, though she had done the best she could on her own. This might have convinced some, but it would be stretching credulity too far to suggest that everyone in the household of Louis Henri was taken in by her portrayal of the young ingénue. She was as miscast in this role in real life as she was when playing much the same part in the performances of amateur dramatics she was forever staging, imagining they were to the household's delight. She was far too experienced, far too aware and far too distrustful to carry it off in real life, while possessing too high an opinion of her acting talent (and, it has been suggested, rather too much weight beneath those muscular shoulders) to be convincing in the role on stage. But the part was hers. Sophie was too sure of her talents to stand wisely aside from any role that took her fancy. She was the centre of attention; she very much liked it that way.

As time progressed, and her hold on the prince tightened, she was less inclined to bewitch and more prone to establishing herself as undisputed mistress of her lover's household. It was bound to upset the Chantilly establishment from top to bottom, but Sophie had the ear of the prince, and a firm claim on just about every other part of his now tiring physique. It was her armour in the battle she, incautiously, had begun to wage in the latest round of her ever-expanding quest for recognition – supremacy in the château as its unofficial queen. It might have served her better had she bided her time, sought genuine friendships and respected the status of those around her. But patience was no longer a virtue. She was in far too much of a hurry.

Haughtiness is often the bedfellow of unbridled ambition. To say she threw her weight around would be a masterpiece of understatement. Violette Montagu paints a vivid illustration in *The Queen of Chantilly* of Sophie's frequently hostile relationship with those in and around the château whose low rank in society she had herself endured not so many years earlier. 'The villagers disliked the woman for her haughty manners and gave vent to their spite by throwing stones at her carriage windows,' the French author recorded in her book. Inside the château, the boot was on the other foot for the erstwhile serving girl of English domestic drudgery; it was she who was now handing out the orders – and *s'il vous plait* seldom came into it! Violette Montagu has this to add of Sophie's savagely scornful distrust of the château staff:

> The servants at the château also looked upon the baroness with disfavour; they, too, felt the lash of her tongue and hated her for it. They only consented to wait upon her because they knew that she was mistress in more ways than one. Certain little traits of avarice had already begun to appear. Sophie, suspecting her servants of stealing her firewood, insisted upon keeping the wood box in her dressing room so that she might keep her eye upon it and see that none was wasted. These habits of suspicion increased until she would allow no stranger to go into her private apartments, and kept the key in her pocket or under her mattress. Scenes of anger and even violence were not rare; on one occasion she flung a coffee-pot full of boiling water at the head of her own maid, whereupon the latter seized the fire-tongs and brandished them in her mistress's face.

This is an interesting passage of text in more ways than one. Not only does it provide a graphic illustration of Sophie's unsophisticated, unfair and unwise behaviour in her dealings with the lower orders, it also clearly implies that the servants had by now correctly interpreted the true nature of her relationship with the prince – even if her husband remained ignorant of, or chose not to believe, the gossip that his wife's 'dear father' was actually her lover.

Of course, her interaction with Chantilly's aristocrats was different – but in its way no less disdainful. She would keep guests to the château waiting, sometimes well into the evening, while she fussed for hours at her dressing table to create what she considered would be a suitably regal grand entrance, arm-in-arm with Louis Henri, her dutiful husband a few paces behind.

This is not a pretty picture. It is far more difficult now to retain much sympathy for Sophie. Her grandly elevated status and its attendant privileges, while hard-won, had not been gathered gracefully by the girl from the workhouse. To paraphrase, at this point there seems little argument that she was more deserving of the 'vulgar, wanton slut from the gutter' image that would later be applied to her by writers seeking to summarise her character. But another part of that character was her undoubted intelligence. She had used it well, if not honourably, on her climb out of the gutter and especially when her intellect was finally wrapped in the cloak of formal education. But her appalling behaviour in those early years of married life at Chantilly was clearly not that of a woman who was using her brain. She collected enemies by the score. Each of them was desperate to bring her down.

One at Chantilly with more reason than most to resent the influence over the prince that Madame de Feuchères too obviously flaunted was Adele, the first daughter born to Louis Henri and his former mistress, Mimi Michelot. Since 1803 Adele had been married to the peer and Condé army veteran, Patrice de Montessus, Count of Ruilly. Another of the soldiers prominently employed in the service of Louis Henri as *aide-de-camp*, he was ranked as the prince's 'first gentleman'. He and his wife had their own suite of rooms at Chantilly where Adele's previously unchallenged high status within the prince's household was matched by the close and affectionate relationship she had cultivated with her father. It has been said that on his return from exile it was she who, with gentle persuasion, 'softened the heavy coarseness' of his manner acquired as an unfortunate, albeit probably inevitable, consequence of his prolonged overindulgence in the London fleshpots of Piccadilly and Soho.[4]

Whether Adele had accepted that Sophie *was* her half-sister, a product like herself of her libidinous father's serial sexual dalliances, or whether she too suspected the true reason for the Englishwoman's presence in the prince's household, it can safely be imagined that the overbearing, clumsy haughtiness of Louis Henri's newly introduced protégé was anathema to someone possessed of the well-groomed, sophisticated and dignified courtly presence of Adele. For her part, Sophie was bound, almost obliged, to bristle with indignation at the temerity of anyone other than herself enjoying the confidence of her princely prey, never mind exerting influence over him. There is no doubt she went out of her way to drive a wedge between Adele and Louis Henri.

Ménage à Trois

There were similar, if less personal, grounds for antagonism between the pushy Madame de Feuchères (as she would have been regarded) and the remaining two women of substance in the prince's household, Madame de Choulot, wife of the Governor of Chantilly, and Madame de Quesnay, who was married to another of the Condé aristocrat's principal attendants. The woman of ignoble ascendancy was never going to impress those ladies of noble birth with her lacklustre grace and poise. Hard though she may have tried at first to do so, she quickly resorted to her base tactic – relying on the undoubted strength of the unique hold she held on the prince's weakening resolve to deny her just about anything she wanted. If that upset the ladies of breeding at Chantilly, then so be it. Sophie was in no mood to stand aside.

It was a gamble, but the prince's weakness was a safe hand for her in this game of cards. Safer than many of those she was dealt in the long hours she spent gambling at the real card table. She loved winning at whist, thrived on the risk of losing – and hated it when she actually did lose. Sophie was a very bad loser; she would play on for hours in the hope of averting the ignominy and frustration of paying a loser's debts. Louis Henri, who some say had won her at the card table in London, would sometimes join the game but her insistence on playing for hours on end to seek the ultimate winning hand was often too much for him. As frequently he did when forced to watch her dramatic roles on the stage, the ageing prince was prone to nodding off in mid-game, a source of disdainful irritation to the wide-awake Sophie. 'Oh do go to bed! We can get on very well without you,' she would tell her yawning lover.

But of course, she could not get on without him, not in the grand scheme of her outrageous adventure. It was reckless of her to treat him so unkindly, accord him so little respect in his own home. She was so very sure of herself, her position at Chantilly, her hold over the prince, the undoubted fascination she was still able to exert over those who had not been on the receiving end of her withering tongue (and even some who had been) that she seems to have been quite unable to take stock of her situation, or seriously consider the potential pitfalls of the precarious game she was playing. Sophie was undoubtedly the subject of endless gossip.

It will forever remain a remarkably baffling aspect of her story that it took Adrien de Feuchères so long to confront her with the stories he had heard – by that time from a great many people eager to put the boot in – about her true relationship with the Prince of Condé. But each time he, no doubt gingerly, raised the matter with her, the actress would adopt the role of the cruelly defamed wife, assuring him it was nothing more than slander from wretches jealous of the closeness she enjoyed with her 'dear father'. But the gossip kept coming back to haunt him. Finally, in September 1822, after four years of marriage, he raised the matter directly with the prince, his master. He sent him a letter, dignified in its approach but full of indignant outrage at his wife's 'regal' status and the implications which lay behind it:

> When Monseigneur is not distracted by the hunt, or circumstances do not oblige him to receive [visitors], it is always with Madame de Feuchères that he passes his days. It is she who does the honour of the Palais Bourbon [the reinstated Condé residence in Paris] or Chantilly or Saint-Leu. Everyone knows that only the people she asks are received. At the card table it is always with Monseigneur that she is seated; at the play, or any public occasion, it is always with her that one can see Monseigneur. And what is the title in the eyes of the world that can authorise such conduct? None, Monseigneur, none, and there is the trouble.

Baron de Feuchères must have felt sure of his ground before writing in such forthright terms. Clearly exasperated, he had concluded that there were only two courses of action open to him. 'Either I leave the establishment of Monseigneur with my wife,' he added, 'or I leave without her. Nothing else can be considered. I beg Monseigneur to judge with kindness my cruel position, to satisfy my honour, or to permit that I renounce his service and all its attendant benefits'.

Whether he was then pulled back from the brink by soothing words of reassurance from the prince or whether, as some have implied, financial considerations helped to sway him from his seemingly determined course, the heat appears to have gone out of the situation. For a further eighteen months the baron and baroness continued to live, outwardly at least, as man and wife in the household of the Prince of Condé.

But if Adrien de Feuchères had hoped to see a fundamental change in the behaviour of his wife he was massively let down. Marjorie Bowen, in her well-crafted 1934 biography, suggests that the baron by now probably had lost the last vestiges of desire for any sort of romantic attachment with Sophie. Nothing had changed. His wife utterly dominated the Condé household; the Queen of Chantilly was firmly on her throne, the prince perched, it might be said dutifully, alongside her. She threw her weight around – and in the physical sense there was an increasing amount of it to throw. Never knowing when to stop, she ate far too much, far too often, washing it all down with vast quantities of wine and other beverages. Her appearance, the looks that had ensnared the prince and then her poor dupe of a husband – and a good many more besides – suffered as a consequence. 'No doubt the dwindling of his wife's beauty helped to exasperate her husband's cruel vexation at her conduct and the scandal it provoked', wrote Bowen in *The Scandal of Sophie Dawes*. No doubt she was correct.

The marriage entered into for respectability's sake, at least on the part of Sophie and her conspiring lover, finally came crashing down in March 1824. There had been many quarrels, with very little restraint on either side, between the baron and baroness over the latter's shamelessly unrepentant behaviour since Adrien had sent his imploring letter to the prince. And no wonder – the matter of the extraordinary tripartite relationship at Chantilly was now the stuff of tittle-tattle in the wider sphere of Parisian society, with Baron de Feuchères the unfortunate butt of the jokes. Aware he had now become a laughing stock, openly ridiculed, the honourable soldier had plainly had enough of his dishonourable wife.

The final, indiscreet, confrontation between them was clearly overheard by at least one other person, despite it taking place in the couple's private apartments, for we have a very precise account of what transpired. A furious Feuchères raged at his wife. The row escalated when Sophie ran through her usual deceitful lines of denial, the perverted pleas of an innocent woman victimised by cruel slander. This time her husband would have none of it. He made clear that he believed not a single word she was saying. Angered, frustrated, she hit back, her earlier attempt at forbearance flung rudely aside as she ripped into him with a torrent of foul-mouthed invective until, dramatically, climactically and very loudly indeed, she screamed the words he had demanded to hear from her: 'No! I am not the duke's daughter, I am his mistress!'

Feuchères had wrung the confession out of her. Now he applied the punishment. Some say he already had hold of his horse whip during the row; others suggest he grabbed it from a table. What is certain is that the baron, now out of control, used it savagely, and repeatedly, on his wife. She fought back as best she could, but her fists and nails were no match for the fearsome whip. It will forever remain a matter for conjecture what might have transpired had not the Prince of Condé, who was either alerted to the altercation or had heard it himself, intervened at its height, inserting himself judiciously between the protagonists. If it crossed the mind of Feuchères to turn his whip, some might say deservedly, on Louis Henri, he managed to recover his composure in time to prevent an ugly scene from becoming even uglier.

Adrien de Feuchères, now with firm resolve, turned his back on his sobbing wife and her lover. In his private chamber he took out the handsome dowry he had received from the prince at the time of his wedding to the woman he had believed was the Condé aristocrat's daughter, returning it to the donor via his private secretary. According to some sources, he also left a hastily scribbled note of resignation from his duties as Louis Henri's *aide-de-camp*, although it seems more probable that the letter was sent later. Either way, his mind was clearly made up. It is said that his parting comment to the prince was to warn him of his mistress's capacity for bringing down all around her: 'Beware of her, she is capable of anything'. Within a matter of minutes he had left the château of Chantilly, and his wife, for good.

Sophie had been given a painfully thorough thrashing. She took to her bed for several days to recover from the effects of what would prove her last encounter with her husband. But it is debatable what caused her the most pain – the physical discomfort from wounds that would long afterwards bear scarring reminders or the mental anguish she must have suffered in contemplating the abrupt change in her circumstances resulting from that horrific act of domestic violence. Along with the departing baron, had her grand plans now gone out of the door?

Feuchères' official position in the household had provided her with a legitimate reason for living there. Now that was gone. Married respectability had been sacrificed. Her quasi-royal status as a blood-relative of the prince, one that had accorded her high privilege and considerable influence within the Condé establishment, among polite Parisian society in general and at the court of the king, had been exposed as a fraud. She was surrounded by enemies who, she must have realised as she lay restless in her bed, would rejoice at her misfortune. Whether she regarded any of this as her own fault, or at least partly so, is a moot point.

Ménage à Trois

There is some dispute as to where exactly Sophie's bed was at this point. It is difficult to imagine anywhere other than her own bedchamber at Chantilly in the immediate aftermath of the beating. She surely would have retreated to the nearest place of sanctuary to begin her recovery. But there is an alternative possibility – an address in Paris where she could be nursed back to health in the most reliable and comforting of company. For some time her mother, Jane, had been maintained by Sophie at No. 25 rue de la Ville-L'Eveque. Living with her at this prestigious city centre location was her youngest daughter, Charlotte, who would by then have been in her twenty-ninth year, a probable (given the uncertainty over Sophie's birth date) four years her sister's junior. Even if Sophie did not rush immediately after sustaining her injuries to the recuperative care of her mother and sister, who presumably both felt they owed her an enormous debt of gratitude for lifting them out of grinding poverty, she was certainly at the Parisian address within a matter of days, a tactical retreat for Chantilly's queen.[5]

These were the two familial relationships which mattered most to Sophie, rare links to her Isle of Wight upbringing that she was anxious to hold onto – especially in times of need. This apparent desire to stay close to her mother and younger sister is perhaps one of the more endearing aspects of her character, an indication of insecurity at odds with her usual brash personality. She was certainly in need of this unquestioning support at this juncture in her life.

That her husband viewed his departure as final is clear from his note, dated 6 March, to the prince:

> In order to prove to the public the complete disinterestedness which inspired my resolution, and in order to show that my present position is owing to my own free will, I renounce entirely any favour or benefits I may have received from Your Royal Highness, and I consider myself from this moment having ceased to form part of the household of Your Royal Highness, which for everyone's honour and peace of mind I should never have entered.

This short, dignified statement from a man who, while he cannot be excused from such a savage loss of control, an assault against a defenceless woman, could certainly claim the most extreme provocation in mitigation, was met with a grovelling response from a clearly shaken prince:

> My dear Feuchères, for I shall never address you in any place, under any circumstances, at any time, as other than the truest, the most honourable, the most loyal, friend that I have in the whole world ... my dear Feuchères, in the name of God, for your mother's sake, for the sake of all you hold dearest on earth, come and see me for a few minutes. This visit will not bind you in any way whatsoever, and you will have the satisfaction of knowing you are consoling the heart of a friend overwhelmed by many and various misfortunes. Do not fear that you will, against your wish, meet your wife. The poor unhappy creature is ill in her bed, suffering, and knows nothing of the letter that I am now writing to you. Come, come, my dear friend, Feuchères, come and talk the matter over with your friend who always wishes you well.

This pathetic plea for undeserved sympathy, the hypocrisy of a man portraying himself as a victim to the 'friend' he had for so long deceived, cut no ice with his former *aide-de-camp*, who had no intention of ever speaking with the prince again. There would be no consoling visit. Forced to accept the situation, Louis Henri, dispatched a final note to the resolute baron:

> It is with a lively regret, my dear de Feuchères, that I accept your resignation which you have sent me. As I have always been pleased with your good and loyal services, believe in the constant friendship that I have always promised you.

Meanwhile, the recuperating Madame de Feuchères had also been busy with her pen. Within a day of Louis Henri's acceptance of Feuchères' letter of resignation, Sophie began her fightback. Her strategy was one of breath-taking hypocrisy. She would seek to show the world, Parisian society at least, that she was the innocent, wronged woman, the victim of a scurrilous, disrespectful man. It was all her husband's fault – and he was not going to get away with it. The first of those who, she resolved, must now be reminded of the true facts was Adrien de Feuchères himself. In an apparent state of indignant high dudgeon she wrote to him:

> Your head and your heart have become so perverse that I have no more hope; my impulses of tenderness towards you, you have always treated as sly insincerity; there remains nothing for me to do but to respect your wishes. I know not what happiness you expect to find in the world, but I believe that everyone will find that you might have paid me more generously for years of tenderness. Your poor heart appears to me to be closed to all sentiments for myself, alas – I can only pray and weep that you will see in this last submission to all your wishes unequivocal proof of my true attachment.

Having now got right into the swing of her strategic hypocrisy and righteous indignation, Sophie truly excelled in writing a second letter the same day to her lawyer, a Maître Tripier, in Paris:

> Among the different pretexts suggested to me which might serve as the excuse for a separation between my husband and myself, it would have been kind of him if he could have found one worthy of a man of honour; but unhappily, from the day that he abandoned me, I have only found on his part – as the reward for so many years of affection – persecution and lies.

Since this letter is dated 10 March, it had actually been only four days since Feuchères had, as she put it, 'abandoned' her. No matter, Sophie was now fully in her stride as she told Tripier:

> Meanwhile, to finish everything, he makes me this dishonourable proposition [to admit to adultery with the prince]. I would sooner die than ever confess to recover my liberty by such vile concessions. What! When I am innocent [and] have nothing to reproach myself [for]; am I to submit to fake accusations? No, I prefer to be reduced to beg my bread. With regard to my revenues, if my husband is so indelicate as to forbid me to receive them and even wishes

> to appropriate them for himself, ah well, I will make this sacrifice sooner than I will allow myself to be degraded ...
> I believe that it was necessary to make this declaration to you in writing.

It should be noted that from this early stage of what would be a long, drawn-out process towards legal separation, there is no record of Adrien de Feuchères seeking to terminate, let alone appropriate, his wife's income or to force from her a public admission of adulterous guilt. But Sophie felt it necessary to use any tactic she could think of to repair her damaged social status and hang on to her money, irrespective of the causes of her fall from grace and any further harm she might inflict on her husband. Financially, there was a very great deal at stake.

On 1 April, just a few weeks before Sophie's marriage fell apart, and surely at her prompting, Louis Henri had made the most generous of gestures towards his mistress by bestowing on her the magnificent domain of Saint-Leu and Boissy, earning her revenues from land use and tenancies worth 20,000 francs a year. She had also been promised by him various sums of money from other sources, a seven-figure fortune by all accounts. It is not hard to see why she was desperate to prevent Feuchères doing anything which might threaten this. Legally, it seems unlikely that he could have challenged the prince's wishes, but she was taking no chances.[6]

The marriage had been a bitter experience for Feuchères, the one wrong turning in a life otherwise characterised by honourable distinction as a soldier and, later, politician. Soon after leaving Chantilly, and having in 1823 been promoted to the rank of colonel while still in the service of the prince, he wrote to the War Office in Paris seeking a posting away from the boundaries of his native country, awash with the scandal of his marital break-up. His reputation was at stake. He therefore felt obliged to reveal 'the details of my past life' and recount in his letter the whole sorry chapter of how he had been duped into a sham marriage. Recalling the crooked assurances of a father-daughter relationship given to him, shortly before his wedding, by both Louis Henri and Sophie, he explained how the prince had arranged to pay the bride an annual allowance of 7,200 francs as a token of his parental regard for her, another indication of just how much in financial terms the English adventuress was raking in from both her attachment to the prince and the clearly lucrative marriage to Adrien.

Holding nothing back, Feuchères then explained how he had learned 'from Mme. de Feuchères' own lips ... during a domestic quarrel' of the true nature of the relationship, the revelation that Sophie was really the prince's mistress. This, he wrote, had 'explained certain rumours'. Over a number of years before his disastrous marriage, Feuchères had proved a fine soldier, worthy of a great many high-profile postings as a commissioned officer. But the War Office was unsure whether it could rely on the decision-making qualities of a man who had so spectacularly failed to recognise the murky complexity of his marital status, and for so long.

Much of the French army, under the command of the Duke of Angoulême, was in Spain. It had been mobilised in 1823 by Louis XVIII to aid Spanish royalists in their bid to restore the Bourbon king, Ferdinand VII to the absolutist rule he had lost to a liberal uprising. Popularly recalled as the One Hundred Thousand Sons of Saint Louis,[7] the campaign had been successfully concluded before the end of the year but 45,000 French troops had remained in Spain, effectively as an occupying force. Adrien de Feuchères saw his chance. Spain became his focus.

A Spanish posting would have suited him very well indeed; he was desperate to get out of France and leave the tangled business of legally separating from his wife in the hands of his lawyers. But the vindictive Sophie had other ideas. In her mind, she was the injured party and she wanted revenge. There was no way her husband was going to have it easy. With a little help she determined to see to this – and, as usual, she relied on the aid and feeble resolve of her lover. Just as Feuchères had convinced the War Office that he was worthy of a posting and was about to leave, Louis Henri, at Sophie's insistence, intervened, suggesting to the ministry that Feuchères should be taken off the army's active list and forcibly retired on a miserly pension. The War Office dutifully backed down. The colonel's move to Spain was blocked.

Furious, Feuchères fought back. Again he reminded the army bureaucrats of the facts behind his marital breakdown, his wife's spiteful character and her dominance over the ageing prince. Again he pointed to his proud military record. The War Office blinked – and sent him to Spain.

There is confusion within the historical record about the length of time it took them to allow his request. This is borne out in the biographical works of Violette Montagu, who writes that the application was 'obtained immediately' (presumably without any negative intervention by the Prince of Condé) and Marjorie Bowen, who says it was not until five years later – in 1829. That was the year the baron, after a torrent of mental anguish and hugely embarrassing evidence from a host of eager witnesses to the Chantilly shenanigans which seemed to have eluded him for so long, was finally granted a legal separation from the wife who had betrayed him.

There again, military and other biographical records suggest instead that the newly promoted Colonel de Feuchères was in Spain, with a regional command at Pamplona, between 1824 and 1826.[8] What seems certain is that four years later, in 1830, he was part of the French force which successfully invaded Algiers at the start of his country's long search for Algerian conquest. When, finally, he felt able to return to his homeland in 1832 he had been further promoted to brigadier. Home commands would follow. The soldier was back on top of his game.

But our narrative must now return to Sophie's plight back in the dark days of 1824 following her husband's departure. The reasons behind her sojourn in Paris after the dramatic events of that March may seem obvious – a simple desire to seek repose in the sanctuary of her mother's home – but there may have been more to it than that. It is probable that, in a rare moment of assertiveness, Louis Henri told her she *had* to leave the château. It was simply too embarrassing, too awkward for him anyway, for her to remain there. For an aristocrat of his time to have a mistress was pretty much *de rigueur* but, denied the cloak of marital respectability and no longer able to claim a royal bloodline, Sophie's status was now widely perceived as that of the pretender – the low-born courtesan, the gold-digging girl from the English gutter. The game of cards had drawn to a close, the truth was finally out. She *had* to go.

But the Prince of Condé lacked the kind of resolve so evident in the determination of Adrien de Feuchères to get the hell out of Chantilly. He also lacked the resolve of that of his cheating wife, as she recuperated in her bed, to claw back as quickly as possible the enormous benefits of her life of rich privilege in the prince's household. Louis Henri dithered. It would have been far better had he decided there and then to consign Sophie Dawes to history – his at least. He could have ensured she was very well provided for financially. He was fabulously rich; money was no object. But he was just too weak, her mesmerising hold over him too strong. He invited her back.

Ménage à Trois

Reinstatement was one thing. Respect was quite another. Her banishment from Chantilly had been seen as the right and proper outcome for the hated English interloper. The scandal might have been tamed with Sophie isolated in Paris, away from the glare of hostile exposure at the château. But when she returned to live again at the prince's ancestral home, and under his close protection, polite French society roared its collective disapproval and disgust.

Those she had striven so hard to emulate and then, when it suited her, so foolishly belittle, wanted no contact with her, and no longer felt it necessary to pretend otherwise. With her status so desperately diminished at Chantilly, despite the shield of her lover's exalted status, the inevitable hammer-blow to her hugely inflated ego was struck. Louis XVIII had been alerted by the gossips to the sensational scandal at Chantilly involving his kinsman and Madame de Feuchères. It is said he immediately denounced Sophie as 'naught more than a commoner street-wench, yet tragically bereft of any skills of the trade' – before banishing her from his court![9]

Chapter 5

Power Grab:
Chantilly's Queen Assembles Her Court

It was a desperately bad move on the part of Louis Henri to reinstate Madame de Feuchères in his household. She did not return to Chantilly in chastened mood. As soon as the axe fell on her cherished admission to Louis XVIII's royal court, she began to pester the prince to champion her obsessive desire for speedy reinstatement there too. It must have been uncomfortable in the extreme for the submissive and increasingly enfeebled aristocrat as his mistress sought to nullify the influence of those who might prevent him from bowing to her wish.

The death at the age of 66 of Louis Henri's unmarried younger sister, Louise Adélaïde de Bourbon, in March 1824, had removed one of the principal obstacles to Sophie's advancement. Louise Adélaïde had maintained for as long as she was able a touchingly warm and loving relationship with the prince. This had included a period as the last abbess of Remiremont Abbey in the Vosges Mountains and, later, her years after the outbreak of revolution as an *émigré* elsewhere in Europe.[1]

In more recent times she had tried repeatedly to persuade him to give up his English mistress, particularly after his extravagant purchase of Saint-Leu and his planned transfer to Sophie of its revenues. 'In God's name, do not let Saint-Leu become in your old age the haunts of, I know not of whom, nor of what – you know what I mean, I can say no more!', she had told him in a letter. 'Adieu you who ever were and who always shall be the well-beloved of my heart.'

Sophie's chief target now was Adele de Rully, who conspicuously had refused to sit down to dinner with her father's disgraced paramour, treating her with utter contempt and ill-disguised hatred. When Sophie, for reasons known only to her, called on Adele at the latter's *hôtel particulier*, the townhouse she used when in Paris, the countess refused to receive her there. Sophie returned Adele's understandable dismissal of her with venomous bile. Her bitter, resentful animosity towards the prince's loyal daughter and her husband, Louis Henri's *aide-de-camp* and, in addition, 'first gentleman' in the prince's household, is evident from a letter she wrote to Louis Henri while visiting the spa resort of Aix-le-Bains in September 1824:

> How the Rullys persist in their stupidity and their ingratitude! It makes me ill every time I think of it! I pray God to forgive them both for what they have done, if not towards me, at least towards my "Poor Dear." You are the best of men, often indeed too good! I ask you in the name of my affection to act with firmness ... your dignity is compromised before everyone.

This short extract serves as a perfect illustration of Sophie's determination to force a wedge between the prince and the Rullys who, her letter implies, were scrounging off his generosity. Again, the hypocrisy is staggering from a woman who had long been sponging off her lover. Such things did not occur to Sophie. The ability to divide and rule was what mattered to her.

But it was not straightforward. Arriving back at Chantilly, she found Adele and her husband still enjoying the prince's hospitality, still secure in their private suite of rooms. Louis Henri had not been able to do his mistress's bidding; he hadn't the heart, and certainly not the stomach, to expel from his household the two people he probably most relied upon for succour at the château. It enraged Sophie. She felt she had been let down, betrayed. For the first time – although it seems certain that it had actually been happening long before this – we learn of the latest tactic in her relentless bid to subjugate the prince wholly to her will.

The evidence comes from the memoirs of the Baron de Saint-Jacques, another of Louis Henri's gentleman-ushers. Noticing the prince's exceptionally low spirits, he asked his master what was troubling him. 'If you only knew how she treats me,' he was told by the mournful prince. 'She beats me!' There was no need for the baron to enquire further as to the identity of the cruel tormentor. Nobody at Chantilly would have harboured any doubts about that.

This, if we accept it at face value, is an uncomfortable read. It is perhaps wise to allow the possibility that the baron, like so many other high-ranking officials at Chantilly, was deeply resentful of the English 'interloper,' a woman who wielded so much power at the château. His male ego perhaps deflated, he might have been tempted to 'stick the boot in' when penning his memoirs. Saint-Jacques' words, however, are not at all out of keeping with those of many others when recalling Sophie's harsh treatment of the prince in the subsequent period.

The prince was 68 in 1824, an advanced age for the period, and would therefore have been considered an old man. His physical health was poor. The wounds he had suffered while on military service at Gibraltar – the disabling musket ball injury to his right shoulder – and with the *Armée de Condé* at Berstheim – the sabre slash depriving him of fingers on his left hand – were incapacitating enough in themselves, but to these had been added a third serious blow to his physical condition. He had fallen from a newly acquired black mare, a gift from his mistress, when it was startled by a wild boar while he was riding on the Chantilly estate. The result was a broken thigh, a difficult injury to rectify in the 1820s. After painful treatment and a prolonged consequent period of severe illness, the prince had been left with a permanent limp.

But Louis Henri was enfeebled in mind as well as body, utterly worn down by his life experience and dominating mistress. She was in her early thirties, strong-willed and strong-armed, her tall, muscular frame still awesomely able to carry a clout despite the inevitable results of her over-indulgence at the dining table. It was testimony to her absolute power over her aristocratic benefactor that Sophie, when her temper reached boiling point, as frequently it did, was able and willing to aim those clouts at her unhappy old wretch of a lover without fear of censure. Louis Henri, Duke of Bourbon, Prince of Condé, was master of his house in name only.

That he had thus far managed to retain the dignified and steadfast loyalty to his daughter, the Countess of Rully, in the face of such violent opposition from his mistress speaks volumes for the high degree of affection and esteem he undoubtedly felt for Adele. But his resistance to his lover's cruel demands for the eviction of the countess and her husband from Chantilly was on a knife's edge. As in his life generally, he was now fighting a losing battle against the woman who had become his unrelenting tormentor and had no intention of loosening her grip.

Saint-Jacques recalled 'another painful scene' during which Sophie lashed out once more at the prince's reluctance to remove the Rullys from his household. Louis Henri threw up his arms in abject despair – and caved in. 'Ah well, I will do as you wish', he told her. And what, according to Saint-Jacques, Sophie now wished him to do was to write to the War Office to seek Monsieur de Rully's formal dismissal from his military post as *aide-de-camp* to the prince – and with it his right to remain in residence within the latter's household. It is not known on what grounds, if any, Sophie had dictated this outrageous application should be based.

Saint-Jacques, if we are to accept his word – bearing in mind that his memoirs rather tend to place him centre stage at all important junctures – writes of his disgust at what happened next:

> It was Madame de Feuchères who, on my refusal to do so, drew up a rough draft of the petition and then made the prince copy it. She then wanted to make the prince order me to take it by itself to the War Office. When I refused to do so, she said: "But if Monseigneur orders you to take it you will have to do so." "No Madame," said I, "I shall not disobey Monseigneur, but I shall give in my resignation." "Come, come," said the prince, "we will say no more about the matter – I will give it to my valet." Three days later the prince received a negative reply from the War Office, bearing the king's signature. He went [to fetch] me and, showing me this, said: "You were quite right. What a foolish thing the woman made me do."

Sophie, of course, was never going to accept any blame for the failure of this ill-considered act of spite. Baron de Saint-Jacques adds a telling post-script to his account of the sorry episode:

> On the following Sunday, while I was waiting in the salon for the prince to appear, I overheard someone representing to Madame de Feuchères that His Royal Highness, by his request to have the Count of Rully deprived of his post as *aide-de-camp*, after having deprived him of [the civil post] of gentleman-usher, had created an unfortunate impression

at Court. I pricked up my ears on catching the name Rully and then I heard Madame de Feuchères say very distinctly, "Ah Monsieur, you are perfectly right. If you only knew what tears I have shed over this affair – I even went down upon my knees at the prince's feet in order to try and persuade him to be lenient, but he would not listen to me." Whereupon I could not refrain from exclaiming, "Oh, what a shocking lie." Madame de Feuchères [having heard] then immediately left the salon in great haste and hurried her guests into the billiard room.

While this, if true, may have caused her a degree of awkwardness, Sophie did not stay embarrassed for long, and neither did her resolve diminish to rid Chantilly of the menacingly influential Rullys. Louis Henri may have railed to his confidantes against her cruel dominance but in Sophie's presence he was little more than a bleating lamb – and the bleats weakened by the day. In the end he saw his only chance of any peace, his one possible route to a life less riven by the threat – and reality – of his English mistress's violent volatility was, finally, to succumb to her vindictive desire. He knew he would have to evict his beloved Adele.

It happened in the spring of 1825. Confident that this time her hitherto recalcitrant prince would at last conform to his dutiful norm and carry out her bidding, but anxious not to be around when her despicable scheming had its desired effect, Sophie had contrived to be far away when the Count and Countess of Rully were eventually banished from the prince's establishment. The villainous *femme fatale* had travelled to the Mediterranean coast for what she no doubt considered a well-deserved period of pleasurable relaxation after the struggles she had endured in order to win the long battle – if not yet the war of reinstatement at the royal court in Paris – she had been forced to wage for far too long against her most hated rival. There may also have been a second motivating factor behind her decision to travel to the south of the country that spring, far away from the excited chatter of an aristocratic elite in the north preoccupied with plans for a momentous event guaranteed to rankle with the scorned Englishwoman who remained bitterly resentful of her enforced exclusion from their midst.

Power Grab

Since September 1824 the royal court at the Tuileries Palace, to which she was desperate for re-admittance, had been paying homage to a new monarch. The health of Louis XVIII had been failing for several months. A number of factors contributed to his final period of intolerable suffering. In his sixty-ninth year the king was not only morbidly obese and plagued by gout, he had also developed severe gangrene in both his legs and spine. On 16 September the Prince of Condé had been among members of the king's extended family and State officials summoned to the Louvre Palace on the right bank of the Seine to witness the childless sovereign's death. There they acknowledged the succession of his younger brother, Charles Philippe, Count of Artois, who at 66 was crowned as Charles X.

The ultra-royalist elite had very much welcomed the succession of the reactionary King Charles. Convinced of his divine right to rule, he was resolutely opposed to any notion of handing meaningful power to the people. The succession had seen the pragmatic liberalism of Charles's predecessor replaced by a revived conservatism of kingly ideology which owed everything to the concept of the pre-revolutionary *ancien regime* and paid dangerously little heed to the profundities of social unrest which had fuelled the revolution. A widower since the death of his wife, Marie Joséphine of Savoy, in 1805, Charles X had assumed the throne as a religious zealot, much admired and feted by the Catholic Church and fellow extremists united in the cause of the undiluted privilege of an absolute royal prerogative. While his complex personality allowed for a large degree of charm, wit and a graceful dignity, none of these qualities would ever be enough to endear him to the masses. For the general populace beyond the tight confines of Court and Church he represented a deeply menacing echo of the past.

Louis Henri had more of an affinity with the new king than he had enjoyed with Charles's predecessor. Their youthful duel was an odd stain on a long relationship of usually cordial companionship. In the month of his accession to the throne, the new monarch had conferred on the Duke of Bourbon – as well as on Louis Philippe, Duke of Orléans – the formal title of Royal Highness and had simultaneously named the Condé prince *Grand Maître de France* (Grand Master of France), one of the great offices of the royal court. It was an honorary, rather than a functionary, position which required Louis Henri to appear at the Tuileries on only the rare occasion. Nonetheless, these conferred honours were indicative of the high regard and affection Charles had for his boyhood friend and fellow guest of Britain in royalist exile.

But this had counted for little whenever the vexed subject of the Prince of Condé's mistress was raised at the Tuileries. King Charles had famously sworn a vow of chastity following the death in 1804 of his long-time mistress, Marie Louise, Countess of Polastron, to whom he had been devoted.[2] It was a promise he had kept entirely in accordance with the new breed of France's nineteenth-century ultra royalists, which demanded a liberal outpouring of Catholic piety and morality while eschewing liberalism itself. Charles had long urged Louis Henri to rid himself of his notorious mistress whose very existence was anathema to the king. Eventually, realising the hopelessness of his overtures and loath to upset his kinsman and friend any further, he had advised his courtiers: 'Let us leave him alone; we only give him pain'.

Taking his own advice, the king had then declined to visit the Condé household for fear of implying a royal seal of approval for the prince's relationship with his 'in residence' concubine. And Charles was every bit as adamant as his predecessor had been – indeed he was resolutely implacable – on the matter of Madame de Feuchères. The disgraced English adventuress was now more than ever *persona non grata*. She would not be returning to court.

The kings of France reigned from the moment of their accession. The pageantry of coronation was not a prerequisite to a monarch's rule. On the Bourbon restoration Louis XVIII, wisely, had decided against a coronation. Charles X saw things very differently. He wanted, and no doubt felt he deserved, the full majesty of a ceremonial crowning – and naturally opted for the tradition of a coronation in Reims Cathedral, nearly 100 miles to the northeast of Paris; the tradition followed by all but a handful of French monarchs since early in the eleventh century.

The new king's investiture was set for 29 May 1825. From Reims, on the eve of the ceremony, Louis Henri wrote to Sophie. The coronation, and the serious potential it posed for personal embarrassment, was clearly on his mind. His letter, somewhat touchingly, began with a reference to himself in the third person:

> I do not know if the 'poor dear' will be able to acquit himself with honour tomorrow. Imagine the stairs to the throne which I shall have to mount and descend three or four times.

> They are as steep as a parrot's perch, with twenty-eight little steps, while I shall have the famous mantle [cloak] to wear and to manage. I am still uncertain if I shall take my cane, for what is to become of me if I should lose it? I should be obliged to use my hands to prevent myself from falling on my knees, which would be the most embarrassing of all possible incidents. However, a miracle equal to that of the Holy Ampulla perhaps will come to my rescue.

The prince's letter tells us several things. Its tone is light, despite the understandable anxiety with which he anticipated the great event. It is laced with humour and a mischievous disrespect for one of the key elements of the occasion – his closing reference to the Holy Ampulla, the glass vial containing the sacred oil of anointment at coronations which, according to legend, had originally been brought from Heaven by a dove to anoint the Frankish king, Clovis I in the fifth century. Surprisingly, given Sophie's cruel treatment of him, Louis Henri gives the impression he is writing to someone he still regards with affection as a confidante. His easy manner of expression is not obviously that of the downtrodden wretch. Perhaps it is a reflection of how much better he was able to cope with life, whatever it might throw at him, when Madame de Feuchères was not physically around to beat him down.

Yet his letter also reinforces the notion of a man whose bodily infirmity was a serious worry to him.

As it turned out, the prince was able to tell his mistress a day later that things had gone remarkably well for him during 'the great day' in the cathedral of Our Lady of Reims. Delightedly resorting once more to an account in the third person, he told Sophie her 'poor dear had got through it all as if he were bewitched … he climbed the heights of the throne as if he were a chamois, coming down again in similar fashion without a walking-stick, and without turning a hair, to the entire satisfaction of all the spectators, who were amazed at his agility'.

In the south of France, Madame de Feuchères was in high spirits, too. Ridding herself of foes was only part of her strategy for reacceptance at the royal court. Sophie had also been acquiring friends, or at least people prepared, for whatever reason and probable reward, to side with her in the insatiable pursuit of personal grandeur at the pinnacle of French society. However, whether all three of the companions who had journeyed south with her to Toulon, Florence and the other jewels of the Mediterranean's northern coastline fell into this category is questionable. It may be that the Count of Choulot, Governor of Chantilly, who was accompanied by his wife, and the Marquis de la Carte were present in their capacities as high-ranking, trusted officials of the Condé prince's court and had been dispatched south at the suggestion, if not insistence, of Louis Henri himself. On the other hand, Sophie was highly unlikely to have accepted the imposition of any travelling companion against her wishes.

Whatever lay behind the choice of her fellow travellers, whether they were there at her bidding or not, Sophie was clearly happy in their company – and thoroughly enjoying her holiday in the sun more than 500 miles from the desperate familial malaise at Chantilly she had worked so very hard to create. Writing from Toulon, she enthused to her prince:

> All the authorities here have been most civil to us; we were visited by the Rear-Admiral, the [divisional] *Sous-prefect,* the General Commanding the Department and several other officers.

We have no way of knowing whether the important personages she delighted in listing were paying court to Madame de Feuchères out of respect for her or for her noble travelling companions. Perhaps, if the news of Chantilly's sensationally scandalous *ménage à trois,* and the woman at its centre, had preceded them this far south, it was curiosity, plain and simple. No doubt Sophie was just pleased that here at least she was being treated cordially.

However, the VIPs she claimed had sought her out in Toulon must have paled into comparative insignificance when, travelling on to Florence, she learned that Hyacinthe-Louis de Quélen, Archbishop of Paris since October 1821, was also in the city. This presented her with a golden opportunity. At the time of Sophie's dismissal from Louis XVIII's court in the wake of the shocking revelation of her true relationship with the Prince of Condé, the archbishop, acting on the orders of a morally outraged monarch, had refused an invitation to dine with Louis Henri at the prince's Palais Bourbon. Now, in June 1825, Sophie, the cause of the outrage, put to one side any ill-feeling she felt towards His Grace and set out to charm him.

There are suggestions that she had some years earlier converted to the Catholic faith, although the accuracy of this assertion is clouded

An early photographic image of Upper Green Road, St Helens – as close a representation as is possible of how it would have looked at the time of Sophia Daw's birth there in the 1790s. (St Helens Historical Society)

Although photographed at a much later period, this Edwardian image of Sophia's Isle of Wight birthplace and childhood home shows the cottage in near original condition, its sloping thatched roof a prominent feature. (Author)

The former Isle of Wight House of Industry at Newport as it appears today. The old workhouse is now part of the St Mary's Hospital complex. (Matt Searle)

The thatched roof farmhouse at Cliff Farm, Shanklin, survives today. It was from here Sophia fled her servant's apprenticeship to begin her extraordinary adventure in mainland England and later, infamously, in France. (Matt Searle)

The first known portrait of the future Queen of Chantilly. This miniature of the young Sophia was painted in London by the French artist Jean-François-Marie Huet-Villiers in 1812. (Musée Condé)

Louis Henri Joseph de Bourbon, the last Prince of Condé. This portrait by the Italian artist Vittore Pedretti shows the ill-fated French aristocrat in middle age. (Musée Condé)

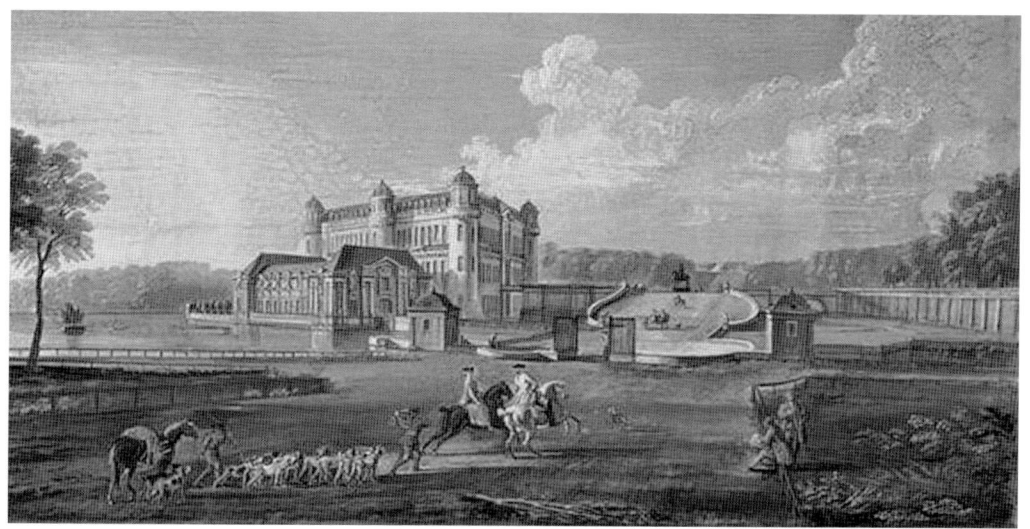

Pictured early in the eighteenth century, this gouache image of Chantilly, the work of French artist Jean-Baptiste Lallemen, shows the château before its partial destruction during the French Revolution. (Musée Condé)

This engraving by H.W. Bond, after a drawing by Thomas H. Shepherd, shows the magnificent church of St Martin-in-the-Fields, venue for the wedding of Sophie Dawes (as she was now known) and Adrien de Feuchères in 1818, before its incorporation in the development of London's Trafalgar Square. (The British Library)

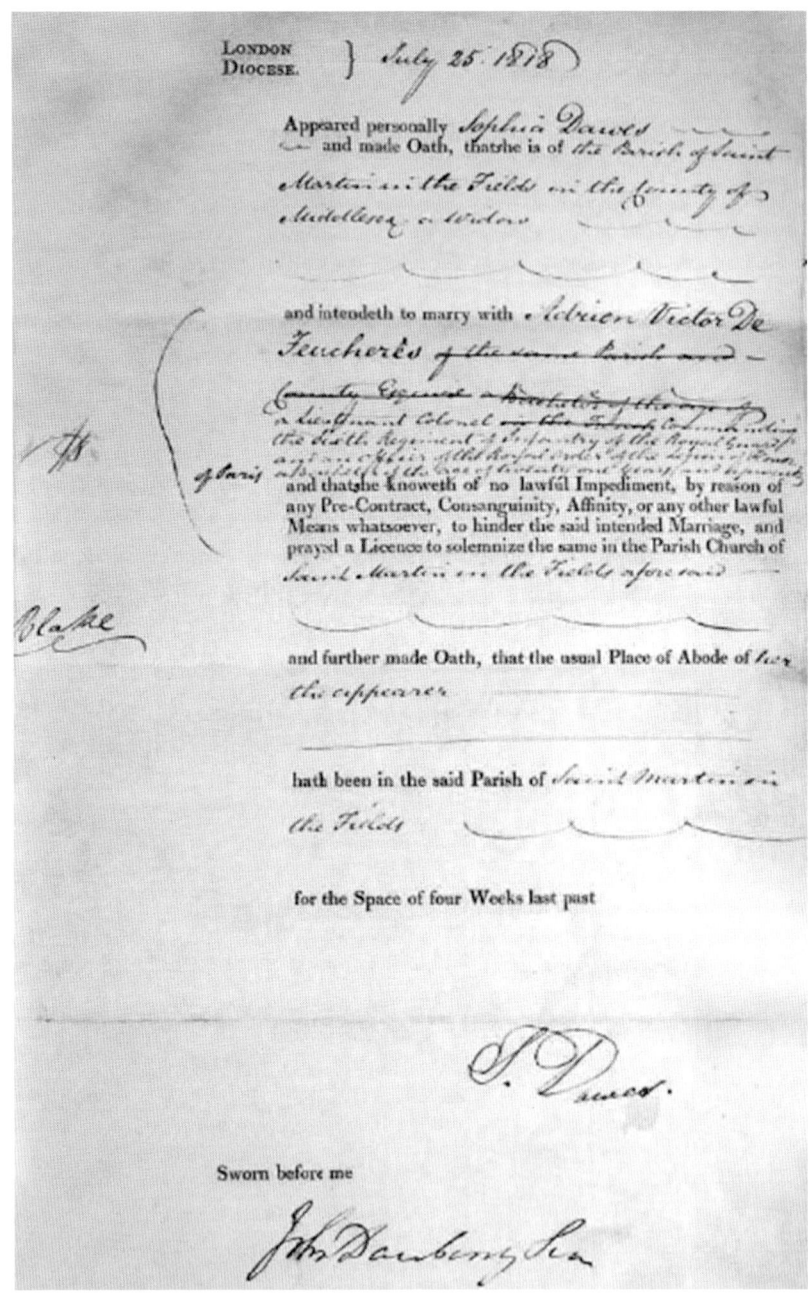

Sophia Daw had become Sophie Dawes by the time the formalities for her forthcoming wedding to Adrien de Feuchères were nearing completion in 1818. However, she reverted to the English form of Sophia with an 'a' when filing her intention to be married by special licence in London – a minor anomaly when compared with the lies she told about her identity in Paris. (Archives for London)

Sophie's husband, Adrien de Feuchères, pictured here in military uniform, was the unsuspecting dupe of his wife's concocted story of a quasi-royal pedigree. (Musée Condé)

Left: Sophie Dawes, Baroness de Feuchères, the domineering Queen of Chantilly, was pictured in riding habit, at the height of her 'reign' at the château, by the eminent French portrait painter Alexis Leon Louis Valbrun. (Musée Condé)

Below: Louis Philippe, King of the French – the country's last monarch – is pictured in this matching set of portraits with his queen, Marie Amélie. The royal couple's pact with Sophie Dawes was a key factor in the suspicious death of the Prince of Condé. (Alamy Stock Images)

Henri d'Orléans, Duke of Aumale, son of King Louis Philippe and inheritor in boyhood of the bulk of the Prince of Condé's vast fortune – a direct result of Sophie Dawes' artful scheming. (Musée Condé)

One of several graphic cartoon images published in the Paris press depicting the discovery in 1830 of the Prince of Condé's body hanging from a makeshift noose tied to a window frame in his bedroom. Sophie Dawes, his mistress, is seen entering the room to view the shocking spectacle. (Alamy Stock Images)

The northern frontage of Bure Homage, near Christchurch, Sophie's palatial country residence following her return to England in 1838. Only the former gatehouse of the mansion survives today. (Christchurch History Society)

London's Hyde Park Square, pictured in 2018. Sophie bought an expensive town house in the exclusive square on her return from France in 1838 and it was at the Hyde Park home (since destroyed in a wartime bombing raid) she died in December 1840. (Sarah Searle)

Its inscribed epitaph long since faded entirely from view, this once fine monument stands forlornly today above the neglected grave of Sophie Dawes in London's Kensal Green Cemetery. (Matt Searle)

The distinctive monument above the grave of James Dawes, Baron de Flassans, in St Helens churchyard. It was erected at Sophie's expense after the body of her nephew was returned to the Isle of Wight following his mysterious sudden death at Calais in July 1831. (Matt Searle)

The inscription on James Dawes' memorial reads that the pillar was erected as 'a mark of affection' by his aunt. But the question remains – was she responsible for his death? (Matt Searle)

Adorned with a commemorative blue plaque, the birthplace of Sophie Dawes in Upper Green Road, St Helens has undergone a noticeable change to its external appearance since her childhood in the 1790s. (Matt Searle)

The commemorative plaque on the wall of her former home records the date of Sophie's birth there as circa 1792. (Matt Searle)

The present owners of Freefolk, the name of the cottage today, have sensitively restored the interior, using many of the original features, in the style Sophie would have known as a girl. (Matt Searle)

An image of Sophie Dawes as the Queen of Chantilly was for many years a popular feature of the famous, but now closed, Osborne Smith wax museum in the Isle of Wight town of Brading. (Author)

The château of Chantilly today. Extensively and elaborately rebuilt by Henri, Duke of Aumale, who inherited it from the last Prince of Condé following his infamous death in 1830, the château is now home to the Musée Condé with the fabulous collection of art amassed by the duke at its heart. (Author)

by later events. If true, it might be fair to conclude that her conversion was not so much on any grounds of faith but was more a stepping-stone to her grand quest for acceptance in French society. This might, however, be doing her an injustice since there are reports that, at one stage and improbable as it seems, she toyed with the idea of becoming a nun, but had then become disenchanted with the Church. Whatever the truth of that, she no doubt convinced herself she had enough in the way of religious credentials, and a raft of deep intellectual questioning, to interest and impress the august cleric, and smooth the way to what she hoped would be a very fruitful discourse with him.

But she had to act quickly. Quélen, visiting Florence 'for reasons of health', as he would later put it, was in the city for only twenty-four hours. Fortunately for Sophie, she had at her disposal a go-between, willing or not, in the person of Madame de Choulot to act on her behalf.

Sophie's travelling companion was a great-niece of the archbishop's predecessor, Cardinal de Périgord. It was a somewhat tenuous link to the prelate but, in Sophie's estimation, good enough to effect an introduction for her to the visiting churchman. She was right about that – Madame de Choulot, staying in the same hotel as the archbishop, went alone to see him and, according to Quélen, wasted no time mentioning that she was travelling with Madame de Feuchères. Then, 'after stammering a few words in praise of that lady', she asked him to receive Sophie during his stay. The archbishop thought it best, however, to return Madame de Choulot's visit and, in the company of one of the vicars who were travelling with him, went downstairs to the countess's apartment where, for the first and only time in his life, he met Sophie.

According to her, the meeting in Madame de Choulot's suite went very well indeed. Quélen, a delighted Sophie would later tell anyone willing to listen, had been effusive in his manner towards her. 'Why, he even presented me with a beautiful bouquet of roses', she would add with a triumphant smile. The archbishop's recollection was different – *very* different. 'This was my only visit [to her]', he remarked, adding that he was 'quite certain that I never presented her with a bouquet of flowers. This story and many others of the same kind are pure invention. After what had happened in Paris, who can think that I should do such a thing!'

Despite her later repeated assertions to the contrary, we may conclude that Sophie's chance meeting with the Archbishop of Paris did not produce for her a miraculous reconciliation with the Catholic Church. Possibly of equal, if not more, importance, neither did the encounter persuade him to put in a good word on her behalf at the royal court. He had clearly regarded her with little more than outright contempt. Her attempts to woo an important ally in her obsessive quest had failed. Not that she was aware of this at the time – Quélen's rebuttal of her version of their meeting would come much later – but, whatever she understood of her situation at this time, Sophie would need to be cleverer, far more imaginative, if she was to achieve her goal.

On returning from her southern sojourn, however, she was able to bask in a smug satisfaction every bit as warming as the Mediterranean sunshine she had left behind. The Countess of Rully had been ejected from the household of the Prince of Condé, summarily it would appear, without even being given the chance to bid her father farewell (though it is easy to imagine just how awkward this would have been for both of them – especially Louis Henri). If that was not cruel enough, Adele had simultaneously been deprived of the dowry the prince had granted at the time of her marriage. The consequential termination of her husband's dual role within the Condé establishment, as the prince's *aide-de-camp* and 'first gentleman' of the household, was only partially achieved when an appalled Charles X intervened to overrule, on paper at least, severance of the Count of Rully's military position and, of course, the salary he received from it.

The humiliation of Adele and her husband, an unspeakable betrayal of the close bond he had hitherto enjoyed with his loyal daughter, paints the Prince of Condé in a very poor light. It was indefensible and yet entirely understandable for a man so completely under the sway of his lover. As Marjorie Bowen memorably puts it in *The Scandal of Sophie Dawes*, 'it was now … quite impossible to save the unhappy prince from himself'. There was no turning back.

The Queen of Chantilly now began in earnest to assemble her own court within the prince's domain. Regardless of their relationship prior to Sophie's vacation on the Mediterranean shores, it seems from the Archbishop of Paris's account of their meeting that she and Elizabeth-Anne, Countess of Choulot, had acquired a friendship of sorts during the trip. The daughter of a marquis, Madame de Choulot was potentially a more than useful ally for Sophie. Her husband, Paul, Count of Choulot, a cavalry lieutenant, was not only installed as Governor of Chantilly, he also held the equally prestigious position of the prince's captain-general of the hunts and, as such, was a man held in particularly high esteem by Louis Henri.

Credited with a close – *extremely* close – relationship with Sophie was the army general, Baron de Lambot. We know for certain that he now served as *aide-de-camp* and secretary to the Prince of Condé. The probability, according to many sources, is that he was simultaneously a lover of the prince's mistress! This clandestine extra-curricular extension of his official duties, it may be supposed, would be an obvious reason for allowing himself to be sucked into her power grab. Events about to unfold would certainly lend support to such a notion.[3]

Her relationship with Louis Frain, recently elevated by Louis XVIII to high-ranking peerage as the Count de la Villegontier, may only be guessed at but he must have pleased her in some way as it was at Sophie's prompting that Frain, a member of a prominent family of Brittany aristocrats, assumed the household position at Chantilly vacated by the departed Count of Rully.

Meanwhile, the imperious English mistress of Chantilly – its prince and, increasingly, his domain – had added two further members of her own family to her rapidly expanding empire of domination. Recently arrived in Paris were the son and daughter of her elder brother, James. Born in March 1799, so only a few years Sophie's junior, her nephew, also named James, was in his mid-twenties when he left his job as a meat porter in London – having already forsaken the life of a fisherman on the Isle of Wight – and sailed to France. Younger sister Matilda, however, born in August 1811, was little more than a child when she made the journey with him.[4] Their father, for whom Sophie seems to have retained a high regard, remained on the island. It is reasonable to assume, given what is known of his character, that he had acquiesced to the departure of his offspring in the justifiable hope that they stood a far better chance of enhancing their prospects under the close aegis of his powerfully enriched sister.

If there was for James and Matilda an element of altruism behind their aunt's invitation to join her in France, this almost certainly was not the principal reason she extended the hand of welcome. Sophie might have held her nephew and niece in familial affection (though she is unlikely to have been that close to either of them given the time she had spent in France), but she was driven by self-aggrandisement. It was as much for her benefit as it was for theirs – indeed, more so – that she had taken them under her wing. James and Matilda might be very useful in the long term to the Queen of Chantilly, strategic pawns on the chequered chessboard of her cherished ambitions. She would have seen it that way, planning ahead as always.

But there was, of course, a problem for Sophie to overcome in order to explain the presence in her midst of the two new arrivals, the progeny of an Isle of Wight shopkeeper and grandchildren of a smuggler. Such low-class origins sat awkwardly with the impression she was still anxious to give – despite no longer being able to claim the Prince of Condé as her father – of a respectable background. She was not going to introduce James and Matilda as her close blood relatives; instead, she claimed they were the nephew and niece of her 'late husband'. For the second time, into the tapestry of tortuous tall stories about her earlier life was woven the name of the mythical William Dawes, who she had insisted at the time of her marriage to Adrien de Feuchères had tragically died in the Cape to leave her widowed and alone.

There were plenty in and around the Condé establishment who believed not a word of this. It was even suggested by some that James and Matilda might actually be Sophie's own children, a theory taking no account of the obvious closeness of age between James and his aunt!

Sophie brushed the doubters aside. Sticking to her story and certain of her unassailable dominance over the prince, she unleashed a plan to bestow on her newly-arrived relatives the grandly elevated status she felt was warranted by her own exalted standing within Louis Henri's household. He seemed happy (or at least prepared) for her to do so, quickly accepting the newcomers in much the same way as he had taken to Sophie's mother (to whom he made frequent visits and rather touchingly referred to her as 'grandmother') and her younger sister, Charlotte. By all accounts the Bourbon aristocrat bonded very quickly with James, the meat porter from London, a city in which the prince had for many years chosen to spend time in the company of the common man. His attachment to the solicitous James rapidly grew. It was not long before Louis Henri had installed Sophie's nephew, willingly it seems but no doubt at her prompting, as his principal equerry, a key, well-paid position within the Condé establishment and one guaranteed to keep him, more often than not, at the befuddled prince's side.

Power Grab

Historically, an equerry's role was not simply that of a personal attendant; he also had responsibility for his master's horses – and in the Condé household that would have been a post of enormous prestige. A veritable equine palace, the stand-out masterpiece of the celebrated eighteenth-century architect Jean Aubert, the stables at Chantilly were the envy of Europe and greatly prized by Louis Henri as a magnificent base for the equally splendid string of horses which underpinned his large hunting establishment. To be placed in operational charge – if indeed that was the case – of this hugely impressive feature of Chantilly's domain was one of the greatest honours the prince could have bestowed on James, whose qualifications for the role appear to have been precisely nil. But whatever his actual duties, James would certainly have been very well placed to keep a close eye on his master.

And no doubt his aunt would have allowed herself a smirk of smug delight at the thought of the large muscular presence of James in the household – primarily there to protect her interests rather than those of a deluded prince who was now firmly in the target sights of a spy network ready to update Sophie on the innermost secrets of their poor old master's mind.

In his interesting work of 1878 recalling the life of Charles X, the prolific French historical author Prosper Vedreme wrote that 'there no longer remained about the prince any but the creatures of Madame de Feuchères. Everyone did her bidding at Chantilly, and the prince most of all'.[5]

Given this grimly succinct assessment of life at Chantilly in Charles X's reign, it is somewhat baffling to find another account, apparently written of that period, which acknowledges Sophie's dominant position at the château yet depicts an aura of relaxed – to say the least – domesticity there. It comes from the memoirs of Jean François Boudet, Count of Puymaigre, a senior French official in the post-revolutionary period and a man who had long enjoyed a close friendship with the principals of the House of Condé. Following the new king's enthronement Puymaigre had been appointed prefect – the State's representative in a department or region – of the Oise, the department in which Chantilly was (and still is) located. Since he refers to himself as prefect at the time of the many visits he made to Chantilly, the assumption is that these cannot have taken place before 1824, the year of his appointment. And yet the count's observations provide little hint of Chantilly's tensions at the time of his visits. In his comments on Louis Henri's demeanour, Puymaigre does not paint an image of the miserable wretch but that of a man determined to grab what joy he could out of life.

Referring, as virtually everyone did, to the prince as the Duke of Bourbon, Louis Henri's preferred title, the count recalled:

> The name of my father [Field Marshal Gabriel Boudet de Puymaigre, a military colleague of Louis Joseph], much beloved of the late Prince of Condé, more than my title of prefect, caused me to be received with welcome, and I took advantage of it the more gladly, because I have never seen a house where one was more at one's ease, and where there was more of that comfortable life known as "the château life" before the revolution. There was little of the prince in [Louis Henri]; he was more like an elderly bachelor who loved to have about him joy, movement, pleasure, a wholly Epicurean life.
>
> The society of Chantilly ordinarily consisted of the household of the prince; that is to say, old servants of his father, some ladies whose husbands held at this little court the places of equerries or gentlemen of the chamber, some persons who were invited or, like myself, had the right to come when they wished – and among this number I frequently saw the Prince of Rohan, relative of the Duke of Bourbon – and finally [there were] some Englishmen and their wives.

The apparently large English presence at the château noted by Puymaigre suggests Sophie had gathered around her not only members of her family but a good number of former companions from her native land. Who they all were was not revealed by the count, who added:

> The tone and manners of these people were quite free and easy, but then the prince set the example. And I well recall that one day he recommended me to be gallant with one of the English ladies, who, he said, would like nothing better than to receive such attentions. That seemed very likely to me, but she was not young enough to tempt me to carry the adventure very far.

It might be said that the only true 'gallantry' here was Puymaigre's decision to omit the identity of the woman who held no sexual appeal for him. The count was not so coy about Sophie:

> The real *châtelaine* who occupied the post of honour – if one can imagine anything honourable about her – was the Baroness de Feuchères, the Duke of Bourbon's mistress. She was exactly like a stout and rather fresh-looking cook, and would have disgusted any decent fellow at the end of three days. She did some good work with the prince's money, hoping thereby to make people forgive her for her scandalous position as the prince's paid mistress at the château of Chantilly. She took me to see the almshouses which had been endowed by the Grand Condé in the town, in which she showed a great interest. I did my best to encourage her in this because good works are good works, and remain so, no matter who their author may be.

Overall, the impression given by Puymaigre is that Louis Henri at this juncture appeared content, outwardly at least, with the literal state of affairs at his château. This begs several questions. Was he so deluded, so lacking in his understanding of Sophie's ever-deepening encroachment on his status as master of Chantilly's establishment, that he was able to implant in his guest the firm notion of a carefree, pleasure-filled life? Or was his apparent demeanour a mere front, masking the bitter realities of his domestic situation? Another explanation, albeit unlikely, might be that Puymaigre was actually recalling visits he made *prior* to his 1824 appointment as Prefect of the Oise, before the prince's English mistress had tightened her menacing grip on events at the château. The count had first become a prefect in 1820, although this earlier prefecture was served in the Grand Est region – as Prefect of the Haut-Rhin – and was thus a long way from Chantilly. It would not have been part of his civic responsibilities to drop in on the château; maybe he was simply there in his capacity as a friend.

Puymaigre again brought the overbearing presence of Sophie at Chantilly into sharp focus when describing in vivid detail some of the social highlights – and lowlights – of his visits to the château. Whether or not he was recalling events before or after 1824, his observations provide fascinating, indeed revelatory, first-hand accounts of everyday life from what were to prove the final years of domestic routine for the House of Bourbon-Condé and its very last prince:

> It was particularly during the hunts of [nearby] Saint-Hubert that Chantilly was a charming abode. The start was made at seven o'clock in the morning, and usually I was in the carriage of the prince with the ever-present Madame de Feuchères. The hunting-lodge was delightful and in a most picturesque situation. There were twenty or thirty persons met [there] to the sound of horns, in the midst of dogs, horses, and huntsmen. The coursing train of the prince was finer and more complete than that of the king. A splendid breakfast was served at the place of rendezvous, built and furnished in the Gothic style of the thirteenth century, and there the chase began. Although I told the prince that I was no hunter, he often made me mount my horse and accompany him; but often, having enjoyed the really attractive spectacle of the stag, driven by a crowd of dogs which launched themselves after him across the waters of a little lake, I hastened back to the Gothic pavilion where the ladies and a few men remained.

In Puymagre's final memoir of Chantilly, Sophie took centre stage – much to the count's dismay:

> Dinner was at six o'clock in the magnificent gallery where the souvenirs of Louis de Bourbon, *le Grand Condé*, were displayed in all their pomp, and the eyes fell on fine pictures of the battles of Rocroi, Seneffe, Freibourg and Nordlingen, inspiring some regret for the life led by the heir of so much glory. After dinner, society comedy was played on a very pretty stage, where the luxury of costumes was very great and the *mise en scène* [the arrangement of the scenery] carefully attended to, [although] this did not make the actors any better! The little plays were tolerable, but with Madame de Feuchères wishing to perform in *Alzire* [Voltaire's celebrated tragedy, first staged in 1736] and to take the principal part – which she doled out with sad

monotony, without change of intonation from the first line to the last, and with a strongly pronounced English accent – it was utterly ridiculous. Voltaire would have flown into a fine passion had he seen one of his *chefs-d'oeuvres* mangled in that way!

Having consigned to print this dismissively trenchant critique of Sophie's acting prowess, Puymaigre closed his colourful account by noting of Louis Henri: 'The poor prince ... if he had neither the virtues nor the dignity proper to his rank, was nevertheless a very good fellow.'[6]

Irrespective of the precise dates of the count's visits to Chantilly, by 1825 the writing on the proverbial wall of the 'good fellow' had become glaringly obvious to anyone who took the trouble – not that it needed this – to read the situation within the confines of his home. His mistress's artful scheming had no time or regard for his life's little pleasures; his death, and the worth of it to her, featured ever more in Sopie's thoughts as she sought to devise a blueprint for achieving maximum reward for years of devotion to her supremely grand design.

Her power base in the gilded corridors of the Condé household was strong, and growing stronger by the day. A second, younger, son of her brother James had arrived at the château. At least, this is what some sources claim today. George Dawes, born in August 1802, the third child of James's union with Mary Crann, presents something of a challenge to historians. He flits in and out of a few biographical accounts of Sophie's life but is entirely ignored in most. The suggestion is that he joined the Condé household in the mid-1820s, apparently employed there as a groom. It might be, however, that he was a much later arrival and the subsequent course of his life – and death – in France may be highly relevant to Sophie's story.

Her resolve reinforced by the virtual omnipotence of her power over the House of Bourbon-Condé, Sophie now sought to stray beyond the environs of its great palaces and to tread into the swamp of *politique royale*. The complex politics of the reinstated Bourbon monarchy and its attendant branches required very delicate handling. Delicacy and Sophie Dawes had never gone hand-in-hand. Luckily for her, she was able to call on a true master of diplomatic counsel.

Frozen out of national office since resigning as Louis XVIII's principal minister in September 1815, Talleyrand, the chameleon prince of diplomats, was, as always, looking to the future and how he might influence it. He had recognised the potential of Madame de Feuchères as a powerful ally, given the huge influence she held over the last of the Condés and was highly likely to wield in the matter of the still-to-be-determined destination of Louis Henri's inheritance. Talleyrand may have been a bishop, as well as a politician and diplomat, but he was not a man to wish eternal damnation upon the unmasked concubine of a wealthy, ageing aristocrat. He had taken many a mistress in his own life and had remained on good terms with several of them. He was not to feel squeamish in the company of Sophie Dawes.

It is unclear who initiated their bond but Sophie and Talleyrand met frequently for earnest discussion. Aided by his artful counsel, the muscular presence of her male relatives and the sycophancy of those who had tied their tawdry colours to her own, Sophie had pursued a sure-footed approach towards achieving her ultimate goals. Yet her initial step along this latest twist and turn on her hopeful pathway to earthly paradise would leave her stuck in the mud.

Louis Henri had ensured more than adequate provision would be made for his mistress after his death, but this would still leave the bulk of his vast fortune beyond her reach. Since the execution of his only son, the prince no longer had any direct descendants; the Bourbon-Condé line would die with him. Among his natural heirs was the House of Rohan, the family of his mother, Charlotte de Rohan. An extravagant settlement in Sophie's favour from the prince's will was, she very much feared, bound to be challenged by the Rohans, who would surely argue, with some justice, that collectively they had the strongest claim to the Condé inheritance. Four siblings – a princess and her three brothers – represented the likely Rohan challenge to Sophie's aspirations. Particularly prominent in her mind was the youngest of the brothers, Jules Armand Louis, usually referred to as Louis, Prince of Rohan, a former soldier in the royalist cause, prominent in post-Restoration Parisian society and – as the Count of Puymaigre had noted in his memoirs – a frequent, and often long-term, visitor to the château of his ageing, enfeebled and hugely wealthy relative without a direct heir, the Prince of Condé.

Born at Versailles in 1768, Louis de Rohan was the archetypal *bon viveur*, a jovial, witty socialite. He was good company for anyone, the last of the Condés included, but Louis Henri's affection for him blew hot and cold – and he was deeply suspicious of the close attention being paid to him by the Rohan noble. 'It is curious how people will leave you alone', he said in an astute observation, 'and then suddenly attach themselves to you, never to leave you in peace'.

It was not just for his Chantilly host that Rohan flattered apparently to deceive. It seems he also sought to ingratiate himself with the prince's English mistress by appearing to grant her both recognition and respect for her undoubted position as the château's unofficial queen. Replying in 1826 from, as he put it, 'an old castle in a deep valley in Bohemia' to a delayed letter Sophie had sent him, he expressed his 'deep acknowledgements' that she had not forgotten him. 'I hoped you could give me some good news of our friend [Louis Henri], for whom my attachment can only vie with yours by reason of its being a little longer', he added before earnestly entreating her to 'look after him carefully always, and, if you think that I can be of the least use to him, write to me a word and I will hasten at once; nothing shall stop me'.

We are left to wonder whether Louis de Rohan, mindful of Sophie's extraordinary influence over her patron, and how he might use this to secure his fortune via the Condé will, was simply trying to retain a place in her affections – a place his letter implies he had firmly secured – or whether, as has been suggested by Marjorie Bowen, among others, the letter was an example of the 'cynical irony' beloved of this 'noted wit'. As Bowen remarked in her fine book, 'this would not have troubled Madame de Feuchères'. Sophie would not have spotted it.

For her part, to protect against all outcomes, Sophie no doubt felt obliged to stay on good terms with the Rohan family – until, that is, she could think of a way to side-step the threat they posed to her own scheming. The apparent solution to this specific dilemma was presented to her when she learnt that Louis Henri, when finally he could be persuaded to talk about it, was not thinking at all of leaving the bulk of his immense inheritance to the Rohans. Although still far from decided, he was leaning towards naming the family of Charles X as principal successors to his fortune – specifically the king's grandchildren, Henri d'Artois, Duke of Bordeaux, born in 1820, and his sister, Louise d'Artois, who was one year older. They were the two children of the Duke of Berry, victim of a Bonapartist assassin seven months before his son's birth.

The murder of Charles Ferdinand, Duke of Berry, fatally stabbed while leaving the opera house in Paris, had deepened the already-close affinity between Louis Henri and Berry's grieving father, four-and-a-half years before the Count of Artois succeeded to the throne. The two Bourbon aristocrats had both lost sons in appallingly awful circumstances. The Prince of Condé had hastened to his kinsman's side at the time of the assassination to offer extended and genuine solace. His empathy and deep affection for the future monarch had endured into Charles's reign. Thus he was now considering seriously the eventual hand-over of most of his huge wealth to the fatherless grandchildren of the king. His words made this clear:

> Berry was a good fellow, he never did any ill to anyone; I liked him very much, he was a companion-of-arms to my son. Well, I will serve as father to his orphans – they shall be my heirs.

The prince, however, could not yet bring himself to turn words into action. He would not commit anything to paper. It has been suggested that he held back in the knowledge that the young Duke of Bordeaux would, in time, succeed his grandfather to the throne as Henri V. If the châteaux, land and millions of francs that made up the Condé inheritance fell mainly to him, all of it, and the very name of Condé itself, would be subsumed within the overall largesse of the monarch, for whom Chantilly's magnificent domain would become a mere add-on. Whatever the truth of this, Louis Henri dragged his heels over the matter of his will.

Sophie saw her chance. If she could secure the inheritance for Charles's grandchildren, and be seen to be the architect of such a pleasing outcome for the royal family, then surely she might expect her own fortune to prosper as a fitting reward. Could she not shelter her own bounty from the will, suitably inflated, behind the shield of the royal inheritance she had engineered, an iron protection the Rohan family, or any other potential claimants, would not dare to challenge? Whether the Prince de Talleyrand was influential in what happened next is arguable. It was far from the shrewdest of moves but Sophie now took matters into her own hands.

Behind her prince's back, she dispatched his secretary and *aide-de-camp*, General Baron de Lambot, by now a regular sharer of her bed, to the court of Charles X. Mistakenly believing Lambot was there under the orders of his master, the king received him at the Tuileries. The general gravely stressed to the monarch his concern for the poor, and worsening, health of the Prince of Condé before moving cautiously – although it is hard to imagine how he managed this – to the delicate matter of the prince's vast inheritance and, more specifically, the fact that he had yet to make a will. If the king suspected by now that Lambot might not be acting on his master's behalf, but on that of the prince's English concubine, he was very soon in no doubt at all. The general reminded him of the great influence Madame de Feuchères enjoyed over the prince and suggested she could perhaps exercise this to bring about a favourable outcome for the royal family – specifically the royal grandson – in the making of the Condé will.

Lambot should probably have noticed the king's less than encouraging demeanour as he outlined what Sophie would expect in return for her intervention: a guarantee that she would herself inherit, without risk of challenge, a very significant share of the Condé estate and a royal promise that she would at last be granted her readmission to court. Lambot had made the case as best he could for Madame de Feuchères' crafty little plot. We have no record of the precise words used by Charles X in response to the entreaties of Sophie's agent. Very few words, it would seem. In essence, the king's reaction can be summed up as a disdainful wave of the hand as a humiliated Lambot was sent on his way.

Possibly fearful of the scorn Sophie might pour on his failure to bring about the desired result, the general tried again – this time with Maria-Carolina, Duchess of Berry, widow of the king's assassinated son. The royal daughter-in-law was asked if she would welcome for one or other of her children, with the emphasis placed on her son, Henri, Duke of Bordeaux, the promise of inheriting the Condé fortune, which was within reach if she would be gracious enough to receive Madame de Feuchères at court. 'She has been judged very harshly and subjected to cruel treatment', he is reputed to have told the duchess, very possibly with tongue in cheek. 'The fact that she is not allowed to appear at Court causes her the greatest anguish'.

The Italian-born princess bristled with indignation. Lambot was told in no uncertain terms, and with typical frankness, that the idea was preposterous. Her son would require no such intervention from the disgraced and reviled English courtesan. 'Henri will be king', she is said to have told the withering Lambot with haughty disdain. 'The King of France needs nothing'.

Sophie's envoy now humbly put forward as an option (although some sources suggest he actually tried this first) that Prince Henri's sister, Louise, might instead be regarded as the potential principal beneficiary of the Condé inheritance under Madame de Feuchères' artful scheme. The Duchess of Berry was equally dismissive about this. The general was shown the door.[7]

Fortune may favour the bold but, as Lambot turned his back on the Tuileries Palace to begin a forlorn retreat to Chantilly, his mission unaccomplished, he may well have questioned, for a while at least, the validity of the old Latin proverb in the grasping hands of the woman he served. She had miscalculated, her outrageous boldness thrown rudely back in her face by royal rebuff. But the resourceful daughter of Dicky Daw would not be shaken off course for long.

And the route had now been opened to the infamous event that ensures her legendary status today.

Chapter 6

Intrigue:
Sophie's Pact with the Orléans Prince

The smuggler's daughter had come a very long way from village life in St Helen's and the forbidding confines of the Isle of Wight House of Industry. From the lowest dregs of English identity she had risen to a position of extraordinary power and wealth among the unimaginable, dizzying heights of post-revolutionary French royalist society. But it was not enough for Sophie Dawes. There was more to be won. She was determined to grasp it, to take her adventure to the limit. Nobody, not even the King of France, was going to stand in her way.

If the main stem of the Bourbon monarchy would not yield to her cunning plan there was still the possibility of shaking its dynastic branches once more and linking her ambitions for the vast inheritance of the last Condé to those of a family with very good reason to covet the harvest of Louis Henri's fortune. The House of Bourbon-Orléans was now the arch-schemer's focus in the duplicitous shape of the man at its head, Louis Philippe, Duke of Orléans, cousin of the king – and detested by the Prince of Condé for his history, politics and character. The Orléans prince was the last of his kinsmen Louis Henri would have wished to benefit from his will.

That Sophie would even contemplate sheltering her anticipated fortune behind the protective shield of the Orléans family by persuading her prince to name them as his principal residual beneficiaries – contemplate and believe it was perfectly possible – is the clearest indication to date of her absolute subjugation of the ailing Condé aristocrat. But to pull it off would require very careful planning, a complex plot and friends in high places. No matter, the determination to succeed would be her driver. Things were about to get a whole lot worse for the Prince of Condé.

To set the scene for Sophie's next move it is necessary to wind back the years in order to understand the vast divide between the Condé and Orléans branches of the Bourbon dynasty, together with Louis Henri's visceral hatred of, and equally deep distrust in, the Orléans duke. The fact that, through the brother-sister relationship of his late father and Bathilde d'Orléans, the Prince of Condé's long-estranged wife, Louis Philippe was Louis Henri's nephew was a matter for regret, certainly on the Condé aristocrat's part, one which gave him no pleasure at all.

It says much about the ideological divergence of the Orléans family from that of their Condé relatives that Louis Philippe was the son of Louis Philippe Joseph d'Orléans who in 1792, at the outbreak of the French Revolutionary Wars and at a time when he was first *prince du sang* (after the sons and grandsons of the royal family itself, the prince of the royal blood closest to the French throne) had changed his name to Philippe Égalité. A demonstrably bold declaration of his, and his family's, leaning towards equality within the French state, it underlined his advocacy of constitutional, rather than absolute, monarchy. It was a position reinforced by his election to the *Convention nationale*, the first revolutionary government,[1] followed by his support – and then vote – for the execution of the toppled monarch, Louis XVI, the absolutist king in whose cause the Condé aristocrats had volunteered to take up arms.

However, in November 1793, within ten months of the king's fateful date with *Madame Guillotine,* Philippe Égalité had met the same fate, a victim of the paranoid suspicions and brutal injustices of the Reign of Terror – and the very fact that he was the father of Louis Philippe, Duke of Chartres, the eldest of his three sons and the prince who would inherit the Orléans dukedom on his father's death. It could be argued that Égalité died for the sins of his son.

The younger Louis Philippe, while still in his teenage years, had been as prominent as his father among the progressive aristocrats who sided with the revolutionary government, becoming a member of the *Société des Jacobin*, staunch defenders of the new republican order, following its formation in 1789 by anti-royalist deputies from Brittany. While Louis Henri, Duke of Bourbon, had campaigned with his father and son in the *Armée de Condé* against the revolutionary forces, Louis Philippe fought on the other side of the French political divide, serving with revolutionary zeal. Soon earning praise and promotion to brigade commander, in September 1792 he had been entrusted with the role of

Intrigue

leading a division in the Valmy campaign, which resulted in the first major victory for the new French army.

Elevated to the rank of lieutenant-general, Louis Philippe, again at the head of a division, had joined the October 1792 march into Belgium of the northern army under General Charles François Dumouriez. Despite suffering heavy losses west of Mons, the Orléans prince, just 19 years of age, had rallied the stump of his division and joined other French units in a crushing advance to victory over the Austrian enemy. Dumouriez was effusive in praise of him.

But then, in April 1793, Louis Philippe flipped spectacularly to betray the republican cause.

Disillusionment at the inability of the revolutionary leaders in Paris to provision properly the Army of the North was partly behind the young officer's defection from its ranks. Jean-Nicolas Pache's incompetence as the newly-appointed war minister had left the northern army almost entirely without supplies. Mass desertions had followed as Louis Philippe considered his position. When the radicals in the *Convention nationale* successfully pushed through the vote to condemn Louis XVI to death, a move supported by Louis Philippe's own father, it was a step too far for the Orléans prince. He had begun to doubt whether he could remain in the revolutionary army, with whom he still felt a bond. But there was no easy way out.

As Louis Philippe agonised over the possibility that he might have to leave France, General Dumouriez, his military superior and close political ally, had been considering his own future. The general had alienated the radical elements in Paris by voicing outspoken opposition to Louis XVI's execution during the king's trial. Notwithstanding his successes on the battlefield, the radicals saw Dumouriez as an old-fashioned, stuck in his ways, war leader and, much worse, no longer saw him as a true patriot. When Dumouriez was decisively beaten at the Battle of Neerwinden in March 1793 his back was well and truly against the wall.

Defeat at Neerwinden, in the Austrian Netherlands, demoralised the French soldiers. A flood of desertions followed as they retreated. Dumouriez gambled, negotiating a deal with the Austrians which would see the French Army of the North pull out of the Austrian Netherlands altogether in exchange for safe passage back to France for the remainder of his troops. The treaty had been struck entirely without authorisation from Paris. Dumouriez was playing with fire. The radicals closed in for the kill, voting to demand the general return to the capital to face trial. Dumouriez knew his options were severely limited. Instead of heading for Paris to account for himself, he turned his back on the revolution he had once championed and threw in his lot with the Austrians. A plan was hatched with the former enemy. The general would march on Paris at the head of his men, overthrow the republic and replace it with a constitutional monarchy. The Austrians, for their part, would simply stand aside.

Reports of the secret talks had then set the revolutionary pulses racing in Paris. Pierre Riel de Beurnonville, who had fought at Valmy under Dumouriez and was now head of the war ministry, arrived with four commissioners from the *Convention nationale* to question the general about his conduct and force his return to Paris under arrest. Dumouriez responded by arresting *them*, handing over his would-be inquisitors to the Austrians. The die was firmly cast.

The general knew he could delay his move on Paris no longer. But he had not bargained for an almost complete lack of interest from his troops in his planned coup attempt. Forced to abandon his desperate plan, the only course left to him was to turn his back on France altogether and ride into the camp of his former enemy. Dumouriez would never again set foot in his homeland.[2] With him on that fateful day in April 1793 had galloped a forlorn Louis Philippe, Duke of Chartres, newly-exposed traitor son of Égalité. Unlike his commander, the young Orléans prince *would* eventually return to France – but it took him twenty-one years to do so.

His defection triggered the bleakest of outcomes for the House of Orléans cadet branch of the humbled Bourbon dynasty. Although he denounced his eldest son's betrayal of the revolution and declared that he should not be spared the wrath of the outraged republic, Philippe Égalité was implicated in the Dumouriez plot, despite the lack of any real evidence against him, and imprisoned. Aged 46, he was condemned to death in November 1793 by the Revolutionary Tribunal in Paris at the end of what was a trumped-up sham trial of short duration. Égalité was guillotined the same day as the extremist architects of *la Terreur* unleashed their vengeful bloodlust against any members of the Bourbon aristocracy still in France.

His younger sons, Louis Antoine, Duke of Monpensier, and Louis Charles, Count of Beaujolais, initially imprisoned with their father in

Intrigue

Marseilles (where they contracted the tuberculosis that would eventually end their lives at an early age), were later removed to American exile in Philadelphia. It was in the USA they were reunited with their older brother, Louis Philippe, whose route to the States had followed an extraordinary series of twists and turns.

After declining the opportunity to take up arms with Austria in the war against his fellow countrymen – a step too far for the young Orléans prince – Louis Philippe had been forced in the months that followed his April 1793 defection to pursue the life of an itinerant outcast, wary of contact with either the French republicans he had betrayed or the scattered *émigré* royalists he had chosen to side against when revolutionary fervour had first reared its head in Paris.

This shadowy existence had taken him first to Switzerland, neutral amid the chaos of European warfare, under an assumed name. While he was able to reunite for a time with his sister, Adélaïde d'Orléans, he travelled for the most part with a single valet, rode the one horse he had not been forced to sell, never stayed in one place for more than forty-eight hours and sought night-time refuge wherever he could find a roof to shelter him and his faithful servant, and a rudimentary bed on which to sleep. The two refugees were hounded as vagabonds, threatened, turned away and frequently exposed to potential capture, injury or worse.

Finally, in what is now the south of Germany, fate dealt the duke a better hand when he secured employment as a teacher of history, geography, mathematics and modern languages in a college at Reichenau, Lake Constance, where he was known by the name of Chabaud de la Tour.

But, within a month, in November 1793, had come the news that Louis Philippe's true status within his aristocratic family had been elevated, at least in the eyes of those who saw him as flag-bearer for an Orléanist monarchical restoration. His father's execution meant he was now the Duke of Orléans – and immediately the focus of intrigue and speculation in France. The intriguers' hopes were soon dashed when Louis Philippe resolutely refused to set himself up as a king-in-waiting, the most likely explanation for this being that he was engaged at the time in negotiations with the French revolutionaries in Paris for the release of his two younger brothers from prison. Leading an Orléanist coup would plainly have put their lives in peril.

So he held back and, after spending time travelling in Scandinavia, he sailed for the USA to reunite during 1797 in Philadelphia with the recently freed Louis Antoine and Louis Charles. In September of that year they learnt of the seizure of power in France by rebel members of *le Directoire*, the country's ruling body since 1795, who had launched a successful hard-line coup to eliminate the rise of royalist influence within the government – a move which established a dictatorship via the annulment of elections, the persecution of royalists and an end to religious and press freedoms. The brothers decided the time was ripe for a return to Europe. They reached Havana, intending to sail on to Spain, but got no further. Expelled from Cuba by the Spaniards, they sailed, via the Bahamas, to Nova Scotia where they were treated cordially by the British military commander, Edward, Duke of Kent, son of George III.

Returning to the USA, it was not until 1800 that the Orléans princes finally made it back to Europe after learning of the event in November 1799 which, in the eyes of most historians today, effectively brought the revolution in their homeland to its close. Napoleon Bonaparte's successful *coup d'état* had seen him seize power in France as the country's First Consul. Sadly for Louis Philippe and his brothers, by the time they disembarked in England early in 1800, Bonaparte and the consulate had established the firmest of grips on French political power. Authoritarian rule – effectively a military dictatorship – had been imposed on the nation.

The chances of an Orléanist-led liberal-leaning intervention in the cause of establishing constitutional monarchy were nil. The brothers were exiled in England and, in the case of Louis Philippe – whose younger siblings were both dead by 1808[3] – exile would remain the case for the next fifteen years. He lived for a long period at Twickenham in southwest London but left England in 1808 to join the Neapolitan royal family in Palermo, Sicily. There, in November of that year, he married Marie Amélie, daughter of King Ferdinand IV of Naples. The marriage sparked considerable controversy in European royalist circles since Marie Amélie, through her Austrian mother, was the niece of Marie Antoinette, whose execution in 1793 had been supported by Louis Philippe's father. Regardless, it would prove a successful union, with ten children born to the couple.

While in exile Louis Philippe, with a hopeful eye to the future, sought an Orléanist reconciliation with the senior branch of the Bourbon dynasty. But, just as he had failed to rally to the cause of the Condé nobility and fellow *émigré* aristocrats in the revolutionary wars – indeed, had taken up arms for their opponents – he played no part in the military campaigns against Bonaparte's forces in the subsequent Napoleonic conflict, despite suggestions that he should fight alongside the British in the Peninsular War against the French empire. The probable explanation for this was the continuing, and entirely unsurprising, mistrust felt by the king-in-exile, Louis XVIII, towards the Orléanist faction and his desire to prevent Louis Philippe, by way of military success, furthering his political cause.

Reconciliation between the elder branch of the Bourbons and the Orléans prince had, at least in part, been reached by the time Louis Philippe finally returned to France at the first restoration of the monarchy in 1814. Bu the royal mistrust of Philippe Égalité's son lingered into Louis XVIII's reign. While the prince was permitted by the king to take re-possession of the estates and forests which had been sold following his father's execution and his own ignominious departure from France in 1793, the monarch had refused to confer on Louis Philippe the formal status of Royal Highness, a right traditionally enjoyed by the head of his family (the title he would later be granted by Charles X). When Napoleon returned briefly to power during the Hundred Days in 1815 Louis Philippe did not follow the royal court to Ghent. Instead, he returned to England until the French monarchy was reinstated for a second time.

Of course, royal wariness of the Orléans prince was bound to be shared by the Condé nobility, whose years of exile prior to extended domesticity in England had differed so fundamentally from those of the man astride the other cadet branch of the Bourbon family tree

On one level the accession to the throne in 1824 of Louis XVIII's brother, Charles X, lessened the tensions between the monarchy and the Duke of Orléans. The new king and Louis Philippe enjoyed each other's company and frequently socialised together. But politics was always going to drive a wedge between the liberal-minded duke and a sovereign enthusiastically endorsed by the far-right ultra-royalists. Louis Philippe made no secret of his continuing allegiance to the cause of the country's liberal opposition. At the Palais Royal, ancestral Parisian home of the Orléans nobility, he played host to a succession of the opposition's most prominent politicians and journalists, openly patronising their principal newspaper, *Le Constitutionnel*. Breaking with royal tradition, he further espoused his liberal tendencies by enrolling his sons for a college education in Paris – albeit at the prestigious Lycee Henri IV – rather than employing private tutors as was the norm among the nobility in France.

Louis Philippe did not, however, stick to the party line when the liberals in the legislative assembly opposed introduction in 1825 of the Law of Indemnity, which set aside a huge amount of money to financially compensate *émigré* aristocrats for the losses they had incurred through confiscation of their land and property during the revolutionary period. Indeed, the duke, though he had not been an *émigré* in the true sense of the term, cashed in on the new law, which significantly boosted his monetary worth at a time when *émigré* influence on French national affairs, while it ranged from restrained royalism to extreme, was at its peak.

However, while his fifth-born child, Princess Françoise, had died at the age of two in 1818, Louis Philippe and Marie Amélie still had nine children to provide for: six sons and three daughters, an inevitable demand on his resources. It has often been suggested that he was struggling to meet this financial obligation (which would only marginally be decreased by another tragic death in childhood, the passing in 1828 of 8-year-old Prince Charles, his fourth son). Yet there is no real evidence that this was the case. He was a man who took his family responsibilities seriously, determined and apparently sufficiently able to care for his children and their mother, to whom he was resolutely faithful. It is, however, true that this cannot have been helped by a sensational, wholly unexpected intrusion into his domestic order.

Bizarrely, he had become embroiled in a costly legal battle to contest an extraordinary claim that he was not a son of the House of Orléans at all, but had instead been fathered by a Tuscan village constable before being switched at birth with the daughter of the man who would later be known as Philippe Égalité in order to fulfil Égalité's preference for a male child. The claim had been made by Maria Stella Chiappini, the putative Orléans daughter, born in 1773, which was indeed the same year as Louis Philippe's own birth. A remarkable life had seen her take to the stage in Florence, where the Chiappini family had settled, and, before the age of 13, become the second wife of the British politician, Thomas Wynn, Baron Newborough, a man nearly forty years her senior. Three years after his death in 1807 she had married into nobility for a second time, becoming for a while the wife of the Estonian Count Eduard Ungern-Sternberg. The eventual collapse of that marriage had not seriously affected her wealth as she was able to continue living off ample revenues from her first husband's estate.

But it was a blood link with the French aristocracy she had determined to prove, much to Louis Philippe's embarrassment. According to her fulsome account of this strange affair, published in 1830 and twice reprinted in the following two decades, the then Duke of Orléans and his wife, pregnant with their first child, were travelling in Italy when the switch of infants took place. The reason for this, it was explained, was the French duke's concern that, in the event of the duchess's death, and with no son to inherit, her vast personal fortune would revert to the family of her father, the Duke of Penthièvre. The switch enabled the newly born baby girl to be passed off as the daughter of Lorenzo Chiappini whose real child was handed over to the Orléans duke and subsequently revealed to the world as Louis Philippe, his natural son.

According to Maria Stella, Lorenzo Chiappini had confessed on his death-bed to the identity fraud and had informed her by letter that she was, in fact, the daughter of aristocratic parents who had been travelling through Tuscany in 1773 under the names of the Count and Countess of Joinville. Discovering that this was a title used by the Orléans princes, she had embarked on her quest, one which would occupy the rest of her life, to establish her true parentage and had become convinced that Louis Philippe, who bore a striking facial resemblance to Chiapinni, just as she did to the famous Bourbon profile, was her assumed Tuscan father's child.

Her case was boosted when in 1824 the episcopal court in the Italian city of Faenza issued a legal judgment which fully supported her account, accepting that she had been baptised under false pretences as the daughter of Chiapinni and that a man calling himself the Count of Joinville was indeed her birth father. But had the Joinville in question really been Philippe Égalité?

In response, lengthy investigations carried out on Louis Philippe's behalf established to his own satisfaction that, whoever the 'Count of Joinville' was, it had not been Philippe, his father.[4] He was able to prove, though his political detractors delightedly denounced it, that his parents had not been travelling in Italy at or around the time of Maria Stella's birth in April 1773 and that his own birth really had taken place at the Palais Royal in the October of that year.

Despite the contrary evidence he was able to present, this story of secret substitution, the portrayal of Louis Philippe as a changeling, was not an easy one for him to shake off. Apart from being a godsend to his many political opponents, it brought him years of exasperation and was a heavy burden on his purse. Whether this latter outcome was in any way a factor in his decision to join Sophie Dawes in her outrageous scheming on the vexed matter of the Prince of Condé's unwritten will is a matter for conjecture, and will probably always remain so.

But when Sophie approached him for help in her quest for readmission to the royal court, and a fortune to underpin the upgraded status this would bring to her, Louis Philippe immediately saw this as an opportunity for a *quid pro quo*. He was perfectly prepared to align himself to her intrigue. It seems safe to assume that, in doing so, he saw the potential for elevating his own position, if not via the vast fortune she dangled temptingly before him, then for the reputational advancement it would bring, reversing the damage caused by the Maria Stella episode.

Sophie lured the Duke of Orléans into her scheming with the prospect of drawing him and his family closer – *much* closer – to his Bourbon uncle, the Prince of Condé. The fact that she was able to persuade Louis Henri that he should allow this to happen against all his instincts was an act of cunning genius on her part, one destined to have vastly differing and very far-reaching consequences for those who, voluntarily or otherwise, shared the centre-stage with her.

The intrigue Sophie fostered with Louis Philippe was, to an extent, a natural development of a cordial relationship between the two stretching back to 1822, the year Louis Philippe's fifth son, Prince Henri Eugène, Duke of Aumale, was born at the Palais Royal. No doubt with her usual eye to self-aggrandisement, Sophie had set about convincing the Prince of Condé that he should stand as godfather to the Orléans infant. At this stage, two years before the scandalous final collapse of her marriage would leave her otherwise socially ostracised in France, Sophie may have thought this a useful insurance policy against any possible challenge to her plans. In the shorter term, she would almost certainly have seen it as the perfect means of effecting an introduction to the fascinations of the Orléans court, a chance to flout her expensive tastes in clothes and the accoutrements of high society fashion her total domination of the Duke of Bourbon had delivered to her. Even before her banishment from the royal court itself, she had, thanks to her prince's refusal to engage

Intrigue

in social contact with the Duke of Orléans, effectively been barred from the bustling salons of the Palais Royal which provided frequent opportunity for entertainment and enlightened discourse between many of the greatest free-thinkers of the day. That openness of invitation had always eluded her.

For his part, while Louis Philippe would have seen the potential advantage to the House of Orléans from such an arrangement, an initial step towards closer ties with his ageing, fabulously wealthy uncle, he must have wondered whether Madame de Feuchères could pull it off. There again, while Sophie's true relationship with Condé was still the stuff of ribald rumour and speculation, Louis Philippe, in line with the rest of Parisian society, would certainly have been well aware of the powerful influence she exerted over his uncle.

As for Louis Henri, the prospect of becoming godfather to the little Duke of Aumale would have gone wholly against the grain. He was as conservative as the family of Louis Philippe were liberal, as attached to the old ideas of monarchy as they were to those of constitutional reform from the monarchy downwards. And yet he *was* persuaded by his domineering mistress to go along with this very public act of apparent inter-Bourbon rapprochement, probably because he simply did not possess the lasting resolve to resist her constant harassment of him on the matter. He must surely have hoped fervently that agreeing to present Prince Henri Eugène at baptism and thereafter guide his religious development would have been regarded as a singular gesture, enough to satisfy all concerned. If so, it was a pious hope.

Almost immediately after Louis Henri consented to his new role, a triumphant Sophie had inveigled him to send a personal missive to his Orléans nephew seeking a letter of formal introduction to the Palais Royal for her on the grand occasion of the infant prince's baptism ceremony. Dutifully, the little boy's reluctant godfather did as he was bid by his mistress. It is not hard to imagine that the approach to Louis Philippe was actually dictated by her:

> You have kindly authorised me to bring whoever I like. You have already been good enough to invite Mme. de Rully. There are three other ladies belonging to my household, Mesdames de Quesnay, de Feuchères and de Choulot, all of whom, although they have been presented at Court, have

not yet had the honour to be presented to yourself and the princesses [Marie Amélie and Adélaïde d'Orléans, Louis Philippe's sister], and are very anxious to witness the ceremony. If it is not contrary to etiquette, you would do them a great honour, and it would be the happiest day in their lives, if you and the princesses would allow them to accompany me.

Louis Philippe probably allowed himself a wry smile on noting the clumsy attempt to avoid drawing too much attention to Madame de Feuchères by squeezing in her name between those of Chantilly's other leading ladies. But he was happy to oblige. It was not long before Dicky Daw's daughter, along with her companions, was acting the part of a pampered, yet pragmatically enlightened, princess amid the engrossing heart of the liberal Orléans court. She would have enjoyed herself immensely. 'The enchanted Sophie had the delight of being received by the pious duchess and the exclusive Madame Adélaïde', Marjorie Bowen dryly noted.

We may well imagine an element of reticence in the welcome extended to her by the duke's wife and his unmarried younger sister. They seem, however, not to have betrayed their innermost thoughts as, according to contemporary accounts, they made a show of 'petting and kissing' the Englishwoman who they believed held the key to the Condé inheritance and had taken what must have seemed potentially a first step towards unlocking its riches for the House of Orléans. It is easier to understand this disturbing preference for family advancement over moral principles when considering the character of Madame Adélaïde, for whom the cause of Orléans progression was rigorously paramount, than it is when reflecting on the virtuous reputation of Marie Amélie, whose own devotion to her family is usually attributed solely to a mother's instinct for protective love, untainted by any hint of a grasping base desire.

Violette Montague, among others, noted that, when rumours of the notorious Sophie's reception at the Palais Royal reached the Tuileries, the Duchess of Orléans found herself the uncomfortable subject of scornful interrogation by Marie Thérèse, Duchess of Angoulême. Under pressure from the straight-talking *Madame Royale*, the only surviving child of the executed Louis XVI, Marie Amélie confirmed that Madame de Feuchères had been received at the Palais Royal. She then felt bound to add that the scandalous Englishwoman, whose true relationship with the Prince of Condé was by then already an open, though still to be confirmed, secret, had subsequently dared to call on her at the Orléans summer residence in Neuilly.

'I hope *you* did not receive that woman?', the trembling Duchess of Orléans is reported to have been asked. 'No', stammered Marie Amélie, too frightened to do anything but lie. 'No, it was my husband who received her.' It is doubtful that *Madame Royale* believed this to be the truth.

The true feelings of the Orléans princesses were probably not something Sophie Dawes would have bothered to consider in 1822. She would simply have been greatly flattered by their public display of affection. The approval, whatever his prime motivation at the time, of Louis Philippe himself was all that mattered to Sophie. The Orléans prince needed little pushing. It is hard not to conclude that his once youthful gallantry, subsequent unblemished domestic probity and open-minded adherence to a modernistic liberalism seems at this point in his middle age to have been submerged, or at least shuffled conveniently to one side, by an unattractive flourish of avarice which perhaps reflected the deterioration in his physique. This had left him looking anything but a majestic presence in public, carrying too much weight, clumsy in gait, heavily whiskered and, in the memorable words of Marjorie Bowen, 'with that crest of hair on the top of his head like a cockatoo's plume so dear to the caricaturists'. None of which mattered a jot to Madame de Feuchères. Having taken this first step in a binding strategic relationship with the Orléans duke, she was determined to run with it.

The Queen of Chantilly was soon using her assumed royal prerogative in cajoling the reluctant Prince of Condé to invite the Orléans hierarchy for grand festive events at his château. Louis Philippe was gushing in his acceptance. The same cannot be said of the welcome extended to his nephew by Louis Henri. A polite nod seems to have been the sum of it.

When the rest of high-society Paris had turned its collective back on Sophie following confirmation of her central role in Chantilly's infamous *ménage à trois* in 1824, and when she had been devastated by banishment from the royal court, Louis Philippe, Duke of Orléans, had refused to join the clamour of condemnation, proving a rare friend indeed to the disgraced baroness. And when, in 1826, General de Lambot had returned empty-handed from presenting to Charles X and his queen the squalid scheme concocted by Sophie for sheltering her anticipated fortune from the Prince of Condé's inheritance beneath an armour-plated Bourbon shield, that plan was quickly re-focussed on the potential offered by the Orléans duke.

Bringing Louis Philippe, the very antithesis of his ageing uncle, into the heart of her devious plot to secure a fabulous Condé fortune and, with it, a renewal of royal favour was not going to be easy for Sophie. She was now in more need than ever before of a huge slice of diplomatic wizardry. We cannot be sure that the Prince de Talleyrand directly aided her at this juncture, but the events which followed strongly suggest the great opportunist had a hand in developing her forward strategy. It is worth remembering that Talleyrand was the man Louis Henri had always held responsible for the death of his son. The fact that he was now a regular visitor to Chantilly underlines still further Sophie's incredible influence over the Prince of Condé, sufficiently powerful to override the extreme distaste he must have felt at some of her actions. Awareness of this no doubt fortified her for the difficult task which lay ahead.

The plan which probably evolved from one of Talleyrand's many meetings with Sophie, would see the dutiful General Lambot despatched by her to the Palais Royal with a proposition for the Duke of Orléans. It seems that at this stage Lambot did not enter into any details but merely suggested to the duke the possibility of securing for one of his sons – and the emphasis here was surely on the Duke of Aumale, Louis Henri's godson – the bulk of the magnificent Condé inheritance. Louis Philippe may have been expecting this and would certainly have been well aware that the trade-off would be guaranteed advancement for Madame de Feuchères. Far from thrown by what Lambot was outlining to him, he told the general he would be happy to discuss the matter with the baroness face-to-face. It would, he said, require very careful consideration and could not possibly be hurried. But then the duke added:

> You know that my dear old uncle still insists on going frequently on horseback. He might in his state of infirmity be killed in an accident and that might very well be without leaving a will.

This was just what Lambot needed to hear. The Duke of Orléans was as fearful as Sophie that, if Condé were to die intestate, his fortune would pass in its entirety to his next of kin, his mother's relatives, the princes of the House of Rohan. Naturally, the duke wanted to discuss it. The puppet-general reported the good news to the puppeteer. Meetings were immediately arranged between Sophie and Louis Philippe to carry things forward. The deluded Prince of Condé, of course, was told nothing of the evolving intrigue concerning the composition of his will.

Louis Philippe was assured by the confident Sophie that the last of the Condés could be persuaded to sign over the bulk of his huge wealth to his little Orléans godson, Prince Henri, Duke of Aumale. A very sizeable chunk of the remainder would be reserved for Sophie herself, a small price, in relative terms, for Louis Philippe to pay. The only proviso was the expected one – that the Orléans duke would agree to mediate with the royal family on Sophie's behalf, using his own royal Bourbon credentials to secure her readmittance to court.

The duke expressed no qualms about Sophie's demand. Unfettered by any moral indignation at being asked to intercede in favour of the socially outlawed Englishwoman, he readily agreed to champion her cause at the Tuileries. Maybe he thought this would be regarded by Madame de Feuchères as enough in itself. He surely cannot have harboured any optimism about the likely outcome of his intervention. No doubt he was diplomatic – but diplomacy was trumped by resolute royal hostility. The court of Charles X remained as closed to Sophie Dawes as Louis Philippe's own court at the Palais Royal had in recent times been opened to her.

Sophie was prepared to wait. While feigning in public a total lack of interest in the destination of the Condé inheritance, she continued to intrigue over that very matter with Louis Philippe as they sought a way forward on both parts of the bargain, behind the back of her browbeaten noble lover. Keeping him firmly in the dark was not a problem. Most of his trusted servants had been systematically replaced by Sophie's imports. Louis Henri was now surrounded by her hand-picked spies, ready to report back to her any inkling that his suspicions might have been aroused. The easy-going Prince of Condé, whether or not he fully understood this, was manipulated into a trap offering little or no chance of escape.

But, with no real progress made on the plot which lay behind his coming torment, help was, somewhat improbably, sought from the Church – specifically from Jean-Baptiste de Latil, Archbishop of Reims. Certainly, given the influence the Catholic Church exerted over the monarch, the cardinal who had crowned him could have been a powerful mediator. Quite what skulduggery lay behind the approach to the archbishop is difficult to determine. Nonetheless, he *was* prepared to intervene. Unfortunately for the plotters, there was a strict condition attached to this. Cardinal de Latil thought it might just be possible to procure for Madame de Feuchères the prize of re-admittance to the Tuileries she so desperately coveted, but only if she agreed immediately to cut entirely her association and ties with the Prince of Condé.

This may have been a moral pronouncement on the part of the archbishop, worthy of his high position in the Church. But it is just as likely, if not more so, that it stemmed from his close friendship with Adele, Countess of Rully, the gravely ill-used illegitimate daughter of the last Condé. Either way, Jean Baptiste de Latil was left in no doubt – Sophie was having none of it.

Frustrating though this must have been for the smuggler's daughter and her noble co-conspirator, lawyers secretly worked on Louis Philippe's behalf in deciding how best to ensure the bulk of Louis Henri's fortune would be passed to his young godson. The make-up of the legal team suggests Sophie had a hand in its selection as it included Maître Tripier, the Parisian lawyer engaged in the matter of her marital split from Adrien de Feuchères. Whatever the truth of the matter, Tripier and his colleagues soon narrowed the options to a choice between naming Prince Henri as the residuary heir (after deduction of other bequests) or enhancing the status of the boy from godson of the Prince of Condé to that of his adopted son.

The latter was thought by all concerned, including the boy's father (who would in effect be selling his son in order a few years later to enrich his family's coffers), to be the better option. It has been suggested since, and may have been at the time, that the idea of adopting Prince Henri might have been welcomed by the last of the Condés. His stubborn refusal to remarry after the death of his estranged wife, Bathilde d' Orléans, in 1822, forty-two years after their acrimonious separation, had left him childless. And by this stage he was almost certainly incapable of producing an heir. Taking the Orléans prince in arranged adoption, it has been argued, would have been seen by the old man in his declining years as compensation for the tragic loss of his own son, Louis Antoine, in the dark days of 1804.

The aim was a 'simple adoption' for inheritance purposes only but it was a tricky one for the lawyers. The laws in France governing this at that time, formulated under the Civil Code of 1804, were very restrictive and allowed only for the adoption of adults. The prime reason was to

Intrigue

prevent couples, or women alone, conceiving children in order to sell them on. It is not clear how the Parisian legal team intended to get round this, but drawing up a persuasive case of very special circumstances for very special people would have been part of it.

Meanwhile, Sophie had been consolidating her power base still further at Chantilly. In 1826, James Dawes, her nephew, staunchest ally and agent in the Prince of Condé's employ, had found his status greatly elevated. Louis Henri had grown ever more reliant on James, for whom he seems to have had the greatest affection, frequently inviting his new companion to accompany him on shooting trips. 'Yesterday, James killed five head of game', he reported admiringly to Sophie in a note. 'They have been sent to Grandmother. I added to them a pineapple, which was served here yesterday at dessert. I know that she likes them very much.'

It is impossible to know whether James felt any genuine affection for the prince. He certainly should have done, but he was first and foremost the puppet of his aunt. She pulled all the strings – and the one she pulled to greatest effect at this stage, though it seems her lover was happy to go along with this, was to seek from the prince a donation of prime land and a noble title to accompany it for the erstwhile meat porter. James duly received a fine estate in southwestern France at Flassans-sur-Isole in the department of Var, with Louis Henri purchasing for him the title of Baron de Flassans. This made James, then aged 27, an attractive catch for one of the three daughters of retired British admiral, Sir Thomas Manby, a veteran of the French Revolutionary and Napoleonic wars.[5] James and Mary Harcourt Manby, chosen by Sophie as a suitable life partner for her ever-obedient nephew, were married in January 1827 at a lavish Paris ceremony, the 16-year-old bride's father receiving from the prince 200,000 francs, a dowry in all but name.

By mid-August of that same year Sophie had conspired to arrange a second marriage of high respectability for her young niece, Matilda. While she was well versed in the art of devious manipulation, in this enterprise Sophie was able to feed off the input from one in her circle who possessed the intellectual capacity to help steer her through the complex maze of her scheming. Artful diplomacy would be the icing on Sophie's cake as she considered how best to use Matilda's marriage eligibility to further promote her family's elevation in French society. Luckily for her, she was able to call on the services of the greatest artful diplomat in the kingdom to sweeten the bitter taste which lay within the ingredients of her self-serving recipe.

This product of the Prince de Talleyrand's amiable alliance with Sophie was something of a family affair, for him at least. In her search for a suitable marriage for the teenage Matilda, Sophie was soon in deep discussion with the obsequious but very well-connected Madame de Choulot, whose brother, Frédéric, held the title of Marquis de Chabannes la Palice.[6] Having forged a highly decorated military career in the service of Napoleon's empire, Chabannes was now a valued colonel in the Royal Guard and was conveniently unmarried at the age of 33.

This meant he was more than twice the age of Sophie's 16-year-old niece. He might not have seen that as a problem but he would probably have needed reassurance that Matilda came from socially suitable stock for a titled army officer. The match-making Madame de Feuchères, of course, had the answer to that and would again declare in all the necessary documentation that the young girl was the niece of her (Sophie's) highly respectable first husband, the late, and entirely invented, William Dawes. But the whole issue of Matilda's marriage eligibility required the negotiating skills of a trusted diplomat. Happily for Sophie, that master of the art, her confidante Talleyrand, just happened to be Frédéric de Chabannes' uncle.

There can be little doubt that Talleyrand played a leading role in the pre-nuptial discussions, convincing his nephew that marriage to Matilda Dawes, niece of the woman who ruled the roost at Chantilly and influenced its ageing master's every move, would greatly enhance his financial prospects. This was no empty promise. Louis Henri, the much-misused Prince of Condé, offered, or more likely was *induced* to offer, a magnificent dowry of 1,000,000 francs.

The forthcoming wedding prompted Sophie to write a few days beforehand to the Duchess of Orléans. But Matilda's marriage was something of a pretext for an update on the progress, or lack of it, of the pact Sophie had struck with the duchess's husband. Writing from the Palais Bourbon, she told Marie Amélie that it was still her 'dearest wish' to see the Prince of Condé adopt the Duke of Aumale. But, converting that wish into a reality was not a simple task:

> Notwithstanding my great desire to see this project realised, a project by which the name of Monseigneur would be perpetuated and would be productive of much satisfaction to the whole of France, I can only hope to influence the heart of my benefactor little by little upon a subject which always

awakens painful memories [of Louis Antoine's death]. However, I can assure Your Royal Highness that I shall do my utmost to obtain a result in accordance with your wishes and to cherish the affectionate interest which Monseigneur always feels in his godson.

Having gushed forth in defence of her, thus far, obviously failed attempts to get Louis Henri to discuss the proposed adoption, Sophie turned the focus on the Orléans side of the bargain:

> Will Your Royal Highness allow me to take the opportunity to inform you of the approaching marriage of my niece with the Marquis de Chabannes? As [the Feuchères] family has the honour of being allied to the House of Bourbon it would give me the greatest pleasure to be able to present my niece to Your Royal Highness as well as to your august family, and to beg you in person to deign to lend us your aid and bestow your favour upon us.

Sophie's appearances at the Palais Royal were by then frequent but, because of her banishment from Charles X's court and polite royalist society, each of her visits to the Orléans palace had been informal by nature. She sought from Marie Amélie formal presentment there for herself and Matilda, a huge step towards the real goal – reintroduction to the court at the Tuileries.

The Prince de Talleyrand was entrusted with the delivery of Sophie's letter to Marie Amélie at Neuilly. The reply from the Duchess of Orléans, as artful as Sophie's own letter – so much so that it is possible her erudite, pragmatic sister-in-law, Madame Adélaïde, or maybe Talleyrand himself, was actually its architect – must have left Chantilly's notional queen in a turmoil of mixed emotion. Marie Amélie expressed how 'touched' she had been to read of Sophie's clearly expressed desire to see the adoption of the Duke of Aumale by the last of the Condés.

She added:

> I have already been informed of your wish to persuade Monseigneur to take this step and so, as you have thought it your duty to write to me yourself on the matter, I, in my

turn, should think it my duty not to leave you in ignorance of the fact that my mother's heart would be overjoyed to behold my son perpetuate the glorious name of Condé, so justly celebrated in the records of our House [of Bourbon] and in the history of the monarchy of France.

This respectful overture out of the way, Marie Amélie's letter adopted a more business-like tone:

> We have heard the scheme of adoption mentioned more frequently than we could have wished. The [duke] and myself have, however, always stated that, if Monseigneur [Condé] should make up his mind to carry it out, and the king should approve, we would strive in every way to carry out his wishes. But we have thought it our duty to Monseigneur, as well as to ourselves, to refrain from taking any steps which might look as if we wished to influence or press him. We feel that, as this adoption would benefit our child so greatly, we ought to preserve a respectful silence. The distressing memories which you have mentioned to us, and which naturally still pain our good uncle, constitute another reason why we should keep silent. We have sometimes felt tempted to break the silence in the hope of being able to heal his sorrow, but we thought it better to wait until his good heart and the affection he has always shown towards us, as well as to our children, prompted him to move further in the matter.

This highly creative slant on the acid relationship between Condé and his Orléans relatives was followed by a promise from Marie Amélie that, 'if ever I have the happiness of seeing my child become [Condé's] adopted son, you will find in us, for yourself and your family, that support which you kindly ask us to grant, which my gratitude as mother shall assure you of'.

And then the duchess's letter reached the sting in the tail. Referring to the upcoming marriage of Matilda Dawes, she wrote:

> The king and the princesses will be pleased to receive her. They hold the family into which she is about to marry in high esteem, but it is my duty to inform you that I cannot

> break the rules of Court etiquette concerning presentations. We can only receive such persons as have already been presented to the king and to the queen – when there *is* a queen – or to Madame la Dauphine and to the princesses who have precedence after her. Neither is it in our power to choose any ladies, or lady, to make such presentations …
> I much regret, Madame, but I am obliged to observe the rules of Court etiquette.

So that was that. There was no chance of formal presentment at the Palais Royal for Sophie to use as a stepping-stone to the Tuileries. Marie Amélie was not prepared to risk another royal telling-off for a breach of etiquette in order to pave the way to meeting the Orléans side of the pact with Sophie Dawes – at least not until the Prince of Condé had been sucked into the squalid scheme of his domineering English mistress and had agreed to adopt the duchess's son.

No doubt for Sophie this disappointing rebuff from Neuilly took some of the shine from the wedding on 16 August 1827 of Matilda and Frédéric de Chabannes, who were married in sumptuous style at the château of Saint-Leu, by now the favoured residence of Louis Henri and his English mistress. Chabannes went along with this but, alarmed by the gossip surrounding the true nature of Sophie's ancestry and probably fearing he had become a pawn in her self-serving intrigues, wasted very little time in removing his young wife from the uncomfortably controlling presence of the bride's aunt. The newly-wed couple had been allocated residence in a handsome suite of apartments in Paris at the Palais Bourbon, a further act of induced generosity on the part of the Prince of Condé. Chabannes saw this as a trap. Refusing to live there, at the earliest opportunity he whisked his bewildered young bride away.

We may imagine Sophie's anger at what she probably saw as a snub. But it made little difference to her overarching plan for the furtherance of personal grandeur. Her prime concern remained the delicate task of persuading the last of the Condés to do what he would consider the unthinkable – sign over the bulk of his immense inheritance to the House of Orléans. Even if the lawyers working on her behalf, and that of Louis Philippe, had not considered this a problem – and if they had, it was surely a case of naivety on their part – winning the agreement of the downtrodden but still proud Condé prince was going to prove enormously difficult. Each time Sophie raised the matter with Louis Henri, it drew a blank response.

'He has not opened his mouth about it yet,' she told the Duke of Orléans in a letter, suggesting that the impasse might be eased if Louis Philippe were to call at Chantilly, bringing little Prince Henri with him. Perhaps the tormented Prince of Condé would soften his hostility if he were actually to meet the boy. Louis Philippe wrote immediately to his uncle asking for such a visit.

The response should not have come as a surprise to either of the plotters. Condé was furious. 'No – never!', he raged. 'Never shall my name – never shall the title of Prince of Condé – be borne by an Orléans!' Louis Henri may have been hampered by failing physical health, his mental stability severely weakened by the omnipresence of his formidable controlling mistress, but he was not a complete fool. He saw right through the plan concocted by Sophie and Louis Philippe. He was not about to hand over the Condé inheritance, its proud titles, its vast monetary worth, its rich heritage, to any member of the Orléans family – and that was that!

Sophie had to bide her time. It was annoying. The prince's health was waning. Time was beginning to run out. He might die suddenly, the destination of his inheritance still unresolved. She would find a way, however, of getting what she wanted – *everything* she wanted – and, despite his obstinacy on this crucial, defining issue, there remained other little prizes to be wrung out of the last in the line of the Condé while he was still around to deliver them.

Louis Henri, so generous a benefactor in the marriages of both James and Matilda Dawes, was now prevailed upon to provide a handsome dowry of 100,000 francs when yet another of Sophie's Isle of Wight family, her younger sister Charlotte, was to be advantageously married in London in September 1828. Sophie had already arranged a finishing school education in the city for the entry into fashionable society of the youngest of Dicky Daw's children. For Charlotte's entry into married life, her sister had engineered a union with French infantry captain Justin Thanaron,[7] a friend and army colleague of Sophie's dutiful confidante, General Lambot. It was a good match for Charlotte, now in her thirty-third year.

In the context of Sophie's match-making, historians and biographers have wondered why, given her huge influence over him, she did not

Intrigue

pursue the ideal match for herself with the Prince of Condé, thus assuring she would inherit the bulk of his fortune with no need for external intrigue with a third party. The probable answer is that she needed the involvement of an influential third party, the Duke of Orléans or whoever else she chose to conspire with, in order to secure her readmittance to court. Making herself the sole beneficiary of the Condé inheritance through marriage to Louis Henri would have cast her so much more firmly in the mould of disrepute, so hated and reviled in royal circles that she would stand no chance of re-entry to the Tuileries. Sophie might have persuaded the prince to marry her – but chose not to.

Her destiny lay in the pact she had forged with the Duke of Orléans. No doubt she became increasingly aware, if she had not been at the outset, that any bargain struck with Louis Philippe was, by extension, effectively one with the woman who, in terms of her influence, counsel and loyalty, mattered the most in his family, the highly intelligent, forthright Madame Adélaïde. The duke's sister would have been consulted closely on the matter of the Condé inheritance. It is doubtful whether he would have gone along with Madame de Feuchères' self-serving intrigue had Adélaïde's highly-valued opinion not supported his own in recognising the immense potential for Orléans advancement offered by Sophie's squalid plot.

Madame Adélaïde's frankness of expression, as well as her strong liberal views, was vastly at odds with the pretentious hypocrisy of Charles X's courtiers who, orchestrated by the monarchy itself, hated her. Perhaps, despite initial reservations about Sophie's moral conduct and motivation, she felt a degree of common cause with the socially ostracised Englishwoman against the prejudice at the Tuileries. If so, it would have been more than Sophie deserved but possibly the Orléans princess recognised in Sophie's dogged determination to pursue her ambitions an empathetic quality worthy of some admiration at least.

Adélaïde, at this stage of her life, remained an elegant, refined woman with a dress sense to match, although her portrait ignores the ruddy, pimpled complexion she shared not only with her brother but also with the would-be Bourbon, Maria Stella. Her face was certainly not that of a classical beauty. As with the over-muscular, awkward Sophie Dawes, the princess's austere looks were routinely mocked at court. Perhaps this helped cement a bond between them.

The Infamous Sophie Dawes

Madame Adélaïde's willing involvement in Sophie's plot, along with that of the Duke and Duchess of Orléans and the wily Prince de Talleyrand, meant that the smuggler's daughter from the Isle of Wight was now embedded in probably the most powerful of alliances imaginable in the third decade of nineteenth-century France. It was true that by 1828, the Orléans side had grown ever more impatient at the lack of progress on the deal, a frustration increasingly shared by Sophie herself. But, the old, weary soldier at Chantilly, though yet to understand how far it had gone, was in the grip of an elaborate pincer movement designed to outflank him and crush all remaining traces of the resistance in his spirit.

Chapter 7

A Will of Infamy:
The Condé Inheritance

Devoid of all but a handful of trusted allies at Chantilly, people like his devoted body-servant (valet) Manoury and his young dentist, Hostein, who had somehow survived Madame de Feuchères' heartless cull of those closest to him – in some cases through a pretence of obedience to his all-powerful English bully of a mistress – Louis Henri, Prince of Condé, cut an increasingly lonely, deeply unhappy figure in the gilded cage of his ancestral home. The mistress he had once, long ago, adored, was constantly on his back, cajoling, pestering and pleading. At times he was physically threatened by her as she attempted to force his agreement to the adoption of his godson, deal with the protracted matter of his inheritance – and secure her pact with the House of Orléans. She did not, of course, refer to it in that way, but he knew full well the truth of it.

But on this one issue he somehow found the strength to resist. No amount of hectoring on her part, none of the spiteful fury, bad-tempered rage, shouting and screaming she lambasted him with, nor the more subtle forms of pressure she sometimes, out of sheer frustration, resorted to, made any difference. In every other regard Louis Henri was reduced in her presence to a submissive, shambling wreck, but on the matter of his unwritten will he simply refused to bend.

Possibly it was Sophie who paid for a notice informing readers in the Parisian journal *L'Aritorque* on 12 November 1828 that 'His Royal Highness, the Duke of Bourbon has made his will, in which he leaves all his property to Monsieur the Duke of Nemours, second son of Monsieur the Duke of Orléans, on the condition that he takes his title of Prince of Condé'.

The subject of the pact drawn up between Louis Philippe and Sophie was not, of course, the 14-year-old Louis, Duke of Nemours, but his younger brother, Henri, Duke of Aumale. Mischief was afoot. The boys' father is said to have exclaimed on reading this: 'We can deny the report without telling an untruth!' He ordered his secretary to send a letter to the Prince of Condé's bailiff categorically denying that he, the duke, had anything to do with the insertion. Nevertheless, good use of it was made with secretary Boroval telling Louis Henri that, 'however gratified he would be to think one of his sons might ever bear the great name of Condé, it would be far from [Louis Philippe] to wish to make such delicate a matter public'.

Whoever was responsible for the press notice, it served to pile further pressure on the last of the Condés, but still Louis Henri refused to budge on the matter of his unwritten will. If the insertion in the Parisian journal was a devious mind game, the prince considered that his wisest move was to treat the whole thing with cold disdain. But in Paris itself the heat on him was being turned up.

The Duke of Orléans, in a bid to force the issue on the Condé inheritance, had redoubled his efforts to secure reinstatement at court for Madame de Feuchères. Why Charles X should now, after years of outright refusal, yield to Louis Philippe's persistent lobbying for Sophie's return to court is uncertain. At the onset of 1829 Charles was a monarch in crisis. Two years earlier, following outspoken criticism during his review of the National Guard of the king's reactionary policies, he had disbanded the State *gendarmerie* which doubled as a military reserve.

In January 1828 Charles had been forced to dismiss his ultra-royalist prime minister, Joseph de Villèle,[1] a man bitterly at odds with the liberal views of the Duke of Orléans, following his defeat in a general election. Villèle had been replaced by Jean-Baptiste Gay,[2] whose far more moderate royalism and personality were much less to the king's liking. It was in the midst of this political upheaval and consequent uncertainty for King Charles that he was urged once again by Louis Philippe to reverse the ban on the infamous English mistress of the Prince of Condé.

With the tide of public opinion flowing ever more against him, perhaps the beleaguered king saw political advantage in coming to the aid of his Bourbon cousin despite, or possibly because of, the Orléans duke's towering status within the liberal opposition. Or was Charles simply too preoccupied with other matters of State to concern himself any further

A Will of Infamy

with the social standing of Sophie Dawes? Whatever lay behind his decision, he agreed to allow her back to court, fully aware that, in so doing, he was paving the way to a massive Orléans boost.

There was a condition attached, however, as General Lambot discovered when he was summoned to the king's presence. 'I charge you, particularly, to talk to Madame de Feuchères on this subject', the king told him, 'and to say to her that if she contrives to persuade the prince to make the will in favour of the Duke of Aumale, she will be doing something that is personally agreeable to me.' This time Lambot had no fear of a tongue-lashing from the woman he served at Chantilly as he made his way back there from the royal palace.

Sophie was triumphant. She could almost touch the reward for her years of scheming. The knife was in her grasp. All she had to do was to twist it into the heart of the Prince of Condé.

Louis Philippe sought to help further by bringing his four sons to visit the old man at the château. From the eldest, Prince Ferdinand, in his eighteenth year, to the youngest, 4-year-old Prince Antoine, they were undoubtedly a brood of charming children. It was a pity for their adoring father that the charm was entirely lost on the sour-faced Condé aristocrat on whose fabled fairy-tale country estate they frolicked. The visit did nothing to soften his bitter feelings towards the family of Philippe Égalité and its descendant representatives. He barely acknowledged the second youngest of the four boys, his godson, Prince Henri, now aged 7.

But the little Duke of Aumale dominated the Machiavellian thoughts of Condé's English mistress as she fine-tuned her strategy to have the boy's name inserted at the top of Louis Henri's will. She knew the onus was now more firmly than ever on her to fulfil her side of the pact.

Still the prince resisted and still he talked of leaving his fortune instead to the king's grandchildren. It was a shame he could not take his resolve a step further and find the courage to end his torment once and for all by writing a will that reflected *his* interests rather than those of his mistress. If he could only have decided just what those interests were, he could have simply told her the matter was settled whether she liked it or not. There was never a chance of that. His firmness only went so far; sadly, he had resigned himself to live out his days in abject misery.

When his sympathetic dentist gently suggested his master adopt a firmer line in dealing with Sophie's cruel treatment of him, the prince who had lifted her out of obscurity, he responded by asking: 'Do you think it is so easy to do that?' According to Hostein, he went on to lament:

> Perhaps when one is young one can do such things. But when one is well past seventy it is impossible to break a habit. I have tried several times, but have always failed. Have you ever observed a fly hovering round a spider's web? If its wing only grazes the web it is caught in the greedy spider's casting net and made a prisoner ... well, that is what has happened to me!

And yet the greedy spider in Louis Henri's tragic story had still to finish off her prey. Face-to-face confrontation with the prince caused her nothing but extreme frustration. A change of tactic was called for. It is interesting how, when corresponding in writing to Louis Henri, Sophie's attitude towards him – implied if not actually based on her true feelings – differed profoundly from her treatment of him in direct conversation. Her letters to him were always grounded on apparent respect and flowered liberally with affectionate words and phrasing. Her purposes were always better served when she took the time to think things through. In face-to-face contact on difficult matters her easily roused anger always got the better of her. And so, on 1 May 1829, while staying in Paris at a grand suite in the Palais Bourbon's Hôtel de Lassay,[3] an early gift to her from her Condé benefactor, she wrote him a long letter, carefully constructed, in the hope that this would finally cause him to throw in the towel.

Louis Henri was recovering at Chantilly from a serious bout of sickness. At this point in his life he was often confined to his bed with one internal malaise or another. His remaining physical strength rapidly deserted him. There are reports, though these cannot be confirmed, that, in addition to the disabling injuries to his right shoulder and mutilated left hand, he had now lost the use of three fingers on the *right* hand.[4] While he was still able to ride his horse, he had to be helped into the saddle. It was the same when he elected to ride his carriage; he could not get in the vehicle without assistance. On foot, his limping gait was markedly more pronounced. It was now virtually impossible for him to use the stairs, up or down. In summary, the physical condition of the Prince of Condé can only be described as decrepit.

He preferred to suffer in silence and increasingly shunned contact with the world outside his bedchamber. More often than not, during the day he sought the solace of sleep rather than being awake long enough to join in prolonged conversation. But sleep at night was difficult for a prince tormented by the demons of a cruel mistress's relentless subjugation of his spirit. Those of his courtiers he was still able to rely on, and by now he had realised just how few remained, were genuinely and desperately saddened by the decline of a man they regarded only as gentle and kind; an aristocrat of the old order who, despite his infirmities, tried always to retain a noble grace.

While Sophie acknowledged in her letter this profound deterioration, she began the lengthy missive in self-pitying manner, portraying herself as the innocent victim of widespread malicious gossip:

> For a long while, my dearest friend, an important matter has occupied me greatly, but up to the present I have not had the courage to open entirely my heart towards you, because I was afraid to distress you. The moment has come, however, when I am forced to fulfil a sacred duty towards you. Badly disposed people do not cease to publish that I wish to profit from the tender friendship that you have for me by obtaining your fortune.

Sophie rose to her own defence: 'Strong in the purity of my intentions towards you in this regard, I have until this moment neglected to take the necessary steps to justify myself before the royal family who would, I cannot doubt, do me justice if they knew the truth about my conduct'.

This outrageously false self-portrayal of a shrinking violet out of the way, Sophie got down to business:

> When I saw you recently, my dearest friend, so indisposed at Chantilly, the saddest reflections came to me. And in truth, if this illness had become graver, what would have been my position?
>
> I, who at such a moment might have hoped to render you the tenderest care, would have been the first to have been sent far from you … because people would have supposed I had interested views upon your fortune! Pardon me, my

dearest friend, if I am obliged to enter here into these details which really tear my heart! But I have already said to you that it is a sacred duty that I impose on myself to implore you, on my knees if it must be, to decide to fulfil the duty imposed upon every man, whatever class he may be, and especially imposed upon a prince who carries a name as illustrious as yours. The king and the royal family wish that you should make choice of a prince of your family to inherit one day your name and your fortune.

People believe that it is I alone who put an obstacle in the way of this desire. They even go as far as to believe that, if I were not near you, this hope of all France would have already been realised. The problem is so painful to me that I really cannot support it any longer and I implore you, my dearest friend, in the name of the tender attachment that you have witnessed from me for so many years, to ease this cruel position in which I find myself by adopting an heir.

In case Louis Henri might have been in any doubt – and he surely would not have been – she added:

After many reflections, my opinion is that the young Duke of Aumale has the best title to this high favour. The young prince is your godson and so is doubly attached to you. Besides, he shows – although his years are so few – every sign of being worthy to bear your name. Do not let yourself regard as an obstacle, I beg you, the idea that this adoption will cause you the least embarrassment. Nothing will be changed in your habitual manner of living. It is only a simple formality that you have to do, then you will be tranquil as to the future, and can let me remain near you without thinking that you would have to send me away.

If, despite all that I have written you, you find your heart still too bruised for you to be able to make this adoption by your own wish, I dare to say that the affection and the tenderness that I have always shown to you should make you do it for me. By doing it, you will assure, my dear friend, the benevolence of the royal family and a future less unhappy for your poor Sophie.

A Will of Infamy

The letter was dispatched to the Prince of Condé and a copy sent to the Duke of Orléans at Neuilly. Suitably impressed by his co-plotter's literary outpouring, the duke acknowledged it immediately, enclosing a supportive letter, dated 2 May, for her to read, approve and forward to the prince. Its content must have delighted Sophie. She could not have asked for more. It read:

> I cannot resist, sir, the desire to express to you myself how I am touched by the efforts – so honourable for herself – that Madame de Feuchères is making on my behalf, and that she has told me of. It does not become me, without doubt, seeing that it rests entirely with you to procure so great an advantage for one of my children, to take anything from her without having it confirmed by you, but I have believed it my duty – and a duty also to the distinguished blood which runs in your veins and mine – to indicate to you how happy I am to see new ties between us, between our two families already united in so many ways, and how proud I should be if one of my children was destined to carry a name that is so precious to all of our family – a name to which is attached so much glory and so many happy memories!

For good measure Sophie sent the two letters to the old man at Chantilly with an appended note in which she told him she would be 'in despair if I found that my efforts had been without effect. Think, dearest, that this is your Sophie who has always loved you so tenderly'. No doubt he read that with scorn as he reflected on the cruel 'tenderness' of his mistress's love.

Subsequent correspondence between them at their respective hôtels in the Palais Bourbon makes clear that the prince was moved only to reproach Sophie for her 'wicked endeavours' with the House of Orléans. She responded to this by telling him by letter that Louis Philippe would be visiting her that same morning in her apartments prior to leaving for a visit to England. 'He wishes to pay his respects to you ... I beg you, do not refuse to lunch with me as usual.'

Ambiguity confronts the reader here. Did she mean that, at this juncture, Sophie's 'dearest friend' was studiously avoiding her, spending time apart from her in different parts of the same palace and refusing to join her for luncheon? Or was she merely expressing her fear that the prince, unwilling to see his nephew, would not fulfil usual practice in joining her for the meal?

'However,' she added, 'if you think it would look better if I was not with you, then [the duke] will wait on you in your own hôtel'. Whichever of these venues he chose, it seems that Louis Henri did meet with his nephew that day – and for the prince that meeting went very badly indeed.

The draft of a complex legal document, drawn up by Louis Philippe's clever team of lawyers was soon delivered to the Prince of Condé, setting out formal details for his adoption of the Duke of Aumale. So it seems that some agreement had been reached on this thorniest of issues.

But, whatever the old prince had agreed to at this point, there was no sign of the tranquillity his pitiless English mistress had promised him. Hugues Acgille de Surval, Chantilly's bailiff (estates and forests manager), who, although one of Sophie's appointees, had grown genuinely fond of his master, recalled a depressed Louis Henri expressing after another sleepless night the 'torments that inflame my blood in the most horrible manner'. Baron de Surval quoted the exhausted prince lamenting: 'Can there be anything more frightful than to find oneself pressed with this violence to do something which is utterly distasteful to one? Nothing else is talked about to me at present ... my death is the sole object that they have in view!'

Taking an enormous risk of losing his well-paid position, Surval offered to confront Madame de Feuchères on the prince's abject misery. 'No, no!' replied Louis Henri, 'that would make matters worse. I know her violence. If you interfered she would make a continual inferno for me!'

But desperate times call for desperate measures. When he felt he could take no more, the prince called for Surval. 'Tell Madame de Feuchères that, if she will leave me in peace on the subject of the inheritance, I will give her the domain of Guise', he instructed the bailiff. Guise, in the Hauts-de-France region, dominated by its historic fortified château, was among the richest possessions in the ownership of the Condé. The rents from its profitable estate would have supported a very comfortable life for Sophie Dawes had she accepted the gift. But when Baron de Surval reported back to his master, it was to inform him that his desperate bribe had failed to sway her from her resolve. Sophie was holding out for a bigger prize than that.

Surval had tried repeatedly to free his master from the tyranny of his tormentor. 'Why will Monseigneur not sign a will in favour of his godson?', he had on one occasion ventured to ask.

'Ah well, I see I must make up my mind to do it, to buy peace if I can, for the few years which remain to me', Louis Henri had replied. But he had not done it; the bullying did not cease.

'Why do you consent to [the bullying] if it causes you so much suffering?', Surval had asked after another scene. 'Monseigneur the Prince of Condé, your father, would never have been so weak'.

The baron probably tried the desperate approach of 'tough love' here in order to shame his master into ending his torment. It didn't work, but certainly struck a chord with the prince. Holding his face in his hands, he had pleaded: 'Don't make me even more unhappy than I am'.

The final days of August 1829 brought the Prince of Condé to his knees. He made one last desperate attempt to thwart the designs on his will of his merciless mistress – a pitiable appeal to the only man who, he forced himself to believe, could intervene on his behalf. On the 20th he wrote to the Duke of Orléans on the 'affair commenced rather thoughtlessly without my knowledge by Mme. de Feuchères and which she has taken upon herself to persuade me to agree to'. It was, he added with stark understatement, 'extremely painful' to him:

> Not only does it grieve me deeply by the sad memories [of his own son's tragic early death] which it awakens and to which I cannot resign myself, but I must confess that other reasons prevent me giving all my attention to the matter just at the present moment. I rely upon your affection for me to persuade Mme. de Feuchères to leave me in peace upon this subject.

Conscious that persuading Sophie to abandon her plan would be hugely detrimental to Louis Philippe's family – especially the young Duke of Aumale – Louis Henri concluded his letter by promising to demonstrate in some other way 'a public and certain mark of my esteem' for the Orléans. The assumption here is that he was hinting at a bequest to his godson of one or more of the fine estates, and the profits attached to these, he owned in various parts of the country.

By now, Louis Philippe would have seen such a gesture as poor consolation for the fabulous riches his son had been brought so close to inheriting from the bullied old man at Chantilly. While he *did* call on Sophie in Paris and asked her, with witnesses present, to stop trying to persuade Louis Henri to make a will so clearly against his wishes, the Duke of Orléans merely went through the motions. Sophie was never going to stand aside and forget the whole enterprise after such a prolonged campaign to achieve her goals. Louis Philippe was of course aware of this – but at least he could tell his uncle he had tried to get Sophie off his back.

This was an act of contemptible deception. It gave hope to the old man when, in reality, there was never a chance of it. Like his uncle, the Duke of Orléans had once been a gallant soldier. Where was that gallantry now? It might be possible to argue that he was motivated by a genuine desire to see his family prosper, but the consequences of his actions in helping to destroy, through exquisite mental torture, a relative who, despite the imperfections of his earlier life, of which there were many, deserved to live out his final decrepit years in peace.

Sophie, of course, ignored the Orléans prince's hollow appeal on his uncle's behalf to stand aside – perfectly sure she was not required to take any notice of it – and continued her relentless assault on the prince's crumbling state of mind. On 29 August, nine days after sending his imploring letter to the Palais Royal, the Prince of Condé and his mistress were together at Saint-Leu. Sitting that evening in the salon, Baron de Surval was disturbed by a series of 'loud cries' from the nearby billiard room where Louis Henri and Sophie had gone to discuss important matters. Clearly, the discussion had descended, as was by now the norm, into a blazing argument. Hearing his name called, the bailiff hurried immediately into the room where his master, as he would later relate, was 'speechless with anger and trembling all over'.

'Just look at how excited Monseigneur is …all about nothing, too!' Sophie declared calmly to the shocked Surval. 'Try and pacify him', she instructed the bailiff as she made to leave the room.

At this point, Surval related, the prince regained his voice. 'Yes, Madame', he yelled at the departing baroness, 'it is an atrocious, a fearful, thing to hold the knife to my throat in order to force me to do what you know is repugnant to me!' Then, in a dramatic gesture, he seized her hand and held it against his throat. 'Well then', he cried, 'thrust the knife in … thrust it in!'

A Will of Infamy

It appears that Sophie was in the habit of carrying the blank, unwritten will with her each time she spoke to the prince on the subject, hoping to find him in a mood of utter resignation and determined not to miss the chance to pounce. This had become apparent to Baron de Surval. Aghast at what he had witnessed at Saint-Leu and deeply moved by the pitiful plight of his employer, a man who had shown him nothing but kindness and respect, he now begged the prince *not* to complete and sign the document his mistress dangled menacingly in front of him at every opportunity. The prince's reply tells us a lot about his addled state of mind: 'But she threatens to leave me if I don't consent', Louis Henri muttered, terror stalking his eyes.

'Well then Monseigneur, let her go!', he was urged by Surval, amazed that his master should spend a moment worrying about losing the woman who had for years made his life an utter misery. The prince looked at his bailiff in astonishment. Leaving Sophie was simply not an option.

Did he realise during the hours – and especially the night – following the appalling scene in the billiard room that he was incapable, and always would be, of breaking the habit of Sophie Dawes? Or had he simply had enough of the awful torture she constantly inflicted on him, and cared for nothing other than an overwhelming desire to live out his life in restful peace? Whatever his thoughts, it seems the last Prince of Condé finally, resignedly, gave up the fight.

On the morning of 30 August, in his own hand, watched over by his triumphant mistress, he made out his will. She may well have dictated it. She would certainly have been pleased with it.[5]

Adoption of his godson, so long sought from Louis Henri by Sophie and the House of Orléans, had not, in the end, been required. The simpler alternative had been achieved. The prince had named his great-nephew and godson, Henri Eugene d'Orléans, Duke of Aumale, 'as my residuary legatee and appoint him at the time of my decease to inherit all my estates and possessions, of whatsoever nature they may be, which I may possess ... to enjoy, with the exception of such legacies as I now bequeath, or shall bequeath at any future period of my life'.

The monetary value of the Duke of Aumale's residuary legacy, which would include the ancestral domain of Chantilly among its possessions, was estimated at between 75 and 80,000,000 francs. To ensure the family of Louis Philippe would not, under any circumstance, miss out on this fabulous fortune, the last of the Condés had stipulated that, 'in the event of the said Duke of Aumale pre-deceasing me, I name and institute as my residuary legatee the youngest male child of my nephew, Louis Philippe, Duke of Orléans'. No doubt this clause had been insisted upon by the gloating Englishwoman who guided the prince's pen.

And what of her own reward for all those years of relentlessly cruel endeavour? How was the Prince of Condé's 'faithful companion', as the will disingenuously described her – no doubt her choice of words – to benefit from his death? The weary old aristocrat had dutifully bequeathed 'to the dame, Sophie Dawes, Baroness de Feuchères, the sum of two millions, which shall be paid *in specie* immediately after my decease, free of a registration fee or of any other fees, which said fees are to be paid out of my estate'. Sophie had ensured there would be no deductions that would eat away at her share of the monetary spoils – and there was a lot more in store for her, too, as the prince's lengthy will listed an extensive inheritance of property.

Not only was Sophie bequeathed the château and park of Saint-Leu, she was also to inherit the forest and adjoining lands of Montmorency, the forest of Enghien (the prince's favourite hunting ground), the château of Gros-bois and estate at Boissy-Saint-Léger, and the domain of Morfontaine. Provision was made, too, for her to assume ownership of the pavilion she and her private household already occupied at the Palais Bourbon in Paris, together with its furniture, the grounds attached to the building, and the horses and carriages kept there for the baroness's use. Together, this handsome pile of bequests – the inherited possessions and money combined – would see her personal wealth increase by approximately 12,000,000 francs.

Again, legal costs arising from the transfer of property into her ownership were to be met by the prince's estate, 'in such a way that she may enjoy the said goods and chattels without having to pay any fees from her private property'. Clearly, Sophie had thought all of this through.

With all this secured for herself, it is not hard to imagine the smuggler's daughter offering no objection to the humbled prince making generous provision in the will for members of his household, amounting to a total of 250,000 francs, and stipulating that his château of Écouen, north of Paris, should be used after his death as a charitable institution for the benefit of the children, grandchildren and later descendants of his former military colleagues in the armies of Condé and Vendée. These were kind, honourable gestures. At least Sophie allowed him those. The will, however, made no provision whatsoever for Louis de Rohan, or for any other member of the family of the Prince of Condé's mother, who had good claim to be his natural heirs.

Baron de Surval was named as executor of the will. It would have been natural for him to have wondered just how long, or short, a period it would be before he was asked to carry out those duties. And, if he did wonder, he would probably have recalled overhearing a recent conversation about the Condé inheritance which took place between Madame de Feuchères and James Dawes, her nephew and loyal lieutenant. The latter had asked his aunt if the Prince of Condé was likely to make his will soon, to which Sophie had replied that 'it will not be long'.

Unconvinced, James had commented: 'Oh, he'll take a long time to die!'

'Bah!', Sophie had retorted, 'he can hardly hold himself together. I have only to give him a push with my little finger and he tumbles down immediately. It would take very little to suffocate him!'

Surval had not forgotten those chilling words – nor the cuts and bruises he and other members of the household had several times noticed on their master's face and body following 'meetings' with Sophie, and which she had once explained away by telling them the tell-tale marks were the result of a failed attempt on the old prince's part to take his own life.

The baron, as much as anyone, knew well the sinister nature of the domination exerted by Sophie Dawes and her cohorts over the household of the last Condé prince. It had been drummed into him when he had first taken up his appointment as bailiff. 'You will have a fine position, but remember – you must always do as my aunt commands', James Dawes had told him. Surval knew the score. As the ink dried on the prince's will the baron must have thought that he would be called upon sooner rather than later to execute the twisted terms of its many pages.

The architect of the will soon basked in the congratulations that flowed liberally from the triumvirate of power and influence within the House of Orléans. Sophie had maintained regular contact not only with Louis Philippe, but also with his wife and sister in the period preceding the signing of the document. Gushing letters of mutual flattery had flown between them as the Orléans establishment awaited confirmation from their English co-conspirator of their young prince's inheritance from his godfather. Deep was their appreciation when the will was satisfactorily signed and sealed. Shallow were the outpourings of warm affection which were showered on Dicky Daw's daughter. It mattered little to Sophie. She soaked up the glory of an astonishing achievement and prepared for the first, longed for, part of her reward.

Having outrageously declared to the Duke of Orléans, and to anyone else who enquired, that the Prince of Condé was now 'more pleased than myself at the composition of his will', Sophie embraced the start of 1830 in a frenzy of excitement. She was to be readmitted to the court of Charles X on Sunday, 7 February. In a hurried note sent to Louis Philippe that morning, seeking guidance on protocol, she wrote that she was 'quite in a state of agitation at the thought of the great event which takes place today'. It is clear, however, that the 'greatness' of the occasion was very much confined to her monstrously egotistical mind alone. 'Madame de Feuchères' reappearance at Court took place without her being able to get much satisfaction from it', recalled one of the courtiers present at the Tuileries, the Count of Menard:

> She was in a very odious position. She was made to swallow many a bitter pill. But she was resolved to play at being a great lady and, provided that she could say, "I am going to the palace," it mattered little to her by which door she entered. She never forgave Madame [the Duchess of Berry] for not having espoused her cause ... Madame, who did not respect her, often said, "I prefer her to appear here as presented by my uncle [referring to Louis Henri], rather than by myself!"

True to her word, the Duchess of Berry was among the notable absentees at Sophie's 'great event'. She was far from alone in decrying the shamed Englishwoman's reappearance at court. Parisian society generally was appalled. The words of the Viscount Sostène de la Rochefoucauld, Charles X's Director of Fine Arts, provide a good illustration of the ill-feeling:

> Madame de Feuchères, who has the worst possible reputation, the acknowledged mistress of the Duke of Bourbon, has been received by the most pious of princes! How then

can one talk of honour, conscience, religion, morality in a country where the Court gives such an example![6]

But Sophie could brush off the bitter words of Parisian society. She was back where she believed she belonged. The Queen of Chantilly had been formally presented to the King of France. And very soon the political tide was turning firmly in the direction of Dicky Daw's girl.

Five months after her readmittance to Charles X's court, the court itself fell apart. The king's principles of rule by hereditary right were finally overthrown in a popular uprising following publication on 26 July of restrictive ordinances which flew in the face of Louis XVIII's constitutional charter of 1814. Angry protests and demonstrations were followed by three days of fighting as Paris was again gripped by revolutionary fervour. By 2 August the Bourbon monarch had been forced to abdicate. A week later the upper bourgeoisie of the liberal opposition were wildly celebrating the accession to the throne of their leader, Louis Philippe, Duke of Orléans. France's July Revolution was over – and Sophie Dawes' pact of self-aggrandisement now lay comfortably with the man who would be styled the King of the French.

But in truth, the bond she now possessed with the throne of France was only comfortable as long as the infamous will at its heart remained intact and unchanged – and stayed that way up until the time of the Prince of Condé's death. While the old man clung to life in a parlous mental state verging on senility, she could not be confident that he would leave well alone. Having no further use for him, she made no attempt at anything approaching civility towards him, barely spoke to him at all and longed only for his demise while fearing constantly that he might yet thwart her cruel designs by having a new, or significantly amended, will drawn up.

She was right to be fearful. In Louis Henri's mind the July Revolution had changed the dynamic of his inheritance. At the time of finally submitting to his mistress's demands and writing the will, he had believed that Charles X's grandson, Prince Henri, Duke of Bordeaux, would one day inherit the throne and have no need of the Condé inheritance. But now Charles's royal family, including the young duke and his sister, had been dispatched into exile. Guilt and genuine grief stalked him. 'What will become of those poor children?', he was frequently heard to say. 'How I wish I could help them … so cruelly orphaned and now in exile!'

Comments such as these – indeed *all* his utterances that could be overheard by Sophie's network of spies – were reported back to her. The prince was several times seen going through his private papers, documents relating to his various possessions, money and lands. Frequent visits were made to his châteaux by the Prince of Rohan for discreet talks. Somehow he managed to hide precisely what he was doing from the ever-watchful eyes of Sophie's army of domiciled agents, but it was obvious he was up to something. The last of the Condés was using his final reserves of mental agility to cobble together a truly desperate plan of escape from his mistress, his home, his country. He hoped to make it to the coast and then set sail once more for England where he could join Charles X in exile – and make a new will.

Chapter 8

Tragedy at Saint-Leu:
The End of the Condé

The key to the Prince of Condé's escape plan was secrecy. In other words, he didn't stand a chance. It was inevitable that Sophie would hear of its every detail – and put a stop to it. That it was one of Louis Henri's most trusted allies, the loyal body-servant Manoury, who gave away the game adds the saddest of ironies to the sheer hopelessness of the old man's bid for freedom. Manoury was devoted to the prince, but he was a trusting soul who placed his faith in too many people. At the château of Chantilly and at Saint-Leu, where most of the despairing prince's blueprint for escape was pieced together, this was, to say the least, unwise.

To provide a firm financial footing for his anticipated retreat to London, the prince instructed Baron de Surval to withdraw, on his behalf, 1,000,000 francs in notes from his bank account in Paris. The next step for Louis Henri was to arrange his journey to the coast. There was, however, an immediate problem. In charge of everything equestrian at Chantilly and Saint-Leu was James Dawes, by now a man the prince had learned no longer to trust. This left him unable to use horses from his stables. Nor could he utilise one of his fleet of carriages. Instead, Manoury would be dispatched to the capital, equipped with 2,000 francs with which to purchase a carriage and pay for the hire of two post-horses. The valet was then to use the newly-acquired conveyance to travel on to Moisselles, a village in the Val-d'Oise, near the north-eastern fringe of the great forest of Montmorency, where the carriage was to be hidden. The Prince of Condé, having excused himself from a hunting party in the southwest of the forest (close to Saint-Leu) and turned his horse in the direction of the rendezvous, would join him there for a dash in the carriage to the northern French coast and onward passage to England.

However, a pre-requisite for the cross-Channel voyage was a passport. Manoury, whose task it was to obtain one, appears to have been flummoxed by this. Not sure how to go about it, he sought advice from a seasoned traveller. Unfortunately for Manoury, and the Prince of Condé, the man he asked, Baron de la Villegontier, was, as noted earlier, a close ally of Sophie's. He alerted his wife, another of Sophie's confidantes, and, inevitably, Sophie was soon made aware of the hapless prince's desperate plan to escape her malevolent hold on him.

Though thwarted, Louis Henri did not immediately abandon his quest. Indeed, he spent the next few weeks planning alternative means of escape. It has been said that doing this was probably the only thing that prevented his fragile mental state from total collapse. But when the exiled Charles X, reaching Edinburgh after a brief stay at Lulworth Castle in Dorset, wrote to his old comrade from the palace of Holyrood, begging Louis Henri to join him in Britain, the former king's letter was never delivered to the prince. Somehow, it seems, Louis Philippe got wind of this and ordered the letter's interception before the prince could react to it.

Madame de Feuchères, too, was racked by anxiety. She tightened the net around the prince, keeping him under constant supervision – and mimicked his stymied bid for freedom by having her own carriage positioned, ready for a quick getaway, at another village near to the forest of Montmorency, conveniently close to Saint-Leu. Marjorie Bowen recorded in her book how Sophie told the obsequious abbé Briant, the grossly overweight yet religiously lightweight priest who was both her secretary and favoured confidante, 'I have decided to accompany the prince wherever he thinks it convenient to go', by which she actually meant that, if he tried again to flee, she would be right on his tail, handily placed to pursue him post-haste.

So fearful was Sophie that her captive prince would get away and leave her very uncomfortably placed in France, having failed to meet her side of the bargain she had struck with the family of the new king, she hastily organised the transfer of 500,000 francs from her account with Rothschild in Paris to the bank's safe keeping in London. A new or revised Condé will might deprive her of the inheritance she had striven so hard to secure, but at least she would not go hungry if this meant she was forced to return to the country of her birth.

Her contingency plan also extended to the hiring of a secret apartment in Paris to serve as a bolthole should disaster strike and leave her, at short notice, otherwise homeless in France. The option of moving, should a move become necessary, to her mother Jane's home in the city was denied to her. Now in her late-seventies and inclined to an ever-deepening piety since her youngest daughter Charlotte's marriage to Justin Thanaron in 1828 had left her in sole residence at the Paris address, Jane had turned her back on society and chosen to enter a convent.

There were rumours, and they may well have been based on fact, that the prince had already made a new will, leaving virtually everything to Henri, Duke of Bordeaux, exiled with his father in Edinburgh, instead of that young prince's Orléans namesake, Henri, Duke of Aumale – and nothing at all to Sophie Dawes. It was said by the rumour-mongers that the revised will had been signed by Louis Henri, witnessed and secretly locked away from prying eyes.

Hearing of this, as she was bound to, a panicky Sophie countered by suggesting to Baron de Surval, and it seems to just about anyone else who she thought she could trust, that, instead of forcing her to wait to inherit the impressive list of property and land earmarked for her in his will of August 1829, Louis Henri should legally transfer the entire portfolio into her ownership while he was still alive. When the difficulties of doing so, and the likelihood that, even if it were achieved, she would immediately need to sell the treasured château of Saint-Leu to cover the enormous legal costs, was pointed out to her by the baron, Sophie backed down.

She was, however, determinedly focused on averting disaster and, true to form, considered the best way of doing this was to terrify her old benefactor into renewed submission so that he would forget any notion of running away. Accustomed though members of the Condé household were to the disturbing physical evidence of Madame de Feuchères' routine bullying of their master, the appalling scene acted out on the first floor gallery of the château at Saint-Leu on the morning of 11 August was in a class of its own. From the door of his first-floor apartments the prince emerged onto the gallery. Contemporary accounts describe him as half-dressed, barefoot and in a clearly pitiful state of distress. Below, amazed household staff on the ground floor stared at the shocking spectacle so unbefitting of the grand environs of its setting.

'Fetch Manoury!', the prince cried, holding a trembling hand to his right eye, on the point of collapse.

Before the valet could be summoned, help appeared from another doorway on the gallery. By chance another of Louis Henri's godsons, his inspector-general of the hunt, Obry, was staying at the château. Having heard the prince's cries, the former cavalry officer rushed to his master's aid. To this young man the prince pointed to his badly bruised and bloodshot right eye.

'Madame de Feuchères is a spiteful woman! Look … look at what she has done to me … she is a wicked woman. I wish I was dead!', he was heard to say between sobs, making clear, though nobody present could have been in any doubt, that it was Sophie who had brutalised him.

Later, no doubt fearing another beating from his mistress, he pretended he had hurt himself getting out of bed, falling against his night-table and striking his head. Then, changing his story, he told Manoury, as the loyal valet tended to his wounds, that he had tripped on a small staircase leading from Madame de Feuchères' apartments to his own, a more plausible explanation than the previous one as he was able, in apparent support of his story, to point to bruising and scratches on his legs. It may be that this was the truth, albeit only partly so. It is not overstretching the imagination to believe that, having taken a facial battering from the powerful fists of his bullying mistress, he *had* fallen down the stairway in a daze, injuring his legs. Whatever the truth of that, the prince was noticeably relieved when Manoury told him Madame de Feuchères would be lunching in her own apartments that day before leaving for Paris.

There are, in fact, several accounts of this unpleasant affair which provide some conflicting detail about precisely to whom the prince was speaking when he offered the various explanations for the causes of his wounds.[1] Sources also differ on other aspects of the incident. Some say a letter was delivered to him during the course of that morning and that it was only after reading this – presumably hurried to him on Sophie's behalf – that he changed his story in favour of the more plausible explanation involving a fall on the narrow private staircase.

One thing, however, does appear undisputed: a fearful Louis Henri asked his valet that day to sleep in future by the doorway in his bedroom. Manoury was devoted to his employer and deeply concerned for his wellbeing and safety. Curiously, however, perhaps out of embarrassment at what people might think, he ventured to suggest that this was really a job more fitting for a servant named Lecomte who had only recently come to wait upon the prince and had quickly assumed attendant duties in the old man's bedchamber as part of his role. 'Oh no!', the prince is said to have replied, shaking his head. Lecomte, formerly a hairdresser in Paris, had been one of Sophie's appointees, a frequently insolent and bullying hired hand Louis Henri distrusted, hated and feared. 'We'll say no more about the matter', he told the valet.

Sophie, of course, had her own explanation for the injuries suffered by the prince. They were, she said, the result of another attempt on his part to take his own life. Fortunately, she had been on hand to prevent him from, almost literally, bashing his brains out on his bedchamber wall.

But there was still hope for the Prince of Condé. While we are left with the impression that Madame de Choulot, wife of Chantilly's governor, enjoyed a friendship with Sophie, whether this was genuine or pretended, there is no doubt that the governor himself, while he may have found it politically expedient to remain on good terms with the prince's mistress, was now a staunch advocate of freeing his old master from her wicked clutches. It was Baron de Choulot who concocted a new escape plan designed to play Sophie at her own devious game.

Aware of the 'carriage dash' schemes of both Louis Henri and Sophie, he suggested to the prince that an old servant of his, a man bearing a close resemblance to him in appearance and build, should be dressed in his master's familiar clothes – his distinctive grey coat, cocked hat, white stockings and black shoes – and sent in pretended secrecy to Moisselles for a high-speed drive to the Normandy port of Le Havre. Alerted, as she was bound to be by her network of spies, Sophie would surely then make for her own hidden carriage and chase him all the way to the coast. The prince could then quietly slip out of Saint-Leu and head instead for Switzerland. Louis Henri was delighted with the outline of the plan. Now it was down to details.

It cannot have been helped (though Marjorie Bowen has a point in suggesting that it would have served as a further incentive for the prince to escape a country which had become so alien to him) that, on 20 August, he was forced to receive the new French queen at Saint-Leu. Along with her husband, who had several times written to Louis Henri with assurances of friendship and security in his dotage, Marie Amélie had embarked on a charm offensive in a bid to win over her elderly relative lest he should be tempted to renege on the terms of his will. It is possible that she was sincere in her overtures of goodwill towards the last of the Condés, to whom she had promised a visit as soon as time allowed. It is probable, however, that the old prince, in the midst of planning his escape, was caught unawares by the queen's arrival at his summer retreat on the 20th. It seems likely that his mistress, growing increasingly fearful of losing all she had schemed for, had urged the queen, with whom she was in regular contact, to come immediately to Saint-Leu – and had not pre-warned the prince.

Marie Amélie arrived bearing gifts. On her husband's behalf she invited Louis Henri to take up his rightful seat in the Chamber of Peers, the upper house of the French legislature, and presented him with the coveted Grand Cross *(Grand-croix)*, the Legion of Honour's second highest order of merit. It is not recorded precisely what the prince said in response to this. We know only that he refused without hesitation both the invitation and the medal. No doubt Her Royal Highness received a far warmer welcome from Madame de Feuchères when the two retired from public view to engage in a prolonged conversation from which the prince was barred.

If this caused him a degree of angst it probably didn't linger. His thoughts lay elsewhere. Late that same evening Baron de Choulot arrived at Saint-Leu on horseback from Chantilly and was speedily, without attracting any unwanted attention, ushered by the faithful Manoury into the prince's apartments. There, well into the early hours of 21 August, the new escape plan was finalised. A smokescreen was devised whereby the prince would announce an earlier than expected seasonal return to Chantilly. He could then be seen openly preparing for a carriage journey, deliberately arousing the suspicions of Madame de Feuchères' spies who would expect a getaway at any time. To add a veneer of authenticity, Louis Henri would instruct his architect to hurry up the completion of repair work and alterations which had been taking place at the great château during the Condé household's summer sojourn at Saint-Leu.

The final detail was to fix the date of Louis Henri's departure. It was decided that he would make his bid for freedom on Friday, 27 August, having first made a point of informing the household that he would be leaving Saint-Leu for Chantilly at the start of the following week.[2] He felt confident his old servant, disguised in his master's clothes, would be seen, as the plan demanded, departing in haste on the 27th for Moiselles and would then be pursued on a fruitless chase to the coast while he, the prince, slipped quietly and unnoticed, out of Saint-Leu.

With the plan finalised, the prince bade farewell to Baron de Choulot as, under the cover of darkness, the governor returned to Chantilly with instructions to return to Saint-Leu on the 27th.

Tragedy at Saint-Leu

The next few days were possibly the happiest Louis Henri had experienced for years. We may imagine the heady emotions of sheer relief and excitement as, confident of success, he prepared for his journey to the border with Switzerland and the prospect of exchanging the twin torments of the hated House of Orléans and the tyrannical Sophie Dawes for an eventual reunion, perhaps in Austria, maybe in Britain, with his boyhood friend, fellow soldier and Bourbon ally, the safely exiled Charles X.[3] With a new will in place, this time solely to his liking and free from any threat of unwanted interference, he could surely live out his life in peace.

On the 25th, the feast day of Saint Louis, the prince hosted a grand fête, happily welcoming Saint-Leu's villagers and civic representatives to his summer residence. The local band added a poignant note to the occasion, entertaining their host beneath the windows of his study with a selection of his favourite music, evoking memories of a time, long past, when his life had been free of constant torment. No doubt a rendition of *Où peut on être mieux qu'au sein de sa famill* (which translates in English as, *Where can one be better than in the bosom of one's family?*), once beloved of the executed Louis XVI, brought a particular lump to the old man's throat.[4]

Poignant, too, was the prince's comment to his doctor, Monsieur Bonnie, on the warmth and evident affection the fête-goers had shown towards him. 'Ah!', he reflected, 'they told me that the villagers hated me. It cannot be true; these people are all my good friends... I have been deceived!' Smiling, he repeated time and again, 'Ah, what a fête, what a fête ... and all for me!'

But there would never be any peace for the last of the Condés from the smuggler's daughter. Her father had once gone to great lengths to prevent his prized contraband from slipping out of his grasp on landing it at St Helen's. Sophie had resolved to do the same at Saint-Leu in the dying days of August 1830. She had redoubled her efforts to keep her prized prince within touching distance, returning to Saint-Leu on the day before the fête from one of her frequent social visits to Paris and, unusually for her, remaining at the château for several days.

Having, in public at least, treated him cordially on the day of the fête, she ruined the prince's reverie by insisting her favourite, the abbé Briant, a man Louis Henri loathed, should be installed as the prince's chaplain in place of the trusted abbé Péller. Probably the only reason the prince did not enter into another major row over this with the demanding Sophie was his expectation of an imminent release from her cruel domination. But a row was not long in coming. Sophie, expensively attired, liberally decorated with jewellery, went out of her way to dazzle the 400 guests invited on the eve of the saint's day to a lavish entertainment in the grand salon of Saint-Leu. But the show she put on for Louis Henri in the morning was of an altogether different character. The dazzle had by then been replaced by the daggers in her eyes.

On that morning of 26 August, the day before Louis Henri's planned escape, a fierce, and very audible, quarrel in the prince's bedroom sent Manoury hurrying to his master's aid. As he approached the room he several times heard a familiar name repeated by an evidently angry Madame de Feuchères. The valet had not been briefed on the details of the new scheme for escape but, knowing something of the kind was afoot, shuddered as he considered the possible implications of the Englishwoman's repeated references to the Governor of Chantilly.

'Monsieur de Choulot is a madman!', he heard her shriek and then, a few moments later, 'Do you not understand me? I wish it so!' There was no time for the valet to mull any further over the meaning of the latter statement. As he reached the door, he was surprised to hear the prince tell Sophie, in a boldly assertive manner, 'No Madame, no, that shall not be!' At this point the door flew open and Sophie tore out of the room before attempting a quick re-entry to continue the fight. The prince yelled at her to 'leave me in peace' and shut the door in her face.

Manoury found his master seated on a small sofa close to a window, shaking uncontrollably, begging for eau-de-Cologne. Though he knew little of the plan for the next morning, the concerned valet wondered if the door to escape had been slammed in his master's face. Had Sophie learnt of de Choulot's involvement in an escape and demanded that he be removed from the position of governor? Manoury thought this probable as his master ordered that a message be sent immediately to Chantilly instructing the baron to bring forward, 'for important reasons', his pre-arranged return to Saint-Leu the next morning from ten to eight o'clock.

An aura of calm then enveloped the Prince of Condé. His demeanour in the aftermath of the altercation with Sophie speaks strongly of a man utterly resolved to make his final bid for freedom. To his few remaining intimates, and especially to Manoury, he was affectionate to the point of tenderness. He was visibly moved by the sight of a young girl, the

7-year-old daughter of one of his courtiers, feeding ducks in Saint-Leu's great park. And he was insistent that alms already promised by him to a woman in Chantilly should be dispatched there and then. This was a man surely saying goodbye, tying up the loose ends of his troubled life in France.

But, in finalising with Manoury the arrangements for delivering the alms in Chantilly's town, he appeared ambiguous as to the precise nature of the freedom he foresaw. 'The money will be safe with you', he told the valet. 'As for myself, I do not know what is going to happen.'

If that was a moment of melancholy, the prince's spirits had lifted by mid-afternoon. For a man hoping desperately to avoid any late obstacles to his planned escape, the knowledge that his mistress's two most feared lieutenants, Baron de Lambot and James Dawes, were off to Paris to secure the sale of 250 horses from the Condé stables, a transaction ordered by Sophie alone, was enough in itself to return his mood to its earlier state of calm. While this significant diminution of his prized stud would normally have upset him greatly, he is unlikely, on what he believed to be the final day of Sophie's bitter hegemony, to have dwelt overlong on the matter. Instead, he took the opportunity to ask Lambot, while in Paris, to look into the case of two young prisoners from the city's fringes which had been brought to his notice during the fête. Was this a gesture of normality to allay the suspicions of Sophie's man?

If so, it was a wasted effort. General Lambot, as well as James Dawes and all the other members of her expanded coterie, would certainly by then have been briefed by Sophie that Louis Henri was planning anew to flee Saint-Leu. Her spies had uncovered the plot, at least in its outline form. Of course they had. On hearing of this, she had immediately alerted the king. 'Prevent the departure of the prince at any cost!', Louis Philippe had quickly instructed her, a remark which today is more often expressed in the rather more terse form of 'stop him at all costs!'

We are left to wonder if Louis Henri knew of this. Had it spurred him to get away at the very first opportunity? Or had he now accepted failure – and was resolved to pursuing another way out?

At least the facts relating to the remainder of 26 August 1830 are clear. Late in the afternoon the prince welcomed an unexpected visitor. The Count of Cossé-Brissac, a staunch royalist closely aligned with the ousted Charles X, and therefore with Louis Henri himself, was probably a man on a mission – but what exactly was it? Opinions vary. Was the count there on behalf of the toppled monarch to encourage the prince to make a new will in favour of the Duke of Bordeaux? Was he merely trying to arrange security and employment with the prince for displaced members of Charles's royal household? Or had he been sent by Charles, or had perhaps volunteered, to urge Louis Henri to make haste to join the former royal family in exile?

If it was the last of these possibilities, and if Louis Henri had not been deflected from making his break-out the next day, it seems highly likely the two men would have used the hour they spent together behind closed doors to discuss the escape plan and what would follow in its wake.

Whatever they discussed in private, at dinner that evening the prince and his visitor appeared happy in each other's company, though Cossé-Brissac declined his host's invitation to stay at Saint-Leu for a few days, or at least remain there for the night. He had, he said with regret, to return to Paris immediately after the meal. It is hard to say whether the invitation was a genuine one, or a verbal feint by the prince, eager to show the normal behaviour of a genial host.

His mood at dinner appeared to be relaxed and cheerful. The one sour note came when Cossé-Brissac referred to the rising number of unflattering caricatures of Charles X circulating in Paris. Clearly upset by this, the prince was heard to mutter, 'Tell him to stop'. Was this a significant moment – a reminder for Louis Henri of the unhappy state of play in the capital? Those at the dinner table possibly had more reason to note a clear reminder of the prince's own unhappy physical state of health when, because of the injuries to his fingers, he was unable to crack open a serving of nuts. Sophie did this for him. He declined to eat them.

That evening Louis Henri did something he had neglected of late. He partnered his mistress in several rubbers of whist, the very game at which, according to many, he had won Sophie all those years ago in London. If we are looking for clues to his mental state at this time, his happy demeanour at the card table betrayed nothing but a man seemingly at peace with himself. Put another way, he must surely have had no reason to doubt his great escape was in prospect. Sophie, too, was in a good mood, apparently confident her own plans for the future were secure. They played cheerfully together, with no hint of the recent animosity between them, against the pairing of the Baron de Préjean, father of the little girl the prince had seen feeding the ducks earlier in the day, and Louis Frann, Count de la Villegontier, who owed his position as 'first gentleman' to Sophie and was in charge of the Saint-Leu household that night.

In some of the earliest accounts of the dramatic events of August 1830 at the château, published in the 1840s, both of these men were quoted as saying that the prince gave his fullest attention to the card game and, according to Villegontier, was sufficiently quick-witted to gently criticise Préjean, 'with more gaiety than was usual' for a revoke, or breach, of the rules.[5] They played for two hours before, around midnight, the whist party broke up. Louis Henri had ended up on the losing side, owing a small sum of money. He made a careful note of the amount on a piece of paper and promised to pay his debt in the morning. Warmly, calmly, he wished those members of his household still in attendance a good night and, helped by a valet, made for his bedroom on the first floor, at one point turning briefly to bow. It looked like a sign of farewell.

Sophie had retired to her apartments as the prince entered his own. Uncomfortably for him, it was the unlikeable Lecomte, Sophie's appointee, who attended to his master's elaborate nightly routine as the clock struck midnight. Lecomte assisted Dr Bonnie as the prince's surgeon cleaned, medicinally oiled and re-bandaged the old man's legs, the constantly swollen and badly inflamed condition of which was a further impediment to his mobility and general wellbeing. With the prince having long been unable to raise his right arm in order to dress it himself, his long, whitened hair was then brushed by the ex-hairdresser and tied, as usual, in a black ribbon. The next task was to help Louis Henri into his accustomed night attire. A detailed description of the various components of his sleeping apparel has survived from the later evidence of those who were familiar with it. Marjorie Bowen summarises it well:

> breeches of white calico, his closely-buttoned flannel waistcoat, shirt of white linen fastened at the neck by a button and at the wrist by [cuff]links of gold, and [knotted] round his head a silk foulard of red and yellow with two rosettes in front – twisted into the form of a nightcap.

It is worth bearing in mind that he could not have undressed himself. His many disabilities had long since put paid to that. This was a man for whom tying or untying knots was no longer achievable while fastening and unfastening buttons, buckles and laces, almost always was a virtual impossibility owing to a combination of missing and paralysed fingers. He was, anyway, incapable of stooping down to reach the fastenings on his shoes. His servants routinely did it all for him and then put him to bed, a slow, laborious process as he always slept on one side of the bed, the least uncomfortable position for his tortured body but one requiring the positioning of a row of folded blankets down the side to keep him from falling out.

He was probably relieved when Lecomte applied this finishing touch. He would certainly have been glad to see the back of his least favourite attendant, leaving him at peace, we may suppose, to contemplate with a heady mixture of understandable sadness and relish his planned getaway. On leaving the room, Lecomte had asked the prince what time he wished to be called in the morning. 'At eight o'clock', the last of the Condés had advised the departing valet.

Now alone, the prince placed on the table beside his bed his hunting watch together with a grandly ornate and, for him, now difficult to manage, dress-watch. Alongside these he positioned the paper on which he had scribbled his debts from the evening's card game. His keys he had already placed on the nearby mantelpiece, having removed these from his waistcoat. As was his custom, he clumsily made a rudimentary loop in his handkerchief, a method he used to remind himself of something he needed to do in the morning. Finally, he extinguished the candles on the table and, it is presumed, closed his eyes to dream of a better life.

The lights went out at the château of Saint-Leu – with a single exception. The candles continued to flicker brightly in the room occupied by the Baroness de Flassons, the wife of James Dawes, as she worked until two in the morning on a letter to her husband, who had left her side only a matter of hours earlier for the horse sale in Paris. When Madame de Flassons finally retired to bed, the prince's once loved palace-turned-prison was bathed in darkness – as the loyal Baron de Choulot prepared to set off from Chantilly on his twenty-mile early hours gallop through the heat of the late-August night to keep his appointment with his master.

Lecomte would later testify that he had bolted from the inside a door between the first floor gallery and the prince's dressing room, which was itself linked to the bedchamber by a narrow passage, thus preventing, or at least deterring, unauthorised access to the bedroom via that route. This was a further nightly ritual for Louis Henri's valets necessitated by the prince's difficulty of late to properly secure himself overnight in his sleeping quarters. It may be wondered why he would have trusted Lecomte, a man he greatly feared, to have done this at such a sensitive time. The fact is he really had no choice. It was a risk, but one he had to take.

Shortly before eight in the morning, just as the punctual Baron de Choulot rode into the courtyard of the château at the end of his overnight journey, Lecomte ascended the building's grand staircase to the first floor gallery and from there entered the ante-chamber adjoining the prince's bedroom. Lecomte knocked on the bedroom door.. There was no answer. He tried the door handle; the door was clearly bolted from the inside. The valet was joined by Dr Bonnie, who had arrived to undertake his usual early morning medical services for the prince. They took turns to hammer on the door. Still there was no response from within. Bonnie and Lecomte went in search of the Count de la Villegontier, the man in charge of the household, only to discover that, two hours earlier, he had left on a visit to the close-by village of Taverny. So they decided instead to inform Madame de Feuchères – and found her still in bed.

Clad only in her dressing gown and slippers, devoid of stockings, Sophie listened to the pair's tale. Quickly, but calmly, leaving her apartments on the ground floor, she loudly proclaimed that she would 'go up at once and see what has happened ... he will reply when he hears my voice! Or, if he doesn't, we must break the door open ... perhaps he has had an attack and requires to be [medically] bled'. With the two men in tow, she promptly rushed up the stairs to take control in the ante-chamber. But there was no reply when she, too, knocked on the bedroom door and repeatedly called out to the prince, 'Open Monseigneur, open the door ... it is I!'

The small gathering behind her quickly became a crowd as Sophie, having failed to elicit a reply, called for Manoury, who until that point seems to have been ignorant of the unfolding drama (possibly because he had been summoned by Baron de Choulot, who slips from the story at this stage, for a last-minute briefing on the prince's planned escape that morning). 'Break open the door,' Sophie ordered the shocked valet. An iron crowbar was hurried to the scene. Manoury used it to good effect, smashing away the lowest panel of the door so that he was able to crawl through the gap into the bedroom, followed by Bonnie and then

Lecomte. They found the chamber in virtual darkness and struggled to make anything out in the dim light.

The principal room in the prince's apartments at the corner of a wing in the château, the bedchamber, large but with a low ceiling, had two sash windows, facing north and east, which normally offered delightful views of the gardens and, further afield, the great park of Saint-Leu, but on this morning were still covered by the interior shutters closed the night before. On the window facing east, the blinds were also drawn. The only discernible illumination came from a night-light still flickering faintly from behind the brass fireplace screen.

To the left of the door through which they had gained entry, it appeared to the three men that the prince's large, heavy bed, positioned in an alcove, was empty and the bedclothes seemingly undisturbed. But then, as they accustomed themselves to the poor light, the grimmest of discoveries was made. The lifeless upright form of Louis Henri, Duke of Bourbon, the last Prince of Condé, could be discerned, framed in the northern window, opposite the door from the ante-room though slightly to the right. The prince was leant against its shutters, his right cheek caressing the woodwork. His head had fallen forward so that his chin rested on his breast. This, according to Violette Montagu's graphic account of the scene, gave the impression that the prince was 'crouching down and apparently listening at the shutters'. Both Louis Henri's knees were slightly bent and his arms hung limply by his side.

A chair stood close to the barely discernible figure. In his agitated haste to reach the prince, Bonnie pushed it roughly to one side. That was the first tampering with this scene of morbid horror.

Manoury, stunned and shaking, gently touched his beloved master's hands and then his face. They were ice-cold. The valet himself was chilled to the bone as the reality of the situation sunk in. Managing to recover his composure, he rushed to the east window, pulling back the blind and opening the shutters before retreating to the middle of the room. Now the bright August sunshine flooded the bedchamber to throw a macabre revelatory light on the dead aristocrat, who was still dressed in the night clothes Lecomte had helped him into hours earlier.

The sunlight revealed exactly how he was suspended in such a vile manner to the tall window. Two of the prince's linen handkerchiefs, each monogrammed with the letter 'B' for Bourbon and a coronet, had been formed into separate loops and then passed one through the other as a two-part noose. Thus intertwined, one of the looped handkerchiefs was affixed to the *espagnolette* (cross-fastening or hasp) of the window and the other was tied around the prince's neck. On closer inspection it was noted that the handkerchief attached to the fastening was anything but taut. Indeed, it was so loose it was possible to pass an entire hand through the loop it formed without touching the neck of the prince encircled by the loop below.

Even in his shocked state Dr Bonnie could not fail to notice the absence of any obvious signs of strangulation. The face was pale, but with none of the discolouration that might be expected, the prince's eyes were half-open and his mouth was nearly closed, with the tongue resting naturally behind the teeth rather than protruding, and with no swelling visible. Louis Henri's hands were half-open, too, not clenched in the more usual manner of a victim of strangulation. And, below the slightly bent knees, the prince's feet were just touching the floor.

Together with the stains on the carpet from the droplets of snuff and mucus which had evidently dribbled from the old man's nose, it was a shockingly ghastly sight which begged a multitude of questions – and was at that moment just too much for a distraught Dr Bonnie to bear.

Rushing forward, he took a penknife from his pocket and was about to cut the makeshift noose, possibly believing there might still be signs of life, when Manoury, with remarkable presence of mind, pulled him back. 'No, Monsieur', he cried, 'what are you doing? This is a matter for justice to decide'. Some say he then pointed out that cutting the handkerchief to free the body would appear suspicious to any subsequent inquiry, 'You'll ruin us all', he told the surgeon. 'We shall be accused of the crime – and we are innocent!' Whatever his precise words, it seems the valet had already assumed the likely involvement of a malevolent third party.

With Bonnie accepting the wisdom of Manoury's caution, the three men now unbolted the bedroom door. Once outside the room they called for assistance and were immediately mobbed by other members of the household, naturally curious to know what had been discovered in their master's chamber. It was now a quarter-to-nine on that dramatic morning of Friday, 27 August 1830, a date destined for a notoriety undiminished by the passage of time.[6]

Chapter 9

Deadly Suspicions:
Suicide or Murder?

Even for many among the household of the Prince of Condé who had witnessed the injurious outcomes of so many earlier acts of violent fall-out in his bitterly soured relationship with Sophie Dawes – and by August 1830 that was virtually all of them – the climactic drama of his death was an astonishing revelation. But this was not the case with Sophie. At first she betrayed not a hint of astonishment, not a flicker of surprise, when she was told of the gruesome discovery in the prince's bedroom. While she expressed a desire to see for herself the body, she did not resist to any great extent when restrained, for what was perceived to be her own good, from entering the room. And then the actress in Sophie Dawes took to the stage.

She sank into an armchair in the ante-room and, according to witnesses, began at last to act the part of a shocked innocent, moaning and wailing, wringing her hands in apparent despair. Some of those present, though not all, later claimed to have seen traces of tears on her face. Perhaps she took her cue from the pitiful sobbing nearby of a distraught Baron de Préjean. Her first discernible comment was not, however, that of a woman grief-stricken by the sudden loss of a loved one: 'Oh, it is indeed fortunate that the prince has died like this!', they heard her say. 'If he had died in his bed someone would have been sure to say that I had poisoned him!'

Evidently, the soon-to-be inheritor of a fortune was keen to portray the death of Louis Henri as a suicidal hanging obvious to anyone who was now able to witness, or had heard of, the awful evidence of the prince's final desperate act. At this stage she had probably not been told of the early cracks in any notion of suicide – the lack of a properly tightened noose, the fact the victim's toes were touching the floor, the absence of tell-tale signs of strangulation. It might have looked, or sounded, like a suicidal

Deadly Suspicions

hanging, but was this actually the result of it being made to *look* like one? That question would be asked increasingly on that hot August day.

As Sophie held out her hand to be kissed by a host of sympathisers, some no doubt more genuinely than others, the chamber from which she had been barred was filled by a shifting crowd of curious courtiers and servants. Nobody took control. Everyone was allowed in, apart from Sophie herself. Later, no-one could quite remember who was there at any given time, what they did and what they said. This scene of a curious, tragic death had been invaded by a mob.

Amid this undignified commotion, Manoury had at nine o'clock led the prince's chaplain, the abbé Péller, who had just returned to the château after celebrating Mass in the town, to the still hanging corpse. 'Look! There is Monseigneur!', he was heard to exclaim. Whether the valet said anything else to the startled chaplain at that time is unclear but he may well have drawn the attention of Péller to three further observations which strongly supported his growing suspicions of foul play and a fatality that was forced upon, rather than sought by, the victim.

The first of these tell-tale signs was particularly glaring. While the principal door from the ante-chamber to the bedroom had been bolted from the inside, no bolt had been slipped across a small door on the right of the room, close to its south-eastern corner, which led to the narrow 'secret staircase', so called because it connected the prince's rooms, via the *entresol* (gallery) below, with the apartments occupied by Sophie on the ground floor. These were the stairs on which Louis Henri had, after reflection, claimed to have suffered injuries in a trip earlier that month. In truth the staircase was anything but secret, but it was still regarded as a private means of communication between the prince and his mistress – and was routinely bolted by a valet from the inside at night

Noticing the doorway had been left unbolted, a significant exception to a rigidly imposed rule, the keen-eyed Manoury enquired of Lecomte: 'Why did you not secure that door last night?' Lecomte's reply was curious. Shrugging his shoulders, he said: 'I didn't pay any attention to it'.[1]

Manoury had also noticed abnormalities with the prince's unwieldly, heavy bed. Despite it being difficult to manoeuvre, it had clearly been moved out of its usual position. Apart from that, although Louis Henri always slept on the edge of the bed, the valet had spotted a deep indentation in the centre. It was as if someone had been standing or kneeling on it.

Finally, although the prince's slippers of green (flexible leather) morocco were always left by the bedside chair to allow him easy access to them in the morning, on this occasion they were found alongside the bed itself, a highly unusual, and therefore suspicious, departure from the norm.

With all this apparent from what had been no more than a cursory inspection of the death scene, it should have occurred to any official investigator that all was not as first it had seemed and that there was a strong possibility, if not probability, that someone had entered the bedchamber while the prince was asleep, had poisoned, suffocated, or otherwise murdered him on his bed and had then 'dressed' the crime to give the clear impression of a suicidal hanging.

But the initial involvement of officialdom in the prince's death did not see it that way. With the chamber finally cleared at 9.45 of its curious crowd by Baron de la Villegontier upon his return to the château, the local legal and medical representatives were shown into the room to begin formal examinations. The little party was headed by the Mayor of Saint-Leu-la-Foret, Pierre Gervais Tailleur, who stared in disbelief at the suspended figure of the prince to whom, just two days' previously, he had been pleased to present a loyal address at the happy occasion of the grand fête. Like his assistant, Leduc, the mayor was a simple man – 'absolutely illiterate' according to some – who, already discomfited in such unfamiliarly splendid surroundings, was overwhelmed by the ghastly spectacle and the responsibility placed on him by French practice, in the absence of a higher legal authority, to produce a *procès-verbal,* an accurate account of any untoward event which seemed to impinge on the law.[2]

Unfortunately for the interests of justice, Tailleur and Leduc could not wait to get out of the chamber, so disturbed were they by the whole affair. Their subsequent report was based as much on supposition than it was on factual evidence. While noting correctly that the prince's toes were touching the floor and that his knees were bent, they wrongly added that his tongue was protruding from his mouth, thereby suggesting strangulation. Equally misleading was their statement that all the doors to the bedchamber had been locked from inside, either by bolts or keys, and therefore no-one else could have entered the room, whereas, according to Manoury's earlier observation, the door to the 'secret staircase' had been left unbolted. The insistence of the mayor and his assistant that the small doorway was closed and bolted when they saw it may well have been the truth. So many people had trampled through the chamber in the ninety minutes between the time of the body's discovery and the formal inspection that somebody could easily have closed and secured the door. Nonetheless, the supposition that the doorway had never at any stage during the night been opened was an error.

The medical examination was carried out jointly by Dr Bonnie and the local village doctor, Letellier, who inspected the prince's body while it was still suspended from the window fastening. It is hard to imagine that Bonnie's suspicions had not been fully aroused by his earlier visit to the scene with Manoury. Perhaps, aware as he was of where the power lay in the Condé household, and the potential threat this posed to anyone who challenged it, he decided to play it safe. That might explain the conclusions he set out jointly with the village GP:

> It is very likely that His Royal Highness rose soon after he had gone to bed, mounted on the chair which we found near the window, attached the knotted handkerchiefs to the window fastening and kicked away the chair. Then the weight of the body would make the knots in the handkerchiefs gradually pull tighter until that which was round the prince's neck would draw him off the floor, causing strangulation. The body would then remain in the position it was found. The *rigor mortis* would then have caused the bending of the knees and, also, as it was very advanced, prove that the prince had been dead about ten hours when we examined him.

All very straightforward, it had been a classic case of suicidal hanging – except, of course, it was nothing of the sort. Bonnie knew full well the extent of the prince's infirmities. Louis Henri was able to struggle out of bed unaided; he did so every morning to unfasten the main door. But he would certainly not have had the strength, intentionally or otherwise, to move the bed, would have found it impossible to climb onto the chair and stand upright, would have been unable to raise his right arm above his shoulder to affix the handkerchiefs and would have lacked the dexterity in the fingers of his badly mutilated left hand to tie the knots above his head tightly enough to ensure fatal strangulation. It was highly unlikely, indeed, practically impossible, for the aged prince to have died this way, quite literally by his own hand.

Though they did not, of course, form part of the medical examination, the prince's views on suicide are worth taking into account at this juncture. Only twelve days before his death Louis Henri was visited by his dentist, Hostein. They discussed the recent arrest of Jules de Polignac, Charles X's prime minister at the time of his overthrow, the man who had signed the infamous 'July Ordinances' which had led directly to revolution and the crowning of Louis Philippe as King of the French.[2] Hostein commented that, had he been in Polignac's place, he would have committed suicide, a remark which earned him a stern rebuke from the prince:

> How can you say such things? I would have you know, M. Hostein, that an honourable man never takes his own life; it is only a coward who could do such a thing. What an example to set to society! I do not speak to you from a Christian's point of view, although I ought to have from the start ... you know that suicide is the worst of all crimes in the eyes of the Church, and how can we possibly appear in God's presence if we have not had time to repent of our sins?

It seems reasonable to conclude that a man who felt so strongly that suicide was both cowardly and sinful would have been unlikely to have taken his own like just over a week later unless something of hideously immense proportions had forced him into the act. The possibility he had been told Sophie had thwarted his escape and had become resigned to death being the only way out cannot be entirely eliminated, given the troubled state of his mind, exacerbated by his undoubtedly deep concern about the change of political power in France. But was his seemingly carefree, playful demeanour the evening before really that of a desperate man determined to overcome a multitude of physical deficiencies in order to kill himself?

Although it was not raised as a possibility at the time, and not for years to come, even less likely was a cause of death which has recently gained considerable currency – the theory of an accident. The suggestion is that the prince was 'pleasuring himself' in an act of what today would be called auto-erotic asphyxia, a method of increasing sexual excitement during masturbation by restricting the supply of oxygen to the brain, usually by tightening a noose around the neck. As several recent high-profile cases have shown, it carries a high risk of death.³

Often mistaken for suicide, auto-erotic asphyxia in its various forms has been documented since the early seventeenth century. The Prince of Condé was known in his younger days to have had a voracious sexual appetite, though nothing emerges from the historical record to suggest any masochistic leanings or involvement in any other deviant sexual practice. It is difficult to imagine how the enfeebled 74-year-old prince would have been physically able to engage in an act of this nature. The theory of auto-erotic asphyxia probably emanates from contemporary references to the prince being only 'partly dressed' when his body was discovered – but nobody can be described as being fully clothed when in their night attire. Far too much has been read into this by sensation-seekers who continue to present the theory as a fact.

Suicide was always the only realistic alternative to murder. The Baroness de Feuchères was anxious to remind everyone that Louis Henri – according to her – had attempted to take his own life only a few days earlier and had been seriously depressed about the collapse of Charles X's reign. The prince's suicide at some stage, she insisted, had been 'quite likely'. But she seemed preoccupied by the possibility her aged benefactor had left a clue which might counter her statement on the matter. She knew he had been working furiously on some kind of document for days. Had he made, or had he been in the process of formulating, a new will with a view to countermanding the original one after fleeing France? If so, where was it now?

Clearly agitated by this threat to her plans, she repeatedly asked: 'Have any papers been found?'

Sophie's many agents at the château were keen to reinforce her unequivocal verdict on the prince's death. 'The good old man had a moment of delirium, which is not astonishing seeing how distressed he was by the fall of the monarchy', the abbé Briant was heard to say in supporting the theory of the prince's apparent suicide. Briant's main concern, however, seems to have been to warn, time and again, all those he came into contact with against touching any of the palace's valuable treasures, especially the silverware, all of which, he emphasised, would soon be the property of Madame de Feuchères as the château's new owner.

It was only Manoury who challenged the prevailing view of suicide. 'I and the Baron de Choulot know better than that. Monseigneur would not have committed suicide because he was preparing to leave the country. M. Choulot and I were his confidantes', said the faithful valet.

It was, of course, an incautious remark. Overhearing it, a startled Sophie told him sharply: 'Take care! If the king were to find out that you were talking like that, you would get into trouble.'[4]

She was right about that. King Louis Philippe had made it clear he wanted any attempt by the last of the Condés to flee from France prevented 'at any cost'. To have done the opposite, to have actually aided the prince's planned escape, was clearly courting severe royal disapproval, especially as Manoury's remark directly rebuffed the theory of suicide and suggested strongly that his noble master had been murdered. It hardly needs saying how bad that would look for the king if it were widely repeated, whether Louis Philippe had actually meant to encompass the murder of the prince or not when issuing Sophie with his dramatic edict.

Louis Philippe no doubt was relieved when told later in the day of the prince's death that a series of further examinations had not cast any doubt over the notion of suicide – at least not in the eyes of those officials who carried out the work. First to arrive early in the afternoon had been the justice of the peace from the town of Enghien-les-Bains, five miles to the south of Saint-Leu. Monsieur de la Roussliere-Clouart's first act on seeing the still-suspended corpse was to order that it should be cut down and laid on the bed. Manoury and a fellow valet, Romanzo, were detailed to carry out the task. Immediately, a crucial discovery was made.

At least, it *would* have been crucial had any official notice been taken of it at the time. The valets found it extremely difficult to untie the knots in the handkerchiefs. One had been tied in a weaver's knot (also known as a sheet bend), a knot quick and easy to tie once mastered, less easy to unpick and considered very strong if applied properly. The other was far more complicated and skilfully tied. Perhaps, as would soon be suggested, the kind of knot that a fisherman might use – and one both unfamiliar and unmanageable to an elderly aristocrat whose badly deformed hands meant he needed help to tie his own cravat and do up his shoe laces. Manoury knew this, of course, but had maybe decided by now that it was better to keep quiet.

Roussliere-Clouart made no further examination, preferring to wait until the arrival of magistrates from Pontoise, twelve miles to the northwest, but he did – and not before time – order the sealing of the doors into the bedchamber. Two hours later, at 4pm, the Pontoise JPs arrived. Their examination was as cursory and as careless as those which had preceded it. MM. Foret de Boisbrunet and Dinet quickly concluded that both doors to the room had been securely bolted overnight and nothing had been disturbed in the chamber – no sign of any struggle – prior to the body's discovery at 8am. It was, they were certain, a clear case of suicide.

When a pair of doctors arrived from the hospital at Pontoise, they at least found scratch marks on the prince's face and a large bruise between the shoulders but concluded these could not have been caused by the noose around the neck, which had left no marks at all. They found nothing to dissuade them from the now widely-held official view of a suicidal death.

Throughout these various inspections of the death scene, the prime concern for Madame de Feuchères and her cronies was an increasingly frantic search for the papers the prince had been working on. 'There must be something somewhere', she insisted, 'he was working on it for days ... keep searching!' But the search revealed only a pile of cinders in the hearth of the old man's bedroom which appeared to be the remains of burnt paper. This was a curious find. The hearth was cleaned every day so it was assumed the cinders had been left the night before.

The search was re-energised with the return to the château from Paris of Baron de Flassans. Sophie's nephew seemed as agitated as his aunt at the failure to find any evidence of the documents the prince had been so keen to keep from the prying eyes of his mistress's army of spies. But when Baron de Surval was dispatched in the opposite direction to inform the king formally of the prince's death, that exhaustive hunt for the dead man's papers had drawn a blank.

There is some confusion as to precisely when the king was told of the tragedy. De Surval had a ride of fourteen miles to undertake. Bearing that in mind, the best guess would be around midnight on the 27th. Whatever time it was, Louis Philippe seemed genuinely shocked by the news, immediately ordering the *Chancelier de France*, Baron Pasquier, with his *aide-de-camp* and chief of police, Colonel de Rumigny, at the head of an official delegation, to Saint-Leu. Travelling with them was General Baron de Lambot, Sophie's much-favoured agent, who had spent the night in Paris at the Palais Bourbon and so, like James Dawes, had, as

Marjorie Bowen, adroitly puts it, 'a strangely good alibi'. They arrived in the early hours of the 28th.

Behind them they left a deeply troubled monarch who had yet to achieve any sense of stability on his throne, but was about to see his family fabulously enriched through a mighty inheritance from an old, enfeebled man, his Bourbon uncle, who he was well aware had been mercilessly hounded to death – whether by his own hand or not – to satisfy the grandly avaricious intentions of Madame de Feuchères, the king's partner in the hunt for the Condé fortune. Louis Philippe could have prevented this tragedy, but, instead, had been a party to it. Even if we regard as highly unlikely that the King of the French, so recently enthroned, expressly intended to order the death of the prince, he had done nothing to prevent it. That was a crime in itself.

That said, his choice of Etienne Denis Pasquier as principal member of the team sent to Saint-Leu seems entirely correct. Pasquier, recently installed as President of the Chamber of Peers, was legally trained, honourable, thorough in everything he did and a past holder of several key State offices since the second Bourbon restoration.[5] Having ordered in peremptory manner the immediate evacuation of the bedroom, which had again been filled with a stream of those apparently eager to gawp at the prince's corpse, he wasted no time in writing to the king.[6]

'On arriving at Saint-Leu I found the tragic end of the Prince of Condé, with all its frightful circumstances known to everyone', he wrote, adding that he had also found 'a *procès-verbal* drawn up by the mayor with the greatest possible care', a curiously complimentary assessment of the report compiled by a man most at the château had regarded as illiterate. It was completely at odds with a letter sent to the king by police chief Rumnigny, who wrote that 'the official statement and *procès-verbal* has been made the care of M. de la Villegontier who has done it as clumsily as possible'. For the two officials to have reached such conflicting views on the same documents is certainly odd but, if Rumigny was correct, it would appear, or at least suggest, that the mayor's report, and probably that of the visiting magistrates, were drawn up under the supervision of Louis Frann, Baron de la Villegontier, the confidante of Madame de Feuchères. He was the man in charge of the château, both at the time of the prince's death and during the initial inspections of the death scene carried out by local officials – the mayor and the magistrates – completely overawed and totally out of their depth.

While Pasquier and Rumigny were out of sync on the reliability of the *procès-verbal* and the non-contradictory statement of the JPs which followed it, they were very much in agreement that things were not as straightforward as they were being painted at the château of Saint-Leu. 'The circumstances of the death are too extraordinary not to require a very careful study. I think it would be useful if the king were to send immediately two doctors, such as Drs Marc and Marjohn, who are accustomed to such tragic investigations', wrote Pasquier to the royal court. He added a short post-script, taking the trouble to underscore the final seven words: 'It is said that not a single document has been found, though a search has already been made [of the château].'

Rumigny was far more direct than Pasquier in expressing his concerns in his own letter to the king:

> Sire, I think it will be impossible for me to leave here for the moment. I shall stay unless I receive orders to the contrary ... No suspicion has so far fallen on anyone, but God knows what we shall learn, for I must say that this death has not to me the air of a suicide. It is important that nobody should be accused who is likely to benefit by the will. I shall certainly not leave Saint-Leu till the doctors Marc and Marjohn have told me the results oi their investigation.

We may assume that the chief of Louis Philippe's secret police was fully acquainted with the terms of the Condé will. He was a trusted agent of the monarch and had attended Saint-Leu very much as the king's man. The only two people who stood to benefit in a major way from Louis Henri's last testament were Sophie Dawes and the young Duke of Aumale, the king's own son. Rumigny would have seen it as his duty to warn his royal master of this lurking peril.

At nine o'clock on the evening of the 28th the two doctors requested by Pasquier arrived at Saint-Leu. Drs Marc and Marjohn, the king's personal medical attendants, carried out an immediate post-mortem examination of the body, assisted by Dr Bonnie and watched over by Colonel de Rumigny. The eminent physicians from Paris were in no doubt – death had been caused by strangulation. There had been no sign of a struggle, no hint of inflicted violence and no disturbance to the prince's clothing. No-one else was involved. He had hanged himself. Given his feeble physical state, it had probably needed only the mere act of his head 'stiffening' into the admittedly loose noose to finish him off. It was suicide – no doubt about it.

But Bonnie, having recovered from the shock of finding the body in the first place, dared to disagree. He had changed his mind and he now asked about the scratches and bruises on the body, the marks on the neck – why had these been ignored? The king's physicians argued that the small wounds were insignificant and were quite compatible with the theory of suicide. Bonnie was not put off. He raised the matter of the prince's infirmities – his inability to raise his right arm above his shoulder, his badly deformed fingers, useless for tying knots, his unstable gait – shouldn't these be noted in the autopsy report? Again, his concerns were ignored. Dr Bonnie was outranked. Reluctantly he signed his acceptance of suicide.

The prince's mental state was, of course, key. Jacques-Charles Dupont de l'Eure, Louis Philippe's Minister of Justice, and Louis Désiré Bernard, the Attorney-General, duly arrived in haste from Paris to interview those who they thought could, or rather, should speak of this. Sophie, her nephew James, her agents Villegontier and the valet Lecomte, among others, gushed forth on their master's deep unhappiness at the political upheaval in Paris and how he had previously attempted to take his own life. The king's men were not interested in questioning anyone who, had they felt able to speak out, could have offered a contrary view. No attempt was made to speak with those who had spent time in the prince's company the evening before his death.

The most glaring omission among the list of potential interviewees was the Count of Cossé-Brissac, who had shared a lengthy private conversation with Louis Henri on the evening of the 26th. The count, above all, might have offered an insight into the prince's concerns and intentions. He was never asked to do so. Neither was the Baron de Choulot. Bernard was satisfied with what he had. The information he had gathered from this shabby one-dimensional investigation was now summarised by the king's legal officer in the following terms:

> The witnesses we have heard have declared that His Royal Highness, the Prince of Condé, particularly since the political events of July, was a prey to profound melancholy, and to fears which were shown in the expression of his

countenance, by his conversation and sometimes even by convulsive movements. He was heard several times to say that he would not survive the last revolution, that it was too much for him to have seen two, that he had lived too long. Several distorted and exaggerated reports of the disturbances in Paris had given him the liveliest alarm for the fate of the reigning dynasty, that of France, and for his own safety, besides that of the people attached to his house. He appeared continually self-absorbed and sad.

The spark of hope for a proper investigation into the prince's death, ignited by the suspicions of Pasquier and Rumigny, appeared to have been wholly extinguished by a shoddy report, superficial and screaming of bias. This was a report penned very much in the service of the king.

Bernard, however, was anxious to make the suicide theory as watertight as possible; his royal master would have demanded it. The attorney-general was therefore delighted when later he searched the château alone and found what he considered was the decisive evidence he needed. 'Scattered like snow', as he later described it, on top of the pile of cinders in the hearth of the prince's bedroom were torn fragments of paper, only slightly scorched and clearly covered with handwriting. Bernard had no doubts. 'We shall find the truth here!', he said.

Painstakingly, Bernard and Armand Guillaume, one of the king's secretaries who had travelled earlier to Saint-Leu in the party headed by Pasquier and Rumigny, pieced the fragments together. Their efforts revealed what appeared to be two versions of the same document, one with several words crossed out, the other a cleaner copy. Both were in the prince's handwriting. Although incomplete, the first of these sheets revealed the following text:

> Saint-Leu belongs to the King Philippe ... neither pillaged nor burnt ... the château nor the village do no harm to anyone ... neither to my friends nor to my people. You have been deceived about me. I have not in writing ... heart the people, and the hope of happiness of my country.

The many gaps made interpretation difficult. It seemed that the Prince of Condé was drafting his intention to leave his beloved château to

Louis Philippe rather than to Sophie Dawes, the nominated inheritor in his will of August 1829. It appeared also that he was pleading for the preservation of the château, the village and its residents, and his friends – perhaps fearing all were threatened by the political upheaval in Paris and the rise of liberal democracy under the country's 'Citizen King'. These two elements appeared, and still do today, as wholly incompatible. Why would the prince want the king, the head of liberalism, to inherit Saint-Leu? Did he view this as a form of insurance against a notion of perceived Orléanist threat? In effect, did he mean: leave Saint-Leu and my friends in peace and the king can have it for himself?

The second copy offered a little more indication of Louis Henri's mindset at the time of writing:

> Saint-Leu and its dependencies … belong to your King … Philippe neither pillaged nor burnt … the village … nor hurt anyone … Neither … my friends nor my people. … You have been deceived on my account. … I have only to die wishing happiness and prosperity to the people of France and to my country. Farewell for ever L. H. J. de Bourbon Prince of Condé. P.S. – I ask that I may be buried at Vincennes near my unfortunate son.

Neither General Lambot nor James Dawes, who had also helped to piece the fragments together, could contain their excitement when the task was finished. 'Nothing could be clearer!', exclaimed Sophie's nephew with an air of triumph. 'There is no question of a crime now. This precious discovery clears everything up. There is no longer the least doubt – it *was* suicide!'

But, if that were true, why did the prince leave only these fragments of paper? They hardly amounted to a suicide note. Why were they torn to shreds? They were really no more than apparently discarded drafts of a letter or document. Certainly they carried an element of farewell, but there was nothing on them to prove the farewell would be by means of suicide. When did Louis Henri write the notes? They were undated; there was nothing to say they were penned on the night the prince died. It was just as likely those scraps of paper were the remnants of notes he was working on prior to drawing up a new will once he was free. Or, as has also been suggested, the drafts of proclamations he was planning to affix to the gates of the château when first he had heard of the civil disturbances in Paris and feared the worst of outcomes.

Most importantly, it seemed not to have occurred to Bernard – either that or he chose to ignore it – that the fragments, clearly visible on top of the cinders when he found them, had not been discovered earlier during those repeated searches of a room that had simultaneously been invaded by deeply inquisitive crowds. How was it that they had suddenly appeared now? A fire had been lit in the room on the night of the 27th to comfort the prince's servants as they sat in silent vigil with his body. How was it that the scraps of paper had escaped the flames?

These questions were never asked. The attorney-general was not interested. He concluded that:

> His Royal Highness's resolution to put an end to a life that continual terrors and fearful fancies had rendered insupportable is manifested so clearly in this writing that it ought by itself to be sufficient to attest the truth, which is, nevertheless, confirmed by every other channel of information.

There is no doubt the Prince of Condé had long suffered from 'continual terrors'. The reason for this can be summed up in two words: Sophie Dawes. The king's men stayed well clear of that.

The official verdict was always going to be suicide, whatever the evidence or lack of it, and despite an advertisement placed in all the principal newspapers by Baron de Surval and the Baroness de Préjean, out of kindness to the late prince, which stated that he had died from apoplexy (a stroke). Below stairs, however, servants loyal to the prince, deeply suspicious of the official finding, were not in the least assuaged by the loud claims of Madame de Feuchères about the prince's favourable tendencies towards suicide and how he had many times spoken of this. The servants scoffed, too, at the abbé Briant's story that he had seen the prince measuring with his cane the distance of the window fastening from the floor in his bedroom. They were convinced their master was merely freeing the curtain, caught up in the frame.

Meanwhile Lecomte, supposedly the last person to have seen the prince alive, was repeatedly pressed by his fellow attendants on the last minutes he had spent with his master. He said little of note until Louis

Henri, his face uncovered, his body draped in a richly embroidered pall, was finally permitted the dignity of being allowed to lie in state in the village church of Saint-Leu. When it came to Lecomte's turn to join the candlelit watch in the church he was moved to an unusual unease, commenting to his companions: 'I have such a weight on my mind'.

There was unease, too, at the court of the king. When well-founded rumours of foul play and claims of a cover-up by the king's men quickly reached Paris, the enemies of the unstable monarchy, from the 'legitimist' royalist adherents to the cause of the ousted senior Bourbon line under Charles X to the more extremist anti-royalist factions, delighted in making hay, eager to spread the news of this bountiful harvest of political fortune as loudly as they could. The will of the last Prince of Condé, which had been in the possession of the king's lawyer, added considerable fuel to the political fire threatening the king when it was opened at Saint-Leu.

Bearing in mind Sophie had been a menacing presence when the prince had written the will in August 1829, and knew precisely what was in it, her reaction to its reading was, to say the least, strange. The bulk of the Condé estate went, as expected, to the king's son, the Duke of Aumale, while Sophie duly inherited Saint-Leu and the other possessions she had been promised. But on hearing confirmation that she was also being left 2,000,000 francs in cash, she bristled with disrespectful rage at the sum of money she had known all along would be hers.

'The wretch!', exclaimed Sophie. 'He has deceived me – it was *four* million he had promised me!'

It is hard to see why Sophie, in full knowledge of the terms of the will, would have felt short-changed, but the late prince was certainly cheated. His expressed wish to be buried at Vincennes, enshrined in the will and later repeated, would never be fulfilled. Neither would his desire for the château of Ecouen to be used as a hospital for the families of his former military colleagues. These things were not concerns for Sophie. She had her own battles to fight.

Stories of her ill-treatment of the prince continued to spread, particularly the dramatic events of 11 August which had left her old benefactor both physically and mentally drained. Sophie reacted by feigning outrage at the suggestion that she had been responsible for the prince's injuries. 'Everybody knows that I was not there at the time! I demand that the matter be inquired into', she protested. 'I cannot be sure of the date ... but I swear that I was in Paris when M. de Flassans informed me of the incident and told me not to be anxious.' It was true she had been in Paris on the 11th but that was only after she had travelled there from Saint-Leu.

Leaving Saint-Leu and its inquisitors for Paris was now once more a priority for Sophie. But first she had to endure, and it must have been a real test of endurance for the under-fire smuggler's daughter, the formalities of the prince's funeral, which had three distinct stages. Traditionally, the heart of each departed Condé prince was removed for permanent preservation in a chapel dedicated for the purpose at the château of Chantilly. On 4 September Louis Henri's heart was solemnly taken to the château where the abbé Péller said a mass for the repose of the dead man's soul. Some sources say that it was in the course of this that Péller, as he raised the silver-gilt vase containing the heart, sensationally told those present: 'I swear upon my faith as a Catholic priest that the prince is innocent before God of his own death.'

It was because of the controversy surrounding the tragedy and the hostility of ecclesiastical law towards suicidal death that the funeral service itself took place on 9 September in the modest surroundings of Saint-Leu's village church. The King of the French kept his distance but was represented by his four sons, led by Ferdinand, the new Duke of Orléans following his father's succession to the throne, and including the principal inheritor of the prince's vast fortune, his 8-year-old godson Henri, Duke of Aumale. The simple ceremony was conducted by the village priest, assisted by the abbé Péller. The Prince of Rohan was among the notable mourners as, of course, was Sophie, although, uncharacteristically, she played no active role.

But the villagers and the prince's loyal household retainers turned out in force to bid him farewell. 'When the cortege started to leave the château for the church of Saint-Leu it was impossible not to be struck with the sorrow – I would even say, in some cases, the despair – of the old servants of the household', wrote an evidently moved Baron Pasquier in his memoirs.

During his funeral oration, the abbé Péller was again determinedly, and riskily, outspoken in his belief that the prince's death had been no suicide. 'No!', he exclaimed, fiercely indignant of the prevailing view of many seated in the small church. 'The prince did *not* take his own life.'

Following the simple service the cortege turned southwards for the twelve-mile journey to the Abbey Church of Saint-Denis, north of Paris, final resting place of so many French kings and princes. Louis Henri was laid to rest in the crypt, in what today is known as the Bourbon chapel, adjacent to his father but separated forever, and against his wishes, from his beloved son.

If Péller's were the most dramatic remarks from the prince's funeral proceedings, and they were sufficiently sensational to earn a ban from high authority on their publication in sections of the Parisian press, one other statement is worthy of mention, though also of scorn. On the funeral procession from Saint-Leu to Saint-Denis the valet Lecomte was pressed by fellow servants to explain his earlier comment about having 'such a weight on my mind'. His explanation was that, having promised the man who had taken over his hairdressing business in Paris that he would not practice the art again in the city, he had now been left without money or the prospect of work anywhere else because of the prince's death, a heavy burden to bear. Few believed a word of it, suspecting he might soon be cashing in on his master's demise.

The formalities completed, the woman who had ruled the prince's life for so long prepared to leave the febrile atmosphere of Saint-Leu for Paris and sanctuary in the Palais Bourbon. Perhaps she thought being closer to the king, her partner in the despicable matter of the Condé inheritance, would offer her protection. She left in her wake a vacuum for suspicions and theories to fester among those at Saint-Leu who refused to accept the official 'proof' of suicide.

The abbé Péller was convinced the main door to the prince's bedroom could have been bolted from the outside even though the bolt itself was on the inside. With the help of one of Louis Henri's inspectors of forests, Mery La Fontaine, the theory was put to the test on a similar door. It was found a loop of horsehair or silk thread could be fed through the keyhole and used to fasten the bolt. It was not easy, but it was possible. Another theory concerned the possible involvement in the death of a mysterious army sergeant, a swarthy character known to James Dawes who, before the tragedy, had been placed in charge of some of the guards at the château. According to some sources, he had then quickly found his way into Sophie's bed and, after the funeral, had been seen leaving Saint-Leu for Paris in her carriage. Where had the soldier been in the interim? Had he been in hiding?

Deadly Suspicions

Meanwhile, with what many in Paris regarded as indecent haste, the king had taken the necessary legal steps in the name of his youngest son to secure possession of the boy duke's Condé fortune. It would have been wise of Louis Philippe to have made a similar effort to honour those parts of the will that were so dear to his uncle, not only his unfulfilled wish to be buried at Vincennes but also his bequests to loyal servants Manoury, Bonnie and several others, none of whom received a franc. Sophie's allies, on the other hand, people like her nephew James, General Lambot and Louis Frann, all benefited from a clause in the will which guaranteed each man for life the generous salaries paid to them while in the prince's employ.

This was inarguably both pitiless on the part of Louis Philippe and rash in the extreme, inflaming the growing unrest at the official acceptance of suicide which was now being openly questioned as news of the tragedy spread widely across France and elsewhere in Europe. The king had not helped his cause by attending a race meeting on the Champ de Mars just three days after the prince's funeral. For once the normally sure-footed monarch misjudged the public mood. The Prince of Condé may have been regarded as a somewhat remote figure by many in France – he had not been seen widely in public for several years – but there was a feeling, fuelled by the king's enemies, an injustice had occurred. Louis Philippe boxed himself into a difficult position. Continuing to ignore the rising calls for an inquiry into the matter, when one was clearly needed, was asking for trouble.

The abbé Péller, tireless in his efforts on the late prince's behalf, stirred things up by demanding from the king an audience. His letter formally requesting this was very much to the point:

> Having vainly waited for someone to question me on the death of His Royal Highness ... and seeing that there is to be no inquiry into so extraordinary a death, I ... implore His Majesty to listen to me. I shall have the honour to place in His Majesty's hands my written declaration. I believe it to be of too high importance to be used as mere inclusion in the history I am writing. Everything ... I hear on this matter inspires me with a desire to express myself directly to the king, who I believe is, above everyone else, interested to know the truth of this horrible murder committed on the

person of his unfortunate relative. To revenge his memory and retain his honour to the last of the Condés cannot be an indifferent matter to the family of Bourbon.

The king refused the audience, referring Péller to the attorney-general. Instead, the abbé sent his twenty-page declaration to the queen in the hope of a more positive reply. Whatever Marie Amélie thought of this, and the abbé's direct reference to 'murder' must surely have shaken her, Péller waited in vain for any kind of response to his second approach to the royal household. But there was no way the royal family could keep a lid on the matter for much longer.

The king was left exposed by a legal challenge to the Condé will from the family who had most cause to feel cheated by it. Making a point of toadying up to Madame de Feuchères during the many visits he had made to Chantilly and Saint-Leu had not served the purpose Louis, Prince of Rohan, had hoped to gain from the power behind the House of Bourbon-Condé. On learning that nothing was to come the way of his family, regarded with good reason by many as the rightful heirs to the Condé inheritance, Louis de Rohan was incandescent with rage. 'This devil of a woman has betrayed me!', he exclaimed to friends, 'but she had better watch out – she is not in Paradise yet! I shall raise the law against her – yes, and against the king himself!' Within days he had filed a case in the civil court for annulment of the will on the grounds of 'undue interference'. It was brought in the name of his brothers, his sister and himself as representatives of the wider House of Rohan-Guéméné, which had absorbed the House of Rohan-Soubise following the extinction of its male line. The Rohans posed a real threat. The case was filed on 7 September, ironically on the same day as a tribunal in the town of Pontoise had formally declared no further investigation into the death of the Prince of Condé was necessary. In its opinion, it had been a tragic case of suicide.

At her apartments in the Palais Bourbon, Sophie had, for once, led a quiet life of almost paranoid unease. Terrified that her life was under threat, she had asked James Dawes' wife, the Baroness de Flassans, to share her bedroom at night while the abbé Briant, in very un-priestly fashion, slept in the adjoining library, fully armed with a pair of pistols! Eventually recovering her composure, Sophie re-engaged in a flamboyant social whirl, extravagantly dressed and bedecked in jewels, displaying an aura of superiority befitting, to her mind at least, that of a very well connected, and very well financially endowed, lady of stature.

The king and queen, Madame Adélaïde too, received her warmly, at least in public, but most of those she sought to impress were disgusted by her ostentation and longed to wipe the smug smile of satisfaction from her face. Her downfall seemed a huge step closer with the news of the Rohan challenge to the Condé will. And then Sophie was hit with a devastating second blow.

An anonymous pamphlet began circulating in Paris, The *Appeal to public opinion on the subject of the death of Louis Henri Joseph de Bourbon, Prince of Condé* pointed the finger of suspicion clearly at Sophie and her cronies, denouncing her character, ridiculing her mannerisms and conjuring up the ghost of Louis Henri to accuse an unnamed individual of carrying out an infamous murder. 'I have a great repugnance to keep him in my palace', said the prince's ghost. 'He remains there against my orders, and through him I died a frightful death'. Many who read this thought it a veiled reference to General Lambot, Sophie's lover and envoy. In truth, it could have been any number of her army of make agents.

Lambot, of course, had an alibi for the night of 26 August. He had been with James Dawes in Paris for the horse sale and had returned the next day with Pasquier, Rumigny and the remainder of the delegation sent to Saint-Leu by the king. The Paris alibis were piling up. Many were now questioning whether they were just too convenient. Had they been pre-planned?

When it was learnt that the Rohan challenge, with all its implications of Sophie-inspired foul play, was to be heard in the criminal court at Pontoise, she responded in the guise of a cruelly victimised, innocent woman, firing off a volley of indignant fury in a letter to the attorney-general:

'Neither patience nor the knowledge of the possession of a pure heart can resist any longer the odious attacks of which I am the object', she thundered before adding:

> In every salon, every day, are passed odious and malicious hints, either intentionally or carelessly. Poisonous insinuations appear in the papers. I have never been named [in the press], it is true, as the perpetrator of the most horrible of crimes but everywhere I am indicated in a manner which leaves no doubt as to who is accused. My honour forbids me to keep silent any longer.

It was, she went on to demand, 'in the public interest that justice should clear up this matter; it is also in my particular interest for I cannot enjoy any of the tranquillity on which I have the right to count'. She had been advised that there were clear grounds for her to seek redress for slander:

> But slander consists in the publication of definite sentiments, true or false. Such a persecution of innuendo as I now endure has no legal redress. I invoke, then, Monsieur, all your vigilance in this matter. I pray you to find witnesses to all the fabulous calumnies, to take the severest measures against them and to seek out the principal authors of these injurious slanders.

The attorney-general, deeply conscious of protecting the king's interests, saw her request to harry her many accusers as akin to opening up a second front on the battlefield. He took no action.

But the Rohan offensive could not be stopped. The proceedings at Pontoise at last provided an opportunity for the Condé loyalists, Louis Henri's friends and trusted retainers, to have their say. They painted a grim depiction of Sophie Dawes' cruel domination of the prince, how so many of his old servants had been replaced by her own appointees, how they, the prince's allies, collectively believed – indeed, knew – he had been forced into drawing up a will he was personally wholly against signing, and how they were certain their master had not committed suicide. They suspected to a man that Madame de Feuchères had conspired to have him killed. She would surely have been arrested had it not been for the intervention of the king.

Suspicions are one thing. Proof is another matter. But there was plenty of evidence to bring before the court. Manoury made clear the prince could never have moved – a foot and a half, he said – his heavy bed from its normal position. He referred to his master's slippers having been left in a place they had never been left before, and to the fact that the centre of the bed had clearly been sat, knelt or stood upon despite the prince always having slept close to one side.

Dr Bonnie, retreating from the suicide theory, stressed how the prince's infirmities would not have allowed him to climb onto a chair in order to hang himself or tie the knots in the handkerchiefs that acted as a noose. The doctor also pointed out, crucially, that it was he who had knocked over the chair in the bedroom, thus accounting for its position near the body; it had *not* been kicked away by the prince in the act of taking his own life. The doctor produced a wealth of medical evidence to prove that death had not been caused by strangulation.

The court was told the door to the 'secret staircase' had been left unlocked on the night of the tragedy and how it was possible to lock from the outside, in the ante-chamber leading to the bedroom, the bolt which was affixed to the inside of the bedroom door. The case for murder was steadily gathering pace.

The abbé Péller, pleased at last to have his say, drew attention to the fact that Madame de Feuchères had used the grand staircase to reach the prince's bedroom on the morning his body was discovered rather than take the much shorter, more direct, route via the 'secret staircase'. The reason, he inferred, was obvious. Using the private stairs would have drawn attention to the fact that its door into the prince's bedroom had been left unbolted the night before.

As for the supposed collapse of the prince's morale and mental capacity in the last days of his life, the Baroness de Préjean, wife of Louis Henri's card-playing opponent on the evening of 26 August, said she had never seen him more cheerful, composed or, indeed, sensible that night, recalling how the prince had playfully revoked her husband during the final game of whist.

The evidence from the 'other side' in the courtroom amounted to little more than a host of conflicting stories and downright lies. Lecomte, for example, in a ridiculously foolish attempt to distance himself from the woman who had appointed him, claimed he had only once come into contact with Madame de Feuchères during the three years he had been employed by the prince!

Intriguing evidence was provided by members of the Dupré family whose room on the *entresol* was immediately below the prince's bedchamber. Sophie had brought them to the château to join her army of spies. They were well-placed in their room (formerly occupied by Manoury) to hear much of what was going on in the room above. It was suggested at the Pontoise hearing that, whether the prince had hanged himself or had been murdered, the Duprés would surely have heard something. Unconvincingly they claimed not to have heard a thing. But it was something several witnesses had heard M. Dupré say that made the most impact.

Following a quarrel with Madame de Feuchères, apparently over money, he had loudly exclaimed: 'Damn that woman! It's lucky for her that I kept my mouth shut and didn't let out all I knew!' Challenged in court as to the meaning of the latter part of this statement, he said it had concerned a 'love affair' of Sophie's he had discovered. This was greeted with general disdain.

The evidence that the prince's death had not been a suicide, that a terrible crime *had* been committed by persons unknown, but probably orchestrated by Sophie Dawes, seemed overwhelming. But then the hearing was suddenly halted. The Prince of Rohan, acting on the advice of his lawyers, exercised his right under French criminal law to have the proceedings transferred to the Royal Court of Paris. As one of the parties to a contested lawsuit, he was entitled to do so under the French criminal code if he believed justice was unlikely because of the capability, or honesty, of the magistrate hearing the case. It was a gamble but one the prince must have thought worth taking in his determined bid to prove a case of murderous guilt.

In January 1831 the case, together with a written record of the evidence heard at Pontoise, was transferred to the Paris court. Instructed to take on the role of examining magistrate was Antoine Edmé de la Huproye who, in his sixty-sixth year, was one of the oldest, most experienced and highly respected judges on the Bench. His appointment to the case would not have pleased the king. Huproye was a legitimist, a staunch supporter of the exiled Charles X who saw Louis Philippe as a usurper and was therefore closely aligned with the politics of the late Prince of Condé. It is assumed that Louis de Rohan pulled several strings to influence Huproye's selection, which was achieved despite attempts by the attorney-general to thwart it.

The king had more than enough on his plate. The Paris press, re-energised under Louis Philippe's reforms, had in turn given a powerful voice to the republican and anti-clerical elements in the capital. At first the government, reluctant to repress former allies, was inclined to turn a blind eye as crowds attacked legitimists at a memorial service. Then the civil unrest boiled over in February when the rebels sacked the palace of the Archbishop de Quelan, smashing his furniture, profaning his chapel and throwing books and just about anything else they could get their hands on out of the windows to fuel their bonfires and barricades. Not for the first time, the archbishop was forced to flee for his safety.

Deadly Suspicions

Against this turbulent backdrop, Huproye began his examination into the suspicious death of a royalist prince.

He worked assiduously on it for four months, re-examining the evidence given earlier, cross-examining the evidence of more than 100 witnesses and taking the trouble to delve deeply into the background, character and behaviour of all the key players in the drama, especially Sophie Dawes. Three times the baroness was called before the judge, whose severity of tone when addressing her was met with ill-disguised scorn and contempt that she, the ultra-fashionably dressed lady of society, should have to face such indignity. Marjorie Bowen's description of the elaborate outfits Sophie chose to wear at the inquiry cannot be bettered:

> The opulent charms of the woman of thirty-nine were set off by tight bodices, full, low-set sleeves, thick ankle-length skirts with frills, huge hats or *capote* [hooded cloak] covered by ribbons and flowers, and weighed down with long, heavy veils. Her jet-black, thick, glossy tresses were divided in bunches over either ear, and the outlines of her massive figure were softened with organdie scarves, lace fichus [triangular shawls], clusters of flowers at the breast, long elaborate gloves, drop earrings and floating cloaks, richly ornamented. Her beauty was rapidly coarsening into an odious vulgarity; her lips [had tightened] into a mere thread.

Thus armoured, Sophie was ready to perform. 'It was terrible for me, who was honoured with the confidence and the kindness of the prince, who would have given my life to conserve his, to find myself the object of these suspicions', she declared before, with dramatic bravura, she spoke the line which would have brought the house down had she been in a theatre. Bristling at Huproye's clear inference that greed had driven her to orchestrate a murder, she told the judge: 'Money is nothing! Honour is everything!'

She refused to accept the evidence of Baron de Choulot, among others, that Louis Henri was planning to escape on the night he died. She argued that the prince had long had a tendency towards suicide and stressed he had become 'very sombre and morose' after the July Revolution of 1830. She tried to explain why she had been so anxious to maintain a thorough search for any papers left by the prince. This was because, 'I could not reconcile myself to the idea that he had left me in such a cruel manner without a word'. She contradicted herself more than once, conveniently forgot details – 'oh well, that escaped my memory; one cannot recall everything,' she said – and then resorted to the emotional rage of the victimised, innocent woman:

> How can I express the indignation that I feel at these odious insinuations? Why should anyone try to fasten on me this horrible crime? If the prince was murdered, who was the murderer? How could he have entered the château? Was not Monsieur de la Villagontier in charge of the château, was there not a valet who slept in the room beneath? Who could have entered the prince's room – were there not guards outside, continually making their rounds? The apartment that I occupied was a long way from that of the prince. Between my room and his was the *entresol* in which several people slept. Monsieur de la Villagontier slept near the prince – he must have heard the least noise!

Sophie denied everything. It cut no ice with the judge.

With each passing day the evidence against her grew. Even Villagontier, now wishing to distance himself from the woman who had appointed him to the Condé household, turned against her, denying her story that she had not been at Saint-Leu on 11 August when the prince had been injured. And, while the doctors sent by the king to carry out the original post-mortem examination remained faithful to their verdict of suicide, Sophie had to endure the evidence of a doctor brought to the court by the Prince of Rohan's lawyer who supported the theory that the prince had been stifled in his bed and then carried by two people to the window.

Huproye was thorough in every way. He had visited the château to see for himself its layout and particularly how the 'secret staircase' directly connected Sophie's ground floor apartments with the prince's bedroom. The judge also had a small model of the building made in plaster by a Paris architect. It was brought to the court to help him interpret the evidence. He listened intently to every word and painstakingly reached his principal conclusion: the Prince of Condé had secretly made a second will, revoking the original of 1829, and was about to flee the country in order to escape the malign power of Sophie Dawes. She had discovered this and had resorted to murder in order to stop him. Using the secret stairs to gain access to the prince's bedroom, she and an accomplice had entered the room at about two in the morning, had smothered the old man on his bed and then fastened him with the two handkerchiefs to the *espagnolette* to create the impression he had hanged himself.

As to the identity of Sophie's accomplice, the judge opted for the abbé Briant as the most likely suspect. He had three reasons for believing this: Briant's muscular physique and extraordinary strength; his overly obsequious manner towards Madame de Feuchères; and the fact that she both relied on and confided in him. In truth, this reasoning could have been just as easily applied to James Dawes and General Lambot were it not for their convenient Paris alibis.

Honest and brave, Huproye had reached his judgment despite repeated reminders from the new attorney-general, Persil, who was frequently at the inquiry, that no action was to be taken against the Baroness de Feuchères, further proof, as if it were needed, that Sophie enjoyed the protection of the king. She had already been helped by the fact that none of the correspondence between her and the Orléans family, potentially damaging for both parties, was made available to the inquiry and neither were the reports sent to the king from Saint-Leu by Pasquier and Rumigny which clearly would have diminished the case for a suicidal death.

Even without this, Huproye was convinced that a murder had been committed and that Sophie Dawes' guilt in the affair was obvious. Before submitting his report formally to the attorney-general and public prosecutor, the judge summarised his findings for Persil who immediately informed the king. Before long, an indignant Huproye heard that his hard work and dedication had been in vain. 'Your report, for reasons of State, must be suppressed', Persil told him.

The smuggler's daughter had escaped the certainty of a criminal trial, the likelihood of a conviction for murder and the probability of a date with *Madam Guillotine*. Other members of her family would not be as fortunate as the story of Sophie Dawes descended further into infamy.

Chapter 10

End Games:
The Scarred Spoils of Victory

Judge Huproye's long inquiry into the death of the Prince of Condé drew to its inevitable conclusion on 21 June 1831 when his report was formally shelved and a judgement which reeked of convenient ambiguity was issued. In essence, it amounted to a ruling that, as it had not been proved the death was the result of a crime, proceedings were now closed. A statement like that was never going to stop the tongues from wagging. There was now outright hostility in Paris towards the Englishwoman who most felt sure had murdered the prince.

Louis de Rohan had not given up his fight for justice, turning to the civil court to challenge the validity of the Condé will. The case was brought by his family lawyer, Monsieur de Harlequin, who had kept a close eye on the affair for a year. He had reached exactly the same conclusions as Huproye and, in effect, made public the learned judge's report in a robust *tour de force* of legal argument. The case for the defence, in which the king's lawyers took centre stage, was, frankly ridiculous. At its heart was a claim that, angered by not benefiting from the prince's will, his loyal retainers had conspired to frame Madame de Feuchères in a murderous plot. There must have been a great many wry smiles among the audience in the courtroom of the Tribunal of the Seine when Louis Philippe's advocate rose to address the hearing:

> The murder of the Prince of Condé on the part of Madame de Feuchères would have been a patricide! No ... good sense alone would reject such an odious supposition! Until some witness comes forward who has seen her actually do the deed, I shall refuse to believe in [her] guilt.

End Games

Patricide? Everybody in the courtroom knew full well that Sophie Dawes was not the illegitimate daughter of the prince. That shabby pretence had been smashed nearly a decade earlier.

Harlequin argued his client's case well. It was, of course, a strong one. But it was not as strong as Louis Philippe's resolve to save the House of Orléans from embarrassment and shame. Royal command again weighted the scales against the Rohans. The case was thrown out.

The Prince of Rohan refused to give up. In February 1832 he circulated a pamphlet which effectively summarised the address Harlequin had given at the tribunal. It sold in huge numbers. The opening retraced the many past glories and more recent tragedies of the House of Condé. It is unlikely that too many of the pamphlet's readers wasted much time ploughing through this often tedious preface. Most would have turned directly to the lawyer's far less flowery prose on the death of the last of the Condés, a man 'who was so completely governed by a will stronger than his own that it was his sole desire, by sacrificing his own personal feelings and real wishes, to purchase a little rest in his old age [and make the will of August 1829]'.

In the pamphlet Harlequin laid bare the rewards 'the Englishwoman' had gained from her domination over the old prince – a very long list indeed – and stressed Sophie's need for 'the protection of some persons no less powerful than enterprising' to guarantee she got a whole lot more from the will than she would otherwise have inherited. Pulling no punches, he turned his fire on the king:

> We can easily understand that a certain powerful and prolific family wanted to see this post of heir to the Condés filled by one of its sons. But what difficulties had to be surmounted? Did not the prince's entire political career place an insurmountable object in the way of such a project?

Thus, Harlequin built the case against the inheritors of the Condé fortune – the pact which had led to murder. He carefully re-presented all the evidence supporting the invalidity of the famous will and the lengths the prince's tormentor had been willing to go to in order to force it through to her, and the royal family's, immense benefit. In a truly brilliant passage, he wrote:

> The most cruel, the saddest, part in the whole affair, the fact that has made the deepest impression on my mind, is that

the prince begged his valet to sleep outside his door. See what the old man thought of his position. Certain persons have tried to make out that Monseigneur wished thereby to guard himself from the temptation to commit suicide – as if the servant sleeping outside his door could have saved him from himself!

In that paragraph Harlequin had exposed the absurdity of the whole case for the defence. It did not stop Sophie suing the Prince of Rohan for publishing a libellous pamphlet. She won the case. Louis de Rohan was fined and ordered to serve two months in prison. He evaded both penalties by fleeing to Bohemia where he and his eldest brother, the Duke of Montbazon, both died in 1836, tired out no doubt by the struggle to wrest justice from the claws of Sophie Dawes.

But Sophie, who had yearned for respect in high places, now found herself vilified in French society. She may have come out on top in her legal battles but she had simultaneously been wholly exposed for the grasping, lying, cruel, stop-at-nothing, selfish woman she had become.

Away from the courts the ill-feeling towards her had already markedly intensified in 1831 when news had filtered through in quick succession of a series of ominously curious events guaranteed to paint her in the worse possible light. The first, during the closing stages of Huproye's inquiry, was a fire which broke out mysteriously at the château of Saint-Leu shortly after one of her brief visits as the building's new owner. The flames engulfed the apartments formerly occupied by the late prince, destroying virtually everything in their path. The old man's bedroom, the infamous window where his body was found hanging, the 'secret staircase' and all the other features of what just about everyone considered had been a crime scene were destroyed, ruling out any further examination in a future quest to seek out the truth.

Then, in July 1831, Sophie and James Dawes had left France for a short visit to London. The reasons for the trip are difficult to verify. Sophie may have been there to discuss investments with her bankers. Or she may have been renewing her friendship with Prince Talleyrand, now representing the interests of Louis Philippe's France as the country's ambassador to Britain.[1] Travelling back to France from Dover on the 18th, she and James stopped off for the night at the port of Calais. The *Gazette de Calais* soon reported on a dramatic incident in its town:

The famous Baroness de Feuchères arrived in our town, coming from Dover, on Monday the 18th at four o'clock in the afternoon. She was accompanied by [Madame] Becquey, a servant, M. Darmaign, editor-in-chief of the *Gazette des Tribunaux,* and one of her nephews, James Dawes, Baron de Flassans, a young man of 32 years who, under the auspices of his aunt, filled the office of squire with the unfortunate Prince of Bourbon-Condé. The crossing, which had taken place on board the English steamer *Sovereign*, had been long and the baron, incommoded by seasickness, had made some efforts to vomit [but was able to leave the ship] no longer in a state of discomfort, and had been at the Customs to have his carriage [released].

He had distinguished himself by his [fine] manners and had dined at the Hotel Meurice[2] with taste and appetite. Madame de Feuchères congratulated him [on this] and offered him cheese. He stretched out his plate and fell down at the same time. A few minutes later he was dead, without being able to utter a single word. It was then eight o'clock. Before ten o'clock Madame de Feuchères and M. Darmaing rode together on the road to Paris. Madame Becquay was commissioned to have the last duties rendered to the remains of the unfortunate young man. Messieurs Arnaud, Souville and Cognon carried out the autopsy. The rupture of a vessel had caused death. A rather singular [problem with confirming this] has been remarked upon since then: the lungs were [so to speak] strangled by two bones which crossed each other.

The *Gazette* did not attribute this last comment to any named individual but there are reports from other sources that a doctor, equally anonymous, declared that 'death has not been due to the causes to which it has been attributed'. The cause of death was officially put down to either apoplexy or a severe case of colic, but the contrary view of the unnamed doctor does raise the possibility that James Dawes had suffered some sort of spasm induced by a strong poison.

Why Sophie was travelling with the editor-in-chief of the Paris-based *Gazette des Tribunaux* (Court's Gazette) is something of a mystery, but having an esteemed journalist with her, able to spread the word of a death by natural causes, might well have suited her down to the ground.

It was known that James had quarrelled with her before they had left France, apparently because he had been talking rather too loudly and too publicly about his relief at not being at Saint-Leu on the night of Louis Henri's death, 'otherwise I would have been accused of the same crime she has been'. It is also believed that the pair had argued over money. But if Sophie was involved in her nephew's sudden death, in an attempt to silence him, at least she gave him a good funeral, returning with his body to the Isle of Wight on 20 September, probably for the first time since she had left it as a young girl, to see him buried in the churchyard at St Helen's beneath a memorial stone bearing on its west face the following text:

> To the memory of James Dawes, Baron de Flassans, who died suddenly at Calais on landing from England on 18th July 1831 in the 29th year of his age, leaving his widow, his family and friends to weep and lament their loss. "In the midst of life we are in death." Erected as a mark of affection by his aunt, the Baroness de Feuchères.

Strangely, James' 'affectionate' aunt had not bothered to get his age right. Born at St Helen's in March 1799, he was, as the Calais newspaper correctly reported, in the thirty-third 'year of his age'.

No doubt Sophie did weep in the village churchyard. But were these the crocodile tears of the practised actress? Were they shed to hide the true emotions of a woman who would resort to even the most despicable of crimes to preserve the riches and status she had devoted her life to secure? There were many in France who needed no encouragement to subscribe to that theory.

Apparently healthy young men can, of course, die suddenly of natural causes, and this was certainly true in the 1830s, but for two seemingly healthy young brothers to die without warning within weeks of each other is another matter altogether. At six in the morning of 31 August a servant discovered the dead body of his master at 102 rue Saint-Lazare, Paris. The dead man was the 29-year-old George Dawes, the younger brother of James. There is no doubt about this; legal documents held privately today in the Isle of Wight confirm the relevant facts. What cannot be confirmed is the date of George's arrival in Paris and, of course, how he died, although the official view, once again, was that it was from natural causes.

The really big question, given the date of George's sudden demise, just six weeks after his brother's in Calais, is: can this also be linked to the August 1830 death of the Prince of Condé? We now have two shadowy characters in this story – George Dawes and the mysterious 'Sergeant X' (as he is mostly described in accounts of the Condé tragedy), the handsome, muscular guard commander who arrived at Saint-Leu shortly before the death of the prince and left very soon afterwards with Sophie. Is there a possibility that these two enigmatic individuals were actually one and the same person – a man masquerading as a soldier whose true identity was known only to James and Sophie, his close relatives at the château?

We can certainly link 'Sergeant X' with the prince's death if we are to believe the deathbed confession years later of the valet Lecomte, testament which also serves as the strongest indicator of Sophie Dawes' murderous involvement – and not merely as orchestrator of the crime:

Lecomte wrote: 'On the night of August 26th and 27th 1830, towards two o'clock, Dupré, Madame de Feuchères' footman, came to wake me. He said that his wife and he had heard footsteps above, in the room of Monseigneur. Madame de Feuchères was not in the habit of going to visit the prince at this time of night – what then was happening?' Rising swiftly from his bed Lecomte hurried to Louis Henri's private apartments, opened the door to the ante-chamber and peered through the open doorway ahead into the bedroom.

Immediately he could see by the light of his candle two people hurriedly making their way to the private stairway. Rushing into the bedroom, he accosted them and then stood back in astonishment as he recognised who he was confronting – Madame de Feuchères and 'Sergeant X'. The latter disappeared quickly down the secret stairs, throwing the door to behind him. For a moment Lecomte and Sophie Dawes stared at each other, unsure of what to say. Then Sophie, recovering her composure, ordered the valet to go back to his room. He did as he was told, too afraid to do anything else despite fearing that something awful had taken place.

Lecomte's wife would later add that her husband had said nothing of this during the judicial hearings because, having seen what she was capable of, he was simply too terrified of the potential consequences of crossing Sophie. Madame Lecomte's own memories of that hot

August night were as vivid as her husband's. She recalled seeing on the morning of the 27th Madame de Flassans' maid with a torn and twisted handkerchief in her hand, stained with mucous and blood, just as the shirt of the prince had been when his body was discovered. The Lecomtes had assumed that this linen handkerchief had been used to smother the master.

The couple had nothing to gain from making this up late in their lives. There seems no reason to doubt the veracity of their statements. Sophie Dawes and her mysterious accomplice surely *had* murdered the Prince of Condé. At the time of his own death, General Lambot would leave papers which also named Sophie and Sergeant 'X' as the murderers, though he claimed 'X' had been the actual killer and suggested the prince had been strangled, not stifled, to death.

And so we come back to the identity of the man known as 'X'. He is never given a name in historical accounts or in the legal records of the judicial process. Why was this? If he truly was sharing Sophie's bed, as some claimed at the time, then there might well have been good reason, for her at least, to shelter his identity and protect both of them against allegations of an incestuous relationship, but it is hard to see how they could have got away with this at the inquiry before the incorruptible Huproye. Strings must certainly have been pulled from very high places.

Since we have no name for the reputed male assassin, and because George Dawes never features in any contemporary account of Sophie's story or, indeed in most of those published since, and yet was definitely in the employ of the prince for a period, it does not seem fanciful to point the accusatory finger at him. It is difficult not to suspect that this was the reason he too lost his life in the summer of 1831. Or maybe, like his brother, he simply knew too much. It is probably safe to say that, one way or another, the prince's death was a family affair.

Unlike his brother, the unmarried George was not taken back for burial in the island of his birth. He lies today in Paris' largest cemetery at Père Lachaise, having taken his secrets to the grave.

Together, these three events and the legal suits in Paris had diminished Sophie. Slowly but steadily, the King of the French began to distance himself from her. Increasingly, she became isolated, shunned by the royal court she had striven so hard to be accepted at, and generally hated. She sought solace in travelling, taking with her the little daughter of her sister Charlotte who had lately fallen prey to insanity. Born in

1832, Sophie Thanaron, named after her aunt, was possibly the only child Sophie Dawes ever really took to. Mostly she kept children at arm's length. Having never given birth herself, some say because of a reproductive malfunction, she formally adopted little Sophie and treated her with kindness and affection.

In 1833 Sophie had the once glorious château of Saint-Leu razed to the ground and put its park up for sale as building plots. Had the château's fire-ravaged presence begun to haunt her? Did she want to banish the memory of the Prince of Condé's death from her thoughts? It would be impossible for anyone to do that when visiting the site today. The one thing that remains is a stone memorial to Louis Henri. It is purported to stand precisely beneath the position of the window where the prince's suspended body had been discovered on that hot late August morning in 1830.

Sophie had endured enough. She sold her remaining portfolio of properties and lands and in 1838, the year of Queen Victoria's coronation in London, the Queen of Chantilly left for good the country from which she had taken so much. Fabulously wealthy, she could afford to pay for the refurbishment of the magnificent mansion at Bure Homage, near Christchurch in present-day Dorset, adding French-style Corinthian columns to its architecture and furnishing it in the French style. She also bought a stylish town house, No. 5 Hyde Park Square, in London's fashionable Paddington district.[3]

A home was found on the Isle of Wight at Carisbrooke Priory for her mother, Jane, who had travelled back to England with her. The old woman died peacefully there a few weeks later in August, two years short of her ninetieth birthday. Sophie seemed as delighted to inherit a pair of Jane's spectacles as she had been determined to get her hands on a large slice of the Prince of Condé's fortune. The death records for Jane described her as a spinster as if Dicky Daw had never existed, giving birth to the notion that Sophie had been born to common law parents.

Sophie's health, once so robust, was failing. Grossly overweight, she had developed the symptoms of what in those days was known as dropsy and today is referred to as oedema. What was going on in her mind at that time we may only conjecture but a quite remarkable change had occurred in her behaviour. She lived quietly, donating large chunks of her fortune to charity, with a particular emphasis on assisting the poor. This had once been politically expedient in France, but in England it was apparently born out of a genuine desire to help those less fortunate than she. Can we attribute this to a guilty conscience? Probably. Sophie had followed her mother into a late acceptance of piety. As the 1830s drew to a close she was a changed woman, trying, we may assume, to make her peace with God and atone for her crimes.

On Tuesday 15 December 1840 Sophie Dawes, Baroness de Feuchères, suffered a sudden heart attack at her London home. At the probable age of 48 her incredible life was over.

Ironically, her own will became a lengthy matter of legal dispute. She had left it unsigned. Under the terms of his marriage settlement, Adrien de Feuchères[4] was entitled to a portion of her estate. The honourable soldier refused to accept a penny and offered his share instead to hospital charities in his home city of Nimes, which were then forced to go to law in order to secure their inheritance in the face of challenges from lawyers representing Sophie's English relations and Sophie Thanaron. A compromise eventually settled the matter. The charities in Nimes received 3,295 franks while James Dawes, father of the late Baron de Flassans, and his one surviving sister, Mary-Ann Clarck, shared 3,000,000 francs between them. The remainder, a considerable sum running into several millions, was inherited by Sophie Thanaron.

Sophie Dawes also left a highly emotive written protest at the failure of King Louis Philippe to honour the Prince of Condé's wish for the future use of the château of Ecouen, declaring this 'the worst of all the sorrows that poisoned a certain period of my existence'. It counted for nothing. The bequest never was honoured. Sophie called upon the Duke of Aumale, 'if ever he remembers the zeal with which I promoted his interests', not to refuse to exercise the last wishes of his benefactor so that [by safeguarding the future of the château of Chantilly] the children of France may profit by the legacy of a generous French prince'. In this she was not thwarted. The Duke of Aumale would eventually do more than simply safeguard the historic château. Returning in 1871 from extended exile in England, he rebuilt the Grand Château to its present magnificence as a lasting memorial to the great princes of the House of Condé. When he died, heirless, in 1887, the château and its fabulous domain was handed over to the French nation together with Prince Henri's vast collection of paintings which today, bettered only by the collection at the Louvre, continues to fascinate as the centrepiece of the *Musée Condé*.[5]

End Games

Henri's father, Louis Philippe, survived several assassination attempts before, following a severe economic crisis in 1847, he was forced to abdicate the throne the following year. France had seen the last of its monarchy as the ousted king fled to exile in England. Louis Philippe, at the age of 76, died at Claremont House in Surrey on 26 August 1850. His remains now lie in the Chapel Royal Saint-Louis at Dreux in northern France, having been moved there from an original grave in Weybridge. His queen, Marie-Amélie, passed away at Claremont on 26 August 1866. She too is now buried at Dreux.

As for the Queen of Chantilly's own 'royal family,' her brother James died on 2 December 1843, probably in his sixty-seventh year, his heart broken by the sudden loss of two of his sons in France a decade or so earlier. His wife, Mary, had died in 1827. The couple's daughter, Matilda de Chabannes, remained in France until her death in 1854, in her forty-third year, having given birth to four children. Another son, William, who remained on the Isle of Wight, did well enough for himself, taking possession of Wydcombe Manor, in the south of the island, where he died in 1853, aged 57. He shares his older brother James's churchyard grave at St Helen's.

It is believed Charlotte Thanaron, Sophie's younger sister, having spent years in an asylum, died in London around 1841, probably in her forty-sixth year. Her daughter, Sophie (full name Marie-Charlotte Sophie) Thanaron, helped by her good fortune in inheriting the bulk of her aunt's millions in 1840, married Frenchman Henri Corbin, with whom she had a daughter in 1854. Sophie Thanaron survived to witness the onset of the twentieth century, dying in 1901, aged 69. Sophie Dawes' other sister, Mary-Ann Clarck, died in 1853 in her seventieth year.

Over the course of time the location of Sophie's final resting place seems to have been something of an elusive biographical element as early-twentieth-century writers in both France and England rose to the challenge of piecing together the variegated mosaic of her extraordinary life. Information on the burial would obviously have proved of immense value to authors such as Marjorie Bowen, who admitted to the lack of this key segment of detail in her otherwise extensively researched 1934 book. 'It is not known where Sophie Dawes is buried, nor if she had any monument', wrote Bowen, leaving readers of *The Scandal of Sophie Dawes* to conjecture over the precise extent of graveyard magnificence which, if a monument had been erected, might possibly have represented a final revealing statement 'from the grave' as to the true sentiments, and maybe even remorse, of Sophie at the end of her life.

The grave's generalised location, however, had never been a secret. Contemporary reports of Sophie's passing had clearly identified the site. 'Her mortal remains were interred in the cemetery on the Harrow-road', reported *The Gentleman's Magazine* in its February 1841 obituary, a clear reference to Kensal Green Cemetery in northwest London. The cemetery had been founded only seven years before Sophie's death as the first in a series of grand, privately-run burial grounds – colloquially known today as 'The Magnificent Seven' – established by Act of Parliament between 1833 and 1841 to alleviate overcrowding in the capital's existing parish graveyards. Considering the abiding influence of the French nation in Sophie's story, Kensal Green's burgeoning cemetery can be regarded as an appropriate site for her burial, inspired as it was in both concept and design by the established Père Lachaise Cemetery in Paris, which had opened in 1804 and is now the largest in the heart of the city. There is a further symmetrical quality when reflecting on the similarities of the two cemeteries in the context of Sophie's tale – Adrien Feuchères was buried at Père Lachaise in 1857 following his death in Paris at the age of 72.

But precisely where in Kensal Green Cemetery's seventy-two acres, home to the graves of an impressive host of celebrated historical figures, had Sophie Dawes been interred? What *was* inscribed on her gravestone or memorial, if indeed the grave had been graced by a memorial at all? Written and online references to her burial place referred only to the broad-brush location of the cemetery and photographic evidence was wholly conspicuous by its absence. Historical record appeared to have decreed the final resting place of the smuggler's daughter from the Isle of Wight was of little consequence – not worth the bother of investigating further.

Fortunately, the General Cemetery Company, which still runs Kensal Green's facility under the authorisation of its original founding Act of 1832, retains the handwritten records of its burials from the earliest days. In 2017 I sought the help of staff there in a bid to pinpoint the exact position of Sophie's grave through the pages of the preserved record books. This was not the straightforward task it had appeared to be. While the records listing burials in 1840 included that of Sophie, cataloguing it, as expected, under her aristocratic married name of Feuchères and annotating a reference number of 2779, the French surname did not appear alongside the details for grave 2779 in a second book, listing the burial plots in numerical order. It took considerable effort on the part of staff to decipher the surname that *was* listed – Dawes.

So, were we looking for a memorial with her family name on it or one with her married name and, probably, the French title? A search of the relevant area in the cemetery proved fruitless until ground staff familiar with the layout were able to point at last to the grave. It is in the main, Anglican, part of the cemetery rather than in the adjoining St Mary's Roman Catholic Cemetery, but as the latter was not established until 1858 it could hardly have been there. When erected, the monument clearly had been impressive but had since seriously deteriorated (see picture). Cracked stonework and broken iron railings at its base were clear evidence of decades of neglect, intentional or otherwise. Obviously there had been an inscription but not a single letter could be discerned. And so there is no longer any kind of message from the grave.

We have no window into the soul of the smuggler's daughter. The facts will have to speak for themselves.

Endnotes

Chapter 1

1. The apostrophe in the name St Helen's is generally not used today but was the accepted norm in the eighteenth and nineteenth centuries.
2. While it is generally accepted that the longer form of the name – expressed as Dawes – was an adaption of the earlier form – Daw – some surviving documentary evidence suggests that the two forms may have both been in use during Sophia's childhood on the Isle of Wight.
3. Together, the various components of the village green are said to be second only in size to the green at Duncan Down, near Whitstable in Kent, although Great Bentley at Tendring, north Essex, has a similar claim.
4. Source: *A Companion to the Isle of Wight* by John Albin, 1799. By the time the census of 1851 was taken, the population of St Helen's parish had risen to 1,948.
5. The workhouse pre-dates Parkhurst (later Albany) Barracks which were completed on the opposite side of the Newport-Cowes road in 1798 and later became part of the prison complex known today as HMP Isle of Wight.
6. Some early biographical accounts incorrectly assumed that 'Cliff' was the surname of the farmer rather than the name of the farm.
7. One theory – locally anecdotal but sometimes referred to in online references – about Sophia's relationship with the Shanklin farmer, that she first married and then left him, can certainly be ruled out despite it being suggested periodically in fanciful online accounts.
8. Records indicate that Dicky Daw died in Newport. Probably the specific location was the workhouse just north of the town.
9. Replaced today by the George Court apartment block, the only other visible reminders on site of the George Hotel are an illustrated panel depicting its unique history and the two gas lamp-posts

Endnotes

which stood outside the main entrance and survived the 1941 German bombing raid.
10. Kirsty Carpenter is Associate Professor of History at Massey University, New Zealand. Her work on the French *émigrés* who fled the Revolutionary and Napoleonic wars was published in 1999.
11. Violette Montagu credits Monsieur Daufresne, former steward of the Princes of Rohan's civil list, as the originator of the story about the legendary game of whist in which Sophia Daw was the prize. Other versions of the card game legend maintain that it was played only between the Duke of Kent and the Duke of Bourbon. Whatever, the outcome was the same!

Chapter 2

1. Protestant convert Louis I de Bourbon, the first Prince of Condé (1530–1569), was the fifth son of Charles de Bourbon, Duke of Vendôme. Initially a soldier in the French army, he later commanded Hugenot forces opposed to the Roman Catholic monarchy and was killed at the Battle of Jarmac during the third French religious civil war. He was the younger brother of Antoine de Bourbon, husband of Jeanne d'Albret, Queen of Navarre. The couple's son, Louis de Bourbon's nephew, became Henry IV of France.
2. Bathilde was the daughter of Louis Philippe d'Orleans (1725–1785), head of the House of Orléans cadet branch of the ruling Bourbon dynasty and the most senior member of the royal court after the royal family itself. Her mother was Louise Henriette de Bourbon (1726–59).
3. Bathilde's great-grandmother was Françoise Marie de Bourbon (1677–1749), known at court by the courtesy title, Mademoiselle de Blois. Louis Henri was a great-grandson of Louise-Francoise, Duchess of Bourbon (1673–1743), known as Mademoiselle de Nantes.
4. *The Gentleman's Magazine,* published in London between its 1732 founding and 1922, was noted for being the first periodical to use the term *magazine,* meaning 'storehouse' in French, and for being the source of Samuel Johnson's first regular employment as a writer.
5. After a distinguished career with the French Army, Louis, Duke of Crillon, moved to Spain in 1762 and become a lieutenant-general in the allied Bourbon army of that nation.

6. Soon after the Duke of Bourbon's arrival as an exile in London, the artist Henri-Pierre Danloux painted his portrait, depicting the duke in the uniform of the *Armée de Condé*. Initially, Louis Henri's mutilated hand was shown in full view but, at the duke's direction, the artist amended the portrait by covering both hands with military gloves. See *The Gentleman's Magazine*, October 1830.
7. With Napoleon Bonaparte at its head as First Consul, the French Consulate was established as a form of revolutionary government to succeed the earlier French Directory in November 1799. It lasted until its replacement by the Napoleonic Empire in May 1804.
8. Completed in 1722, Wanstead House was the ancestral home of the Tylney-Long family at the time of the exiled Condé nobles' arrival, in the ownership of the young Sir James Tylney-Long, 8th Baronet of Westminster, who died, aged 11, as the last baronet in 1805.
9. The conspiracy to overthrow Napoleon was led by Jean-Charles Pichegru and Georges Cadoudal. After capture both were tried and condemned to death. On 5 April 1804 Pichegru was found dead in his cell, having apparently hanged himself with his own tie, although many believe him to have been murdered. Cadoudal was executed on 28 June 1804.

Chapter 3

1. The works of Huet-Villiers (1772–1813), both portraits and landscapes, are still popular today, several having been sold in recent years at auctions. For example, in the year 2000 his depiction of an extensive river landscape with the ruins of an abbey and shepherds in the foreground was sold at Christie's New York's 'Important Old Master Drawings' auction for $8,625.
2. Roman Catholicism was favoured both politically and financially following its reinstatement as France's official religion. While its lands and endowments confiscated during the revolution were not returned, the Church received salaries and maintenance costs from the government for normal church activities and the bishops regained control of Catholic affairs.
3. Louis XVIII fled Paris at midnight on 19 March with a small escort, headed for safety in Lille, before crossing the border into the Netherlands to reach refuge in Ghent.

Endnotes

4. The occupying coalition force, under the Duke of Wellington's command, was to have stayed in France for five years. In the event, the soldiers were withdrawn after just three years in 1818.
5. Talleyrand's tenure as prime minister lasted only until September 1815 when, under pressure from political opponents and dismayed at the outcome of the second Treaty of Paris, he resigned.
6. In book format, Thackeray's story was retitled *The Memoirs of Barry Lyndon Esq*. In 1975 it was adapted by Stanley Kubrick for the British-American film, *Barry Lyndon*, starring Ryan O'Neal. The website https://pottoingaround.wordpress.com/ identifies Sophie's companion in Paris as 'her lover, Thomas Barry'. <Accessed 6 March 2019.>
7. See https://royalfavourites.blogspot.com/2016/03/bourbon-royals-lovers-mistresses.html. <Accessed 6 March 2019>
8. It was not until the Marriage Act of 1836 that allowance was made for non-religious civil marriages to be held in register offices across England and Wales.
9. The comment on Louis Joseph's final years appeared in Arnaud's 1906 biography, *Adélaïde d'Orleans (1777–1847)*.
10. Commissioned by Louis XVIII, praying memorial statues of the executed Louis XVI and Marie-Antoinette, sculpted by Edme Gaulle and Pierre Petitot, were not completed until the late 1830s. They were installed at the Basilica of Saint-Denis, where they remain a much-visited feature of the cathedral today. The royal couple's re-interred remains rest in the crypt below.
11. To be fair, the source of this theory, the pottingaround website, does admit that the whole idea of an aristocratic Sophie being 'adopted' as a baby by the hard-up Daw family in St Helen's is probably verging on the realms of fantasy, but it is right to add that such an unlikely proposition is no more incredible than the proven facts of the story.

Chapter 4

1. The domain of Chantilly had been dismantled in 1793 and the land sold off. The two-part château was acquired by a syndicate of revolutionary speculators, the Bande Noire, who planned to demolish all the buildings and sell the stones. Only *le grand château* was pulled down. The château had been a Condé possession since 1643 when it was given by Anne of Austria, wife

of Louis XIII, to Charlotte Marguerite, Duchess of Montmorency and Princess of Condé.
2. The couple's first-born son, Napoleon-Louis Charles Bonaparte, was only 4 years old when he died at The Hague in May 1807. Their second son, Napoleon-Louis Bonaparte (1804–1831), reigned for a short period in 1810, while still a child, as Louis II of Holland. The youngest son, Charles Louis-Napoléon Bonaparte (1808–1873) made the most impact, becoming President of France in 1848 and, as Napoleon III, Emperor of the French between 1852 and 1870.
3. In 1811 Hortense had secretly given birth to a fourth son who was illegitimate. He was the product of a relationship with Colonel Charles Joseph, Count of Flahaut, reportedly at a Swiss inn close to Lake Geneva. Hortense was 54 at the time of her death, also in Switzerland, in October 1837.
4. The collection of archives in the *Musée Condé* at Chantilly, where much of the correspondence quoted in this and succeeding chapters is preserved, includes a letter, dated 20 January 1804, from Adele's mother, Mimi Michelot, to Louis Henri which illustrates the affection between the latter and the couple's eldest daughter. Adele would have been 23 at the time and it would seem she was either living with the exiled Duke of Bourbon in London or owed her security to him. Mimi writes: 'I shall forget all the wrong you have done me; that wrong is repaired since it is to you that our child owes her happiness. I shall never speak of it again and I shall only remember what I suffered in order to realise my present happiness.'
5. Rue de la Ville-L'Eveque, in the 8th *arrondissement* of Paris, is part of the Madeleine district and close to L'église Sainte-Marie-Madeleine, the magnificent Roman Catholic church which, in its present neo-classical form, was founded in 1807 by Napoleon as a temple honouring his army.
6. In her book Marjorie Bowen says Louis Henri did not hand over Saint-Leu and Boissy to Sophie, among a raft of other generous gifts, until she returned to Chantilly from her mother's home in Paris. Bowen suggests the prince's 'opulent presents' were given to express his gratitude on her return. However, the likelihood is she had already secured the gifts before the collapse of her marriage.
7. The Hundred Thousand Sons of Saint Louis is something of a misnomer; the French force was nearer 60,000.

8. See *Dictionnaire des parlementaires français* (Dictionary of French Parliamentarians) 1789–1859.
9. There is some dispute as to precisely when the royal edict banning Sophie from Court was issued – and by which king. Some sources suggest the formal ban may have come from Louis XVIII's successor, Charles X. It is, however, likely that she had been an unwelcome presence at Court since the true nature of her relationship with Louis Henri became an open secret in 1822.

Chapter 5

1. Following her mother's death when she was just 3 years old, Louise Adelaide had been raised by her great-aunt, Henriette Louise de Bourbon, Benedictine abbess of Beaumont-lès-Tours. Educated at the convent and then at the royal abbey of Bernardine Panthémont in Paris, she had the Hôtel de Bourbon-Condé built for her personal use in 1780. Six years later she was appointed Abbess of Remiremont. Exiled from France during the revolution, she returned to Paris in 1816 to found the religious institution known as the Bénédictines de la rue Monsieur.
2. Born in 1764, Marie Louise d'Esparbès de Lussan, Countess of Polastron, had served as a lady-in-waiting to Louis XVI's queen, Marie Antoinette, before the revolution and it was at the court in Versailles she first met the Count of Artois, later Charles X. She died of tuberculosis.
3. Lambot was the uncle of the renowned French engineer Joseph-Louis Lambot (1814–1887), inventor of ferro-cement, which led to the development of what is now known as reinforced concrete.
4. Matilda's first name is sometimes spelt Matilde with a final 'e' during her time in France, a close match to the French (as well as German, Dutch, Norwegian and Danish) name of Mathilde.
5. Source: *Vie de Charles X, roi de France* by Prosper Vedrenne, published by J. Lecoffre, Paris, 1876.
6. These extracts from Puymaigre's memoirs were reproduced in Imbert de Saint-Amand's nineteenth-century work, *La Duchesse de Berry et la court de Charles X*, first published in Paris by E. Dentu, 1893, and reprinted in English by the Echo Library, 2009.

7. Violette Montagu places Lambot's approach to the Duchess of Berry at an earlier stage – in 1822 when Louis XVIII was still on the throne – and suggests that the general met only with one of the duchess's officials who reported the gist of Sophie's indiscreet proposal to her. This version, however, does not accord with the more generally accepted timeline of events following the collapse of Sophie's marriage in 1824 and her subsequent banishment from Court.

Chapter 6

1. Set up on 24 September 1792, the *Convention nationale* (National Convention), the first truly republican government from which the monarchy was totally excluded, succeeded the earlier *Assemblée nationale constituante* (National Constituent Assembly, 1789–91) and the *Assemblée législative* (Legislative Assembly, 1791–92). It functioned in Paris until 3 November 1795.
2. Dumouriez spent his years of exile in various parts of Europe before settling in England, where he died in 1823. The five French officials he had arrested, Beurnonville and the four commissioners, were kept captive by the Austrians until released under a prisoner exchange in 1795.
3. Montpensier died on 18 May 1807, aged 31; Beaujolais on 30 May 1808, aged 28.
4. In 1773 the title of Count of Joinville was among those held by Louis Philippe I, Duke of Orléans, the father of Philippe Égalité, who succeeded to it in 1785. Following his execution in 1793 the title passed to his son, Louis Philippe III himself, the man at the heart of Maria Stella Chiappinis's extraordinary story of identity fraud during her infancy.
5. Having retired from the navy on medical advice, Thomas Manby (1769–1834) had settled on an estate in Norfolk and in 1810, aged 41, had married 20-year-old Judith Hammond, the mother of his three daughters. Mary Harcourt Manby was the eldest of the three.
6. While his first name was usually styled simply as Frédéric, this was actually the fifth of the Marquis de Chabannes la Pilace's forenames after Hugues Jean Jacques Gilbert. Awarded the status of chevalier of the *Légion d'honneur* in 1814, he was elevated to that of an officer of the meritorious order four years later and had been installed as a

commander, the order's next degree of distinction, by the time of his marriage to Matilda Dawes in 1827.
7. Full name: Jean-Baptiste Paul Augustin (Justin) Thanaron. The surname is sometimes spelt Thaneron in archival documentation. While he is usually described simply as an infantry captain, some French military and genealogical records refer to him as a captain-adjutant major.

Chapter 7

1. Ultra-royalist Joseph de Villèle (1783–1854), a member of the Chamber of Deputies between 1816 and the July Revolution of 1830, had served as France's prime minister since December 1821.
2. Jean Baptiste Gay (1778–1832), a member of the Chamber of Deputies between 1818 and 1832, served only until August 1829 as prime minister before being replaced by ultra-royalist Jules de Polignac, who himself was in office only until the July Revolution of the following year.
3. Today the Hôtel de Lassay is the official residence of the President of the National Assembly, adjacent to the Palais Bourbon, which is now the seat of the lower parliamentary chamber.
4. It may be that there has been confusion about which of the prince's hands had suffered the loss of use in three fingers – the reports may actually refer to the missing fingers on his left hand.
5. The will, dated 30 August, notes that it was signed at the Palais Royal in Paris. This may be a legal nicety, added later, or may suggest that the prince was taken to the Orléans palace to sign it.
6. Rochefoucauld specifically referred to Sophie having a bad reputation 'in London', presumably to make her sound even more notorious and reviled than she actually was at that time.

Chapter 8

1. Violette Montagu, for example, suggests the prince's injuries were tended to by his private surgeon, Dr Bonnie, when he first made references to the cause of the several wounds.
2. Sources vary on the precise day given by the prince for the journey to Chantilly he never actually intended to take. Some say it was

announced as Monday, 30 August; others say it was Tuesday, 31 August.
3. The exiled Charles X did eventually reach the Austrian Empire, dying from cholera at Görz in November 1836, aged 79.
4. Performed usually in the presence of the royal family, the song became an unofficial national anthem for royalists between the Bourbon Restoration in 1815 and the July Revolution of 1830. The piece was taken from Jean-François Marmontel's play *Lucile*, first performed in 1769.
5. *L'espagnolette de St Leu: calcul rationnel de probabilités sur la fin tragique*, by J. Augustine Chaho de Navarre, Paris, 1844.
6. Many reports of the prince's death, particularly those published by the English media in the autumn of 1830, wrongly gave the date of his demise as 30 August rather than the correct 27 August – an error which is perpetuated to this day in several online accounts of Louis Henri's life.

Chapter 9

1. There are confusing references in some accounts, arising from Manoury's questioning of Lecomte, to the door to the 'secret' staircase being not only unbolted but left open when the body was found. It is probable the valet simply meant that the door was unlocked when he saw it.
2. Known in France as a *procès-verbal*, such accounts of an act or proceedings would have normally been undertaken by a magistrate (or, in modern practice, a police officer), but, in their absence, it could be carried out by anyone holding a position of formal authority in a locality.
3. Probably the first recorded case of auto-erotic asphyxia was that of Peter Anthony Motteux, the English author, playwright, translator, publisher and editor of *The Gentleman's Journal* in the 1690s. In recent times reputed cases have included those of Stephen Milligan, Conservative MP for Eastleigh, in 1994, and the American actor-musician David Carradine in 2009.
4. Violette Montagu suggests that, after this attempt to bully Manoury, Sophie 'tried to buy his favour by promising to give him a place in her own household but Manoury was not to be bought'.

Endnotes

5. Etienne Denis Pasquier (1767–1862) had previously served as President of the Chamber of Deputies under Louis XVIII in 1817–18. His title of *Chancelier de France* was revived for him by Louis Philippe shortly before his appointment as President of the Chamber of Peers in 1830. His famous, and many times reprinted, memoir, *A History of My Time*, has recently (2015) appeared in a new format by public domain publishers, Palala Press.
6. Pasquier dated his letter Friday, 27 August, 'four o'clock at night'. By this he meant 4am on *28 August*.

Chapter 10

1. Talleyrand served as Louis Philippe's ambassador in London between 1830 and 1834. He died in Paris four years later, in May 1838, in his eighty-fifth year.
2. The Hotel Meurice in Calais town centre remains in business today as one of the town's best-known destinations.
3. No. 5 Hyde Park Square was demolished following a Luftwaffe bombing raid in World War Two.
4. Adrien de Feuchères retired from the French Army as a field-marshal and was a member of the Chamber of Peers during the period of Louis Philippe's 'July Monarchy'. Following Feuchères' death in 1857, two days after his seventy-second birthday, the city of Nimes named both its first modern avenue after him and its principal college.
5. The Duke of Aumale was exiled in England between 1848 and 1871. By the time of his return to France he was a widower who had lost his two sons at an early age. His subsequent rebuilding of Chantilly's Grand Château was one of the greatest achievements of a man who was also a distinguished soldier. Retiring from public life in 1883, he died in May 1897, aged 75, in Sicily.

Acknowledgements

In a long quest to unravel the tumultuous life story of Sophie Dawes, examine aspects never before made public and prepare this book for submission, I have been fortunate to receive practical help and, just as importantly, encouragement from a large number of people and organisations. Without their invaluable input it would not have been possible to progress a project which, while always compellingly fascinating, at times possessed the capacity to test to the limit my resolve to keep the quest on track. Sophie had made it difficult, challenging in the extreme, to establish the truth, or at least the *probable* truth, about her scarcely believable life – the record of a woman about whom virtually anything appeared to have been possible. It was never going to be an easy task. I very much appreciate all the help that was extended to me.

Among the principal acknowledgements I must straightaway thank my publishers, Pen & Sword, for entrusting me with this assignment, while special thanks are owed to the ever-patient Laura Hirst, production coordinator, and to my editor, Danna Messer, for her perspective, enthusiasm and kind words of encouragement.

I was, as ever, helped by having a family with a mix of skills highly relevant for a project of this nature. My daughter-in-law, Sarah Searle's diligent research greatly aided my own when looking into the hitherto unearthed records of Sophie's troubled early years, and those of her family, on the Isle of Wight, together with genealogical records relating to the subsequent period prior to Sophie's move to France. The map of the Isle of Wight as it was in the late eighteenth century is also Sarah's work. My niece, Beccy O'Donoghue's fluent grasp of the French language was of immense – and obvious, given the nature of the story – value as was her read-through of the draft narrative. Meanwhile, my son, Matt Searle, somehow found the time in a busy work schedule to take the contemporary photographic images reproduced in the book and help me with the procurement and cataloguing of the book's overall image content.

Acknowledgements

In the context of pictures I am grateful also for the help of the local historical society in Sophie's home village of St Helens who provided from their archives some of the earliest photographic evidence of Sophie's humble birthplace. One of the most pleasurable aspects of research was the chance to visit, at the kind invitation of owners Mark and Rosy Hickman, Sophie's former house in Upper Green Road, a property which delightfully, and deliberately, recalls the era of the girl who lived there, often in abject poverty, during the closing years of the eighteenth century before making her extraordinary leap from obscurity to the riches which lay in wait for her on the mainland of England and, later, so memorably and dramatically, in France. I thank the Hickmans for allowing me to sample the unique atmosphere of their characterful home. I also extend thanks to the many other islanders in St Helens, Ryde and Seaview who have helped with background information on the Dawes family.

I acknowledge the immense contribution of the ever-helpful staff at the Isle of Wight Record Office in Newport to the 'early years' research, and, when it came to examining the facts at the other end of Sophie's story, the patient help and guidance provided by the staff of the General Cemetery Company at London's Kensal Green Cemetery in pinpointing the location of her, now neglected but once splendidly endowed, burial site – an impossible task without them.

In France, the setting for so much of Sophie's story, the principal source of reference relating to the Bourbon-Condé dynasty, the family of her aristocratic lover, Louis Henri de Bourbon, Prince of Condé, was always going to be the prince's former great château of Chantilly, the magnificent present-day location of the *Musée Condé*. I am grateful for the help provided by the curatorial staff there in my search for the relevant original source material among their extensive archives. How interesting it was to reflect while visiting the château on the huge role played by Sophie, albeit as a by-product of her self-serving scheming, in the preservation of Chantilly's breathtakingly beautiful domain under the nineteenth-century aegis of Henri, Duke of Aumale, leading to its current status as a glittering jewel in the crown of French heritage.

I must also acknowledge the guidance provided by staff during my visit to the Basilica of Saint-Denis in Paris, the final resting place of Louis Henri among so many French kings and princes. The abbey church is an extraordinary, hauntingly beautiful place to carry out historical research.

Finally, my thanks to the many genealogists in both France and Britain, too many to mention individually, whose studious compilation of records relating to Sophie's family and other leading characters in her complex story provided a foundation for a great deal of familial context.

Selected Bibliography

Books

Albin, John – *A Companion to the Isle of Wight*, Newport, 1799 (reprinted by Nabu Press, 2019).

Arnaud, Raoul – *Adélaïde d'Orleans, 1777–1847, D'Apres Des Documents Inedits: L'Egerie de Louis-Philippe*, Paris, 1906 (reprinted by Nabu Press, 2013).

Bowen, Marjorie – *The Scandal of Sophie Dawes,* John Lane, The Bodley Head, London, 1934.

Carpenter, Kirsty – *Refugees of the French Revolution: Émigrés in London 1789–1802*, Palgrave Macmillan, London, 1999.

Chaho, J. Augustine – *L'espagnolette de St Leu: calcul rationnel de probabilités sur la fin tragique*, Paris, 1844 (reprinted by Nabu Press, USA, 2012).

Coignard, Jerome – *The Domain of Chantilly: A Home. A Museum,* Musée Condé, Chantilly, 2018.

Cornut-Gentille, Pierre – *La baronne de Feuchères (1790–1840): La mort mystérieuse du duc de Bourbon,* Perrin, Paris, 2000.

Davenport Adams, W. H. – *The History, Topography and Antiquities of the Isle of Wight*, Smith, Elder & Co., London / James Braddon, Ryde, Isle of Wight, 1856.

De Gerainville, Alexander E. Billault – *Histoire de Louis-Philippe* (self-published), Paris, 1871.

Drinkwater, John – *History of the Siege of Gibraltar 1779–1783*, Thomas Nelson, Edinburgh, 1839.

Jones, Jack and Johanna – *The Isle of Wight: An Illustrated History*, The Dovecote Press, Wimborne, Dorset, 1987.

Le Jeune, Raymond – *Beyond Avarice* (self-published), Ryde, Isle of Wight, 2014.

Selected Bibliography

Low, David and Sheila White, Sheila – *Twelve Hundred Years in St. Helens: A Parish History* (self-published), Ryde, Isle of Wight, 1977.

Mackett, John – *The Portsmouth-Ryde Passage: A Personal View*, The Ravensbourne Press, London, 1970.

Montagu, Violette – *Sophie Dawes: Queen of Chantilly,* John Lane, The Bodley Head, London, 1912.

Newborough, Lady – *The Memoirs of Maria Stella* (*Lady Newborough*), Eveleigh, London, 1914 (reprinted by Ulah Press, USA, 2012).

O'Meara, Barry Edward – *Napoleon in Exile or A Voice from St Helena*, Jones & Co., London, 1822.

Paladilhe, Dominique – *Le prince de Condé: Histoire d'un crime*, Pygmalion, Paris, 2005.

Pasquier, Etienne Denis – *A History of My Time: Memoirs of Chancellor Pasquier,* T. Fisher Unwin, London, 1893.

Robert, Adolphe and Cougny, Gaston – *Dictionnaire des parlementaires français 1789–1889,* Bourloton, Paris, 1889.

Saint-Armand, Imbert de – *La Duchesse de Berry et la court de Charles X,* E. Dentu, Paris, 1893 (English reprint by Echo Library, 2009).

Vedrenne, Prosper – *Vie de Charles X, roi de France,* J. Lecoffre, Paris, 1876.

Periodicals

The Gentleman's Magazine, London, October 1830 & February 1841.
La Belle Assemblé, London, October 1830, August 1831 & February 1841.

Principal websites

www.ancestry.co.uk/ (various pages)
www.domaindechantilly.com/fr/ (various)
https://en.geneanet.org/ (various)
https//.en wikipedia.org/wiki/ (various)
www.isle-of-wight-fhs.co.uk (various)
www.pottoingaround.wordpress.com/2017/08/29/sophie-dawes-part-1-from-the-isle-of-wight-to-chantilly/ (& related pages)
www.royalfavourites.blogspot.com/2016/03/bourbon-royals-lovers-mistresses.html

Key original sources

General Cemetery Company, Kensal Green – records relating to burial of Sophie Dawes, 1840.

Isle of Wight Record Office, Newport – Isle of Wight House of Industry record books & other documents relating to Daw(es) family.

Musée Condé, Chantilly – correspondence and other documentation relating or relevant to Sophie Dawes in France.

Index

Algeria, 78
Angoulême, Louis Antoine, Duke of, 77
Angoulême, Princess Marie Thérèse, Duchess of, 114-15, 122
Arnand, Souville & Cognon, Drs (Calais), 187
Armée de Condé, 32-7, 104, 138
Artois, Louise Marie Thérea d', 99, 102
Aubert, Jean, 93
Aumale, Henri Eugene, Duke of, 112-13, 117, 121, 128-9. 132, 134, 135, 138, 145, 172, 173-6, 192, 205
Austria / Austrian Empire, 32, 34, 37, 44, 45, 47, 105-7, 149, 199, 202, 204

Bahamas, The, 108
Batavian Republic, 54
'Barry' (companion of Sophie), 47-8
Beauharnais, Hortense de, 64-5, 200
Beaujolais, Louis Antoine, Count of, 106-8, 202

Becquly, Madame (servant to Sophie), 186
Belgium, 105
Brussels, 32
Ghent, 198
Mons, 32
Belleville, Adolphe de, 19
Bernard, Louis Desire, 168-9, 171
Berry, Maria-Carolina, Duchess of, 101-2. 122-3, 140, 202
Berry, Charles Ferdinand, Duke of, 99-100
Bohemia, 99, 186
Beurnonville, Pierre de Riel, Marquis of, 106
Bonaparte, Louis (& family), 64-5, 200
Bonaparte, Napoleon – see Napoleon I, Emperor of the French
Bonnie, Dr (Condé surgeon), 149, 155-7, 161, 167, 178-9, 203
Bordeaux, Henri d'Artois, Duke of, 99-101, 141, 145, 152
Boudet, Gabriel Jean, 94
Boudet, Jean François – see under Puymaigre, Count of

Bourbon, Adélaïde ('Adele') de, – see under Rully
Bourbon, Bathilde, Duchess of – see under Orléans, Bathilde d'
Bourbon, House of, 31, 37, 104, 106, 108, 109, 122, 176
Bourbon-Condé, House of, 58, 65-6, 93, 96, 97
Bourbon, Louis Antoine de, – see under Enghien, Louis Antoine
Bourbon, Louis Henri, Joseph. Duke of – see under Condé
Bourbon, Louis Joseph, Duke of – see under Condé
Bourbon, Louise Adelaide de, 80
Bourbon, Louise Françoise de, Duchess of Bourbon, 197
Bourbon-Orléans, House of – see under Orléans
Bourbon-Siciles, Louise Charlotte de, 28
Bowen, Marjorie, 20, 39-40, 49, 70-1, 78, 90, 114, 147, 153, 154, 166, 181, 200
Briant, *abbé*, 144, 149, 163, 171, 183
Brignole, Maria Caterina, 31
British East India Company, 54

Cape of Good Hope / Cape Colony, 54, 92
Carpenter, Kirsty, 21-2, 197
Carte, Marquis de la, 88
Chabannes la Palice, Frederic, Marquis de, 120-1, 123, 202-3
Charles II, King of England, 60

Charles X, King of France, 85-6, 90, 93, 99-101, 103, 109, 115, 117, 121-3, 125, 128-9, 140, 142, 144, 149, 151-2, 162, 172, 180, 201, 204
  as Duke of Artois, 26-7, 28-30, 37, 44, 86, 100, 201
Chiappini, Maria Stella (& Lorenzo), 110-12, 125
Choulot, Paul, Count de, 69, 88, 90, 147-8, 150, 154-5, 164, 168, 181
Choulot, Countess de, 69, 88-90, 113, 120, 147
Clarck, Bernard, 56-7
Clemens Wenceslaus, Prince of Saxony, 32
Clovis I, King of the Franks, 87
Condé, House of Bourbon, 24-5, 31-2, 34, 176, 185, 192
Condé, Louis I de Bourbon, Prince of, 24, 197
Condé, Louis II de Bourbon, Prince of, 58, 63, 95-6, 203
Condé, Louis Henri Joseph de Bourbon, Prince of,
  appearance & character, 25-7, 39-40, 41-2, 87, 94, 97, 147, 153
  birth, childhood & marriage, 23, 24-8
  military career, 28-31, 33-7
  English exile, 22-3, 39-40, 64, 80, 86, 198, 200
  early relationship with Sophie Dawes, 23, 24, 40, 41-4 (rumoured, 60)

Index

return to France, 45, 47, 50-63
deceptive relationship with Sophie, 50-1, 53, 54-5, 57, 63-79
open relationship with Sophie, 80-102
Sophie's manipulation & cruel treatment of, 112-16, 120-43, 146, 149-53, 172, 185
relationship with House of Orléans, 103, 112, 116, 122, 124, 129, 135, 147-9, 180
will, inheritance & plans to re-draft, 62, 98-101, 112,-19, 123-6, 127-54, 170-2, 175, 184, 192, 203-4
death, circumstances of & investigations into, 34-5, 155-86, 188-91, 204
Condé, Louis Joseph de Bourbon, Prince of, 22, 24, 94, 135
military career, 31-7, 58
English exile, 39, 44
return to France & death, 45, 57-8
Condé, Marie de Bourbon-, 24
Condé, Louise Adelaide de Bourbon, 24
Corbin, Henri, 193
Cossee-Brissac, Count of, 151-2, 168
Crann, Mary, 9, 97
Crillon, Louis, Duke of, 29, 197
Cuba, 108
    Havana, 108
Cutler, Sir John, 42

Darmaign (editor), 186
Davenport Adams, H., 6
Daw, Charlotte (sister of Sophie), 2
Daw / Dawes, Charlotte Mary (sister of Sophie), 2, 10, 14, 73, 92, 124, 145, 190
Daw / Dawes, George (nephew of Sophie), 97, 188-90 – see also 'Sergeant X'
Daw / Dawes, James (brother of Sophie), 2, 9, 10, 15, 60, 91, 97, 192-3
Daw / Dawes, James (nephew of Sophie), 91-3, 119, 139, 143, 145, 151, 154, 165, 170, 173, 174, 177, 183-9, 192, 193
Daw / Dawes, Jane (mother of Sophie), 1-2, 9, 10, 42-3, 48, 73, 119, 191
Daw, Mary-Ann (later Clarck – sister of Sophie), 2, 9-10, 56-7, 192-3
Daw / Dawes, Matilda (later Chabannes, de – niece of Sophie), 91-2, 120-4, 193, 201, 202
Daw, Richard (brothers of Sophia), 2
Daw, Richard / Dawes, Dicky (father of Sophie), 1-3, 6, 8-9, 10, 14-15, 54, 55, 102, 124, 140,141, 196
Dicky Daws Gut, 3
Daw, Sarah (sister of Sophie) 2
Daw, Sophia / Dawes, Sophie,

appearance & character, 17, 18-19, 41, 43, 44, 66-9, 71-2, 78, 82, 95, 97, 146-7, 177, 181
birth, age & styling of name, 1-2, 11, 51, 54-7, 60, 73, 196, 199
childhood, 5-6, 9-12, 14 (rumoured, 60)
teenage years, 15-23, 40
education, 43-4
early relationship with Condé, 23, 24, 40, 41-4
life in Paris without Condé, 48-9
reunion with Condé, 50-59
marriage to Adrien de Feuchères & elevation to baroness, 51, 53-62
married life, 63-72
revelation of true relationship with Condé & banishment from Court, 72-80
manipulative relationship with Condé, 81-102, 103, 112-14, 120, 127-51, 158, 172, 178, 183, 185
intrigue with Louis Philippe, 103-4, 114-19, 121-6, 127-51, 163-6, 172, 185
beneficiary of Condé will & readmittance to Court, 138-9, 145, 158, 167, 172-3, 176-7
& death of Condé, 155-6, 158-9, 163-9, 172-3, 178, 180-6, 190

& deaths of nephews James & George, 186-92
returns to England, death, will & burial, 191-2, 194-5
Daw, William (brothers of Sophie), 2, 9, 10
Dawes, William (nephew of Sophie), 193
Delille, Jacques, 33
Drinkwater, Captain John, 28
Dumouriez, General Charles François, 105-6, 202
Dupont de l'Eure, Jacques Charles, 168
Dupré family (servants of Sophie), 179-80, 189

Eliott, General George (Baron Heathfield), 28-30
Enghien, Louis Antoine de Bourbon, Duke of,
birth, 25-6
military career, 31, 33, 34, 37
arrest, trial & death, 25, 37-9, 40, 118
England, 1, 3, 35, 55, 108, 109, 142-3, 186, 191-3, 202, 205
English Channel, 6, 35, 48, 60
Dorset, 191
Christchurch, 191
Lulworth Castle, 144
Essex, 37
Hampshire,
Portsmouth (& The Solent), 13, 14, 15-17; George Hotel, The, 15-16, 196-7

Index

Kent,
  Dover, 186
  Duncan Down, 196
London, 17-23, 35, 40, 44, 49-50, 57, 58-9, 91, 92, 124, 186, 191, 194
  specific locations:
    Bloomsbury, 42.45; Chelsea, 43; Covent Garden, 19, 61; Kensal Green Cemetery, 194-5; Marylebone, 49, 61; Newington, 54; Paddington (High Park Square), 191, 205; Piccadilly, 21-2, 40; Turnham Green, 20-1, 43; Twickenham, 108; Wanstead, 37, 39, 198; Westminster, 57, 60-1
Norfolk, 202
Suffolk,
  Samford House of Industry, 6
Surrey,
  Claremont House, 193
  Merton, 16
Wight, Isle of, 1-15, 35, 42, 48, 53 54, 55, 60, 91-2, 188, 193, 196
  House of Industry, 6-9, 10, 11, 12, 13, 14-15, 18, 23, 54, 56, 66, 103, 196
  Record Office, 11, 14
  smuggling, 3-4, 6
  specific locations:
    Bembridge (& Ledge), 3, 6; Brading (& Haven), 3, 6, 14; Newport, 7, 15, 54, 56, 196; Parkhurst (& forest / prisons), 7, 8, 9, 66, 196; Ryde, 13, 15; St Helen's (& Duver), 1-5, 9, 10, 54, 60, 103, 149, 188, 196, 199; Sandown Bay, 14; Shanklin, 11-13, 14, 15, 196; Yarmouth, 60; Wydcombe Manor, 193
Europe, generally, 31, 32, 33, 36, 39, 80, 93, 175

Ferdinand IV, King of Naples, 108
Ferdinand VII, King of Spain, 77
Feuchères, Adrien de,
  birth & parentage, 52
  appearance & character, 52, 54
  military career, 52, 61, 77-8
  marriage to Sophie & elevation to baron, 52-62, 92
  married life, 63-77
  & Sophie's will / later career, 192, 205
Flassans, Baron de – see Daw / Dawes, James (brother of Sophia)
Flassans, Baroness de – see Manby, Mary Harcour
Foret de Boisbrumet (Pontoise JP), 165
France, 1, 16, 18, 23, 28-30, 31-5, 36-7, 39, 41, 47, 54, 56, 57-8, 62, 65, 66, 77, 91, 97, 106, 108, 109, 112, 124, 135, 162, 169, 192-3, 198, 199, 204

regions:
Brittany, 36
Grand Est, 95
Haus-de-France, 134
Nirmandy, 147
departments:
Aisne,
   Guise, 134
Ardennes,
   Rocroi, 96
   Sapogne-et-Feuchère,s, 52
Bas-Rhin, 34
   Strasbourg, 38
Bouches-du-Rhone,
   Marseilles, 107
Eure-et-Loir,
   Dreux, 193
Haut-Rhin, 85
Hauts-de-Seine,
   Neuilly-sur-Seine,115, 123
Loire-Arlantique,
   Nantes, 192
Manche,
   Cherbourg, 3
Marne,
   Reims, 86-7
Morbihan,
   Quiberon, 35
Nord,
   Lille, 198
   Valenciennes, 32
Oise, 93-5
   Chantilly, château & town of, 19, 27, 32, 44, 45, 58, 63-71, 73, 78-9, 80, 81-2, 84, 91, 93-7, 99, 100, 102, 114, 116, 120, 124, 126, 127, 129, 130-1, 134, 136, 143, 148, 150-1, 173, 176, 192-3, 199-200, 203 (*Musée Condé,* 44, 192, 200)
   Morfontaine, château 83, 138
Pas-de-Calais,
   Calais, 186-9, 205 (*Gazette de Calais*, 186-7)
Seine,
   Paris, 24, 27, 31, 32, 37, 44-6, 48-9, 52, 54-6, 58, 73, 79, 80, 91, 105-6, 107, 141, 143-7, 151, 154, 168, 169, 171, 173, 174, 175, 177, 180, 184, 186, 188, 189, 190, 200, 201, 203; specific locations & features: Bois de Boulogne, 27; Élysée Palace, 27; Louvre Palace, 95; Palais Bourbon, 70, 88, 123, 130, 138, 174, 176, 203; Palais Royal, 109, 111, 114, 117, 121, 123, 136, 203; Père Lachaise Cemetery, 190, 194; Royal Court of, 180; Seine, River, 64, 85; Tribunal of the Seine, 184;Tuileries Palace, 64, 85, 114, 125; Versailles, palace of, 25, 31, 32, 98, 201
Seine-Saint-Denis
   Saint Denis, Basilica of, 58, 174

Index

Savoie, 81
Seine-Maritime,
   Harfleur, 3
   Le Havre, 147
Somme,
   Péronne, 32
Val-de-Marne,
   Boissy –Saint-Leger, 76,
     138 (Gros-bois, château
     of, 138, 200)
   Vincennes, 37, 38, 172, 175
Val d'Oise, 65
   Ecouen, 138, 172
   Enghien-les-Bains, 164
   Moisselles, 143, 148
   Montmorency, forest of, 64,
     66, 138, 143-4
   Pontoise, 165, 177-8
   Saint-Leu-la-Foret,
     château & town, 64-5,
     70, 76, 80, 136-8, 143-4,
     145-8; 150-4, 160,
     164-74, 176-7, 186,
     188-9, 191, 200
   Vendée, 35, 47-8, 138
   Vosges mountains, 80
Var, 119
   Flassans-sur-Isole, 119
   Mons, 105
   Toulon, 88
see also French
   Revolutionary / Napoleonic
   Wars
Francis II, Holy Roman
   Emperor, 34
Frann, Louis, Count de la
   Villagontier (& wife), 91, 144,
   153, 155, 166, 168, 175, 182
French Revolution, the, 18, 22,
   28, 31, 33, 45, 58, 63, 104-5
   Bastille, storming of the, 31,
     38, 58
   Convenyion nationale,
     105-6, 202
   First Republic, 33-4, 104-5, 107
   la Directoire, 108
   Reign of Terror, 31
   Revolutionary Wars, 33-6,
     104-6, 119, 197
   specific events: Amiens,
     Treaty of, 36; Berstheim,
     Battle of, 34-5, 39;
     Chouannerie Uprising,
     35; Lunéville, Treaty
     of, 36; Neerwinden,
     Battle of, 105; Valmy
     Campaign, 105-6;
     Vendée Uprising, 35,
     46-8; 1st Coalition, War
     of 32; 2nd Coalition,
     War of, 37

Gay, Jean-Baptiste, 128
Gazette e Tribunaux, 186
Gentleman's Magazine, The, 26,
   34-5, 62, 194, 197, 198
George III, King of Britain and
   Ireland, 18
Gerainville, A.E. Billault de, 19
Germany, 47
   Black Forest, the, 34
   Coblenz (Koblenz), 32
   Ettenheim, 37
   Luftwaffe, the, 17, 196-7
   Reichenau & Lake
     Constance, 107

Rhine, river / Rhineland, the, 32, 37
Gibraltar, Great Siege of, 28-31, 35, 82
Great Britain, generally, 28, 36, 37, 46, 47, 109, 149
see also England / Scotland
Guillaume, Armand, 169
Guy, Monsieur (Condé servant), 22, 40, 41
Gwyn, Nell, 19, 60-1

Hapsburg, House of, 32
Harlequin, de, 184-6
Harris, Sophie, 49-50
Hickman, Mark & Rosy, 5-6
Holy Roman Empire, 32
Horace III, Prince of Monaco, 31
Hostein (Condé dentist), 130, 162
Hudson Lowe, Sir, 38
Huet-Villiers, François, 44, 198
Hulin, General Pierre-Augustin, 38
Huproye, Antoine Edne de la, 180-4, 186, 190

Italy, 111
   Faenza, 111
   Tuscany, 110-11 (Elba, 44, 46)
      Florence, 88-9, 110
   Venice, former republic of, 35-6
   Verona, 35-6

Jones, Jack & Johanna, 7
Joséphine, Empress, 64

Kemp, William, 11, 12
Kent, Edward, Duke of, 22-3, 108, 197

Lady's Magazine, The, 18
La Fontaine, Mery, 174
L'Aritorque, 127-8
Latil, Archbishop Jean-Baptiste, 117-18
La Constititoonnel, 109
Lambot, General Baron de, 81, 100-1, 115, 116, 124, 129, 151, 165, 170, 175, 177, 183, 190, 201-2
Lecomte (Condé servant & wife), 146-7, 153-6, 159, 166, 168, 171-2, 174, 179, 189-90, 204
Leduc (Saint-Leu Mayoral assistant), 160
Letallier, Dr (Saint-Leu, GP), 161
Lorenzo (Condé servant), 163
Louis XIV, King of France, 25
Louis XV, King of France, 24, 27
Louis XVI, King of France, 27, 29, 31, 32, 34, 36, 45, 52, 58, 104, 114, 149, 199
Louis XVII, King of France, 35-6
Louis XVIII, King of France, 35-6, 45-7, 51, 53, 58, 64, 65, 79, 80, 85, 86. 88, 91, 97, 109, 198, 199-200, 201
Louis Philippe I, King of the French, 19, 205
   appearance & character, 136
   as Duke of Orléans, 85, 103-7
   revolutionary military career, 104-6
   exile & marriage to Marie Amélie, 107-9
   return to France, 109-111

Index

Chiappini scandal, 111-12, 202
intrigue with Sophie Dawes, 112-19, 121-6, 127-35, 138, 140
as King,
July Revolution / July Monarchy, 141, 162, 203, 205
continuing intrigue with Sophie, 141, 148, 151, 165-7, 172, 175, 177, 185
& death of Condé, 165-7, 169-70, 172-3, 175-7, 180, 183, 185, 192
abdication, English exile & death, 193
Low, David, 4

Manby, Mary Harcourt, Baroness de Flassans, 119, 154, 190, 202
Manby, Sir Thomas, 119, 202
Manoury (Condé valet), 127, 143-5, 146, 150-1, 155-7, 159-61, 163, 178-9, 204
Marc, Dr, 167-8
Maria Theresa of Savoy, Queen of France, 123
Marie Amélie, Queen of the French, 108, 114, 120-2, 126, 147-8, 176-7, 193
Marie-Antoinette, Queen of France, 31, 58, 199
Marie Josephine, Countess, 85
Marjohn, Dr, 167-8

Menard, Count of, 140
Michelot, Marguerite ('Mimi'), 28, 68, 200
Monpensier, Louis Antoine, Duke of, 106-8, 202
Montagu, Violette, 19, 20, 58, 66-7, 77, 114-15, 197, 202, 203, 204
Montbazon, Duke of, 186
Montespan, Françoise-Athénaïs, Madame de, 25
Morning Herald, The, 37

Naples, Kingdom of, 108
Sicily, 108, 205
Napoleon I, Emperor of the French, 16, 21, 23, 36, 37, 38-9, 44, 45, 46-7, 52-3, 64-5, 99, 108-9, 198
Napoleonic Wars, 16, 44-5, 52-3, 119, 197
Peninsular War, 63, 109
Trafalgar, Battle of, 16
6th Coalition, War of, & 1st Bourbon restoration 44-6, 109
100 Days, The, & 7th Coalition, War of, 46-7 (Battle of Waterloo, 47)
2nd Bourbon restoration, 47-9, 53, 58
Nelson, Horatio, Lord, 16
Nemours, Louis, Duke of, 127-8
Netherlands, The, 47, 54, 65, 105, 198
Austrian Netherlands, 105
The Hague, 65, 200

Newborough, Baron Thomas, 110-11
Nova Scotia, 108

Obry (godson of Condé), 146
O'Meara, Barry, 38-9
One Hundred Thousand Sons of Saint Louis, 77, 200
Orléans, (Louise Marie) Adélaïde d', 107, 114-15, 121, 125-6, 177
Orléans, Antoine d', 129
Orléans, Bathilde d', Duchess of Bourbon, 25-8, 104, 118, 197
Orléans, Charles d', 110
Orléans, Ferdinand d', Duke of, 173
Orléans, Françoise d', 110
Orléans, Henri Eugene d' – see under Aumale, Duke of
Orléans, House of Bourbon-, 26, 103-4, 107-9, 113-14, 137, 170, 183
Orléans, Louis Philippe, Duke of (*le Gros*), 197
Orléans, Louis Philippe, Duke of – see under Louis Philippe, King of the French
Orléans, Louis Philippe Joseph, Duke of (*Philippe Égalité*), 104, 106, 109, 110-11, 129, 202

Pache, Jean-Nicolas, 105
Paladilhe, Dominique, 50
Pasquier, Etienne Denis, Baron, 165-7, 169, 205
Péffer, *abbé*, 149, 173, 174-6, 170
Perigold, Cardinal de, 89

Persil, Jean-Charles, 183
Polastron, Marie Louise, Countess of, 86, 201
Polignac, Jules de, 162, 203
Portugal, 46
Préjean, Baron & Baroness de, 152-3, 171, 179
Prussia, 44, 45, 52
Puymaigre, Jean François, Count of, 93-7, 98, 201

Quelan, Archbishop Hyacinthe-Louis de, 88-90
Quesnay, Madame de, 69, 113, 180

Rochefoucaud, Sostene de la, Viscount of, 140-1, 203
Rohan, Charlotte Elisabeth de, Princess of Condé, 24-5
Rohan, Charlotte Louise de, Duchess of Enghien, 37
Rohan, House of (& branches), 98, 100, 117, 139, 176-8, 185
Rohan, Louis de, Prince of, 94, 98-9, 139, 173, 176-7, 180, 182, 184-6
Roussliere-Clouart de la (Enghien-led Bains JP), 164-5
Rully, Adelaide ('Adele'), Countess of, 28, 68, 80-1, 82-4, 90, 113, 118, 201
Rully, Patrice de Montessus, Count of, 68, 81, 83-4, 90, 91
Rumigny, Colonel de, 165-7, 169
Russia, 36, 44, 46, 47, 52

Saint Helena, 38
Saint-Jacques, Baron de, 81-2, 83

Index

Savary, General Anne-Jean-Marie-René, 38
Scotland, 144
   Edinburgh (Holyrood), 144, 145
'Sergeant X', 174, 189-90 – see also Dawes, George
Seven Years War, the, 32
Southcott, 'Hal', 13, 14
Sovereign, SS, 186
Spain, 16, 28-30, 32, 47, 48, 52, 53, 77-8, 109
   Madrid, 29
   Pamplona, 78
   Trafalgar, Cape of, 16
   see also Napoleonic Wars
Surval, Hugues Acgille, Baron de, 134-9, 144-5
Sweden, 46, 47
Switzerland, 47, 107, 147, 149

Tailleur, Pierre Gervais, 160
Talleyrand-Périgord, Charles-Maurice de, 39, 44-5, 46, 47, 97-8, 116, 120, 121, 126, 186, 199, 205
Thackeray, William Makepeace, 48-9
Thanaron, (Jean-Baptiste) Justin, 124, 145, 203
Thanaron, (Marie Charlotte) Sophie, 190-3
Thirty Years War, the, 33
   Rocroi, Battle of, 33, 97

Ungern-Sternberg, Count Edward, 110
USA, 107-8
   Philadelphia, 107

Vedrene, Prosper, 93
Villegonyier, Count de la – see under Frann, Louis
Villèle, (Jean-Baptiste) Joseph, Count of, 128, 203
Voltaire, 96-7

White, Sheila, 4
Winchelsea, George, Earl of, 22